DISTURBED COMMUNICATION

By Jurgen Ruesch

MENTAL EXAMINERS' HANDBOOK
(*with F. L. Wells*)

CHRONIC DISEASE AND PSYCHOLOGICAL INVALIDISM

DUODENAL ULCER

COMMUNICATION: THE SOCIAL MATRIX OF PSYCHIATRY
(*with Gregory Bateson*)

NONVERBAL COMMUNICATION
(*with Weldon Kees*)

DISTURBED COMMUNICATION

THERAPEUTIC COMMUNICATION

Disturbed
COMMUNICATION

The Clinical Assessment
of Normal and Pathological
Communicative Behavior

By Jurgen Ruesch, M.D.

The Norton Library
W · W · NORTON & COMPANY · INC ·
NEW YORK

152013

W. W. Norton & Company, Inc. is also the publisher of the works of Erik H. Erikson, Otto Fenichel, Karen Horney and Harry Stack Sullivan, and the principal works of Sigmund Freud.

SBN   393   00634   4

Contents

v

Part Two

The Clinical Observation of Communicative Behavior

Acknowledgments

THE CONTINUED support received from the National Institute of Mental Health through United States Public Health Service grants MH-37 and M-534 made it possible to engage in a long-term study of the problems of human communication; and I am grateful to all those who, for a longer or shorter period of time, have contributed to this venture and have participated in the formulation of principles of communication pathology described in this volume. I am especially indebted to Drs. Jack Block and Betty L. Kalis, both clinical psychologists, who emphasized the need for a more systematic approach to clinical observation; and I wish to thank Dr. Lillian Bennett for her useful suggestions in matters concerning group communication and Dr. Emmy Sylvester for her pertinent comments regarding disturbed communication in childhood. Susan West, the secretary on the study, who edited the manuscript and prepared it for the publisher, has as always been extremely helpful in the handling of many technical and administrative details. I also owe an intellectual debt to those of my friends and colleagues—particularly Dr. Roy R. Grinker and Dr. David McK. Rioch—who, at a time when ideas about communication were new and not as yet accepted, provided a forum for open discussion of these problems and thus encouraged the development of approaches set forth here.

J. R.

Preface to the 1972 Edition

MORE THAN FIFTEEN years have elapsed since this book, the second in a series of three volumes concerned with communication in the field of psychiatry, was written. The first volume, *Communication, the Social Matrix of Psychiatry* (with Gregory Bateson) was conceived from the viewpoint of the scientific observer and emphasizes primarily the context in which communication takes place. The third, *Therapeutic Communication,* was written for the therapist and deals with the ways in which communication can be utilized for the benefit of the patient.

The present book, addressed to the clinician, is concerned with the relationship of communication to psychopathology and abnormal behavior. The notion of disturbed communication that is set forth here was based upon three distinct ideas:

First, that communication and its disturbances are learned in a social context—that is, in an ongoing exchange with others;

Second, that the differences between normal and disturbed communication are characterized by quantitative variations and deviant patterning rather than by qualitative or other generic factors;

3 Third, that deviant action and disturbances of communication are linked in a circular way. When the impact of an ineffective action is incorporated in the informational body of the person, it may give rise to additional disturbances of communication and action.

These three basic ideas have withstood the test of time—so far for about twenty years. Of course, this does not mean much when we consider that the nosological and taxonomic efforts of psychiatrists and the psychodynamic efforts of psychoanalysts survived for about seventy years. But a certain dissatisfaction with these older approaches has been felt for some time. Although the descriptive inventories of psychopathological phenomena were indeed objective, they were at the same time too static. The formulation of hypothetical intrapsychic processes, in contrast, was more dynamic, but it was at the same time too subjective. To counteract the shortcomings of these two major approaches, the author originally set himself the task of studying the operations through which both descriptive and psychodynamic psychiatrists obtain their information: they observe normal and disturbed communication in a two-person or a group context, and they experience the effects of communication upon themselves. Since the early 1950's, the conceptual framework and the methods used for observation and recording of disturbed communication have undergone little if any change. What has changed, however, is the emphasis. While the earlier focus circled around output—that is, words or actions—the modern concern is with input—that is, perception and cognition. The scheme of "Who has perceived whom, where, when, in what context, and leading to what definition of self and other" now precedes the basic "Who talks to whom, about what, in what manner, for how long, and with what effect."

A second shift in emphasis in the last fifteen years has been brought about by the introduction of computer models which are capable of simulating normal and abnormal communication. Because symbolic re-enactment of natural phenomena is the path on which advances are currently made, we have been forced into a tighter and more precise formulation of theories. The similarity between a series of logical statements and a computer program has led scientists to believe that a theorem that cannot be operationalized and translated into a computer program has not been properly formulated. To the reader who is unfamiliar with computer models it might suffice to state that simulation of behavior is based not on deterministic but on probabilistic mathematics. Probabilistic mathematics are capable of coping with the "sometimes-true theories of social processes," as opposed to deterministic mathematics, which represent the "always-true theories of physical processes." The "sometimes-true" theories are neither true nor false; instead, they are true under certain circumstances of which the probability of occurrence can be calculated. The second foundation of computer simulation is set theory, which deals with collections or classes of objects. The operations performed upon sets are considered a branch of mathematics called Boolean Algebra. With the help of probabilistic mathematics and set theory, computer programs can be written that simulate the therapist's or the patient's behavior; and interaction between two computers can simulate the exchange between doctor and patient—or between any two people whose conversation is limited to certain topics.

In the second part of this volume, the reader will find a guide to the observation of communicative behavior. This section fulfills several functions. To the clinician, it points out what kinds of observations are relevant for the assessment of normal and disturbed communication. To the computer expert who wishes to write a program or to simulate interaction, it suggests a number of normal and abnormal communicative sets. Although not meant to be exhaustive, this guide is intended to inform the reader of the range of possible observations. Another function of the guide is to illustrate how a single word or symbol can carry a lot of information. Every word derives from a family or set of words. Implicitly, therefore, a word evokes an image of all the other words contained in the set, provided the perceiver is familiar with the language and the relevant culture. Inasmuch as the number of words chosen to express a thought is always smaller than the number of possible choices contained in the original set or sets, the meaning of a word is characterized not only by its overt definition but by all the other words or symbols in the set. The old saying "Tell me what company you keep and I'll tell you what you are" is here quite to the point. Indeed, years are spent in training youngsters to acquire not only a vocabulary but knowledge of the sets from which the vocabulary derives so that they will be able to engage in precise and economical ways of expression.

In considering the topic of disturbed communication and in keeping with the modern requirement of operational definitions, the author steered away from value judgments. Instead of basing the diagnosis of "disturbed" upon a comparison of a given word or statement with an accepted norm, the author defined disturbed communication as messages that occur at the wrong time or at the wrong place, or that are quantitatively not matched to the input characteristics of the other person. Consequently, the receiver either cannot understand the message at all or he misunderstands it. The principal idea that underlies this definition is that no verbal or gestural expression per se is disturbed before it is considered in a social context and is followed by other people's reactions. When the message remains unintelligible and no correspondence of information can be established between the participants, the conclusion can be reached that communication is disturbed. Communication pathology thus is defined not through normative procedures but through the effects achieved. If concordance of information can be established between sender and receiver, even if limited to a small universe of discourse, then communication has been successful. And successful communication is the process that connects one person to another and that enables people to accumulate knowledge and to acquire an identity.

In today's world, however, the citizen not only has to attend to the exchanges with the people he is in contact with; he also has to cope with all those unwanted messages that reach him through the mass media. Thus to the disturbances of communication that are rooted in human interaction we have to add those disturbances that are triggered by unwanted input. Noise, input overload, and message alteration have become progressively more significant as the range and scope of our technical means of communication have increased. Perhaps the most significant change that has occurred in the last twenty years is that the machine has been interposed between person and person, resulting in delay, amplification, repetition, distortion, addition, or omission of messages. While the characteristics of the communication machinery can be blamed for some of the distortions, more often than not these are brought about intentionally or unintentionally by the handmaidens of the machine who edit, censor, or program human communication. This conglomorate of machine, crew, and image-making experts— the message-manipulating industry—intrudes into everybody's life. The disturbances arising through these influences in human communication have not as yet been fully assessed and the description of this type of pathology remains a task for the future.

However, coping with disturbed communication in individuals or small groups is a professional task for today. But above and beyond the professional, all people can exert a normalizing influence upon others by being understanding and by attempting to reply to those who are in distress and who wish to establish communication with another living being. This personal contact serves to balance the distortions of communication introduced by technology. Direct human contact is an absolute must for all people if they wish to retain their sanity and their ability to meaningfully communicate with their fellow men.

JURGEN RUESCH

San Francisco, California
August, 1971

DISTURBED COMMUNICATION

Introduction

MID-TWENTIETH century advances in science and technology have brought about profound changes in our views of man and nature. No longer are we concerned with the transmission, storage, or transformation of energy; instead, we have moved on to problems of control of forces through information and self-regulation, even to the extent of building decision-making machines. Such events have left psychology and psychiatry not unscathed. Our present-day **concern with sociocultural events** and human relations is but one of the repercussions of this general trend, another being the struggle for newer and more effective approaches to the understanding of behavior and the treatment of mental disease.

Following this line of thought, the author made the biosocial function of communication, which seems to be basic to all forms of human relations, the center of his studies. By borrowing from such disciplines as biology, cybernetics, psychoanalysis, social psychology, and cultural anthropology (205), he gradually developed a **theory of human communication** founded upon modern principles of scientific philosophy (210). Within such a framework, it is possible to dispense with a multitude of unnecessary assumptions, theoretical constructs, and scattered observations inherited from older scientific and metaphysical thought which obscure our present vision. The formulation of human problems in terms of communication preserves the immediacy between scientific observation and theoretical considerations, enabling the scientist to carry out the assessment of human communication along a continuum which ranges from normal to abnormal. Disturbances of communication thus are viewed either as quantitative alterations of ordinary functioning or as forms of exchange which do not fit the social situation. Such a view makes possible the inclusion of individual psychopathology, disturbed two-person relations, and group pathology all within one system (203).

The consideration of intrapersonal and extrapersonal events as integral parts of the same system necessarily results in observations and conclusions which overlap and crisscross traditional psycho-pathological formulations. But since the latter have neither explained the origin of mental disease nor contributed toward the development of effective treatment methods, the time has come to try a different approach. New theoretical formulations and emphasis upon communication have led to a different view of what constitutes a basic datum in the consideration of human interaction. The observations made in social situations do not have the characteristics of a scientific procedure in which one aspect is studied in detail while all other variables are held constant. In human interaction, any part function has to be viewed within the framework not only of one organism but of the sum total of all organisms that participate in a given situation, and this sum total is in a **perpetual flux.** Therefore, any attempt to treat a state of affairs at a given moment as if it were fixed usually meets with failure. When a written report is made about a social situation, the inherent characteristics of verbal language introduce a further distortion of the space and time scales involved. In the end, after having been exposed to such verbal reports, we tend to accept the implication that the situation is fixed.

The spoken or written report of self or alter, therefore, cannot be accepted as the **basic datum of psychiatry.** Instead, the total experience of the individual as it is reflected in appearance, word, and action at a particular moment in a particular situation has to be taken as the unit of consideration. This of course involves the assessment of nonverbal events (215) which, in order to be understood, have to be traced to the other participants operative in the social situation.

In no other discipline—and this includes all the social sciences, biology, and medicine—is there a greater need for "knowledge in action" than in psychiatry. The therapist cannot wait for the results of a test; he cannot delay for hours or days his responses to the messages of his patients if he wishes to be effective. The therapies that are built upon the process of communication rely upon immediacy. When the patient makes a statement—be it in word, gesture, or action—the reply or lack of reply on the part of the doctor acknowledges, amplifies, contrasts, or contradicts. The effectiveness of the therapist's operations is based upon the fact that statement is tied to statement within the mind of the patient and from person to person. To achieve such connections, split-second observation and, if deemed necessary, reaction are of the essence. To prepare the clinician to make concrete observations and to scan these against a background of possible alternatives, as well as to help him to make on-the-spot conceptualizations which can be acted upon in reply to the patient, the present volume was written.

This book incorporates the results of a long-term study of human communication involving psychiatric patients and other people. Many of the observations and formulations here reported reflect the personal experience of the author gained in the extended treatment of over two hundred patients in the course of ten years. Their conditions ranged in severity from the acute psychoses to mild character disturbances. The age range of the patients included small children and people over sixty; in terms of diagnoses, all psychiatric categories were represented. In reporting his experiences, the author has not attempted to present detailed case studies; instead, he has concentrated on observable communicative behavior as well as upon on-the-spot formulations, the validity of which has been verified in the later phases of therapy.

Therefore, the **presentation is problem-oriented** rather than patient-oriented. It reflects the fact that in the process of communication at any one instant an individual deals not with the total personality of the other person but with certain salient features in self and in alter which are relevant to that situation at that instant. Events of the past are relevant only in so far as they extend symbolically into the present; events of the future exist in the present only symbolically. Both memories of the past and anticipations of the future may find expression in action, but if they are to shape a social situation they have to be operative then and there—in the present. The many factors which do shape a social situation at a given moment are encompassed in the phenomenology of the communicative process which determines the fate of the message. The message, in turn, is the problem around which this book is oriented.

In the past few decades, many attempts have been made to adapt psychotherapeutic procedures to the specific needs and disabilities of patients. That most of these efforts fail is principally due to the fact that no appropriate concepts or language exist which enable doctors to be aware of or to talk about second-by-second changes which occur in the course of therapy. The conceptual schemes available and the language actually spoken by therapists signify primarily long-term, almost secular changes in the personality of the patients. In this volume, in contrast, an attempt is made to emphasize the actual, **instantaneous communicative behavior** rather than the more time-enduring qualities of people. In any case, the latter represent abstractions which become effective only when a patient acts upon them. The author hopes that the specification of both normal and disturbed processes of communication with an emphasis upon instantaneous happenings in the present will provide the clinician with a workable scheme which will prove useful in action as well as in retrospective reporting. After all, the psychotherapist in his daily and momentary reactions is message-oriented, and only in his over-all attitude is he patient-oriented. Any principle, attitude, or goal of his can be implemented only through an actual communicative exchange. Therefore, precise and relevant observations made in the course of clinical interviews, when supplemented by the therapist's experience of communication shared with the patient, eventually should lead to a more precise formulation of treatment methods which are specifically designed to meet the disability of the patient.

Part One

The Nature of
Communication Pathology

Chapter One

Antecedent and Contemporary
Source Material

MODERN THEORIES of communication grew amidst a matrix of ideas which derived from a multitude of sources. Perhaps the first person to study the role of communication in human relations was the sixth-teenth-century Florentine Renaissance intellectual, Niccolò **Machiavelli**, who is known to the world as the man who formulated techniques and strategy for gaining and keeping political control (154). But to the psychiatrist his work is of interest because he was the first man to describe one aspect of the process of communication: the relationship of conscious intention to social effects achieved. But the enlightenment of that period hardly affected psychiatry. Ancient demonology and magic views dominated the scene until in the late eighteenth century **Pinel** laid the foundations of modern psychiatry (184). By removing the chains from the unfortunate, by prohibiting the exhibition of patients against admission fees as if they were wild beasts, and by introducing general humane methods of approach, he was the first to utilize the element of human relations and communication in the treatment of the mentally ill. Almost another hundred years passed before **Freud,** at the end of the nineteenth century, after having immersed himself in the study of hysteria and hypnosis, gradually evolved the concept of transference (206). His contribution marks a milestone in the history of communication inasmuch as it emphasizes the fact that the content of a message is a function of the human relationship. We owe to Freud the notion that messages have to be interpreted in the light of a person's expectancies of role assignment. The next decisive step in the definition of the function of communication in the field of psychi-

9

atry occurred nearly fifty years later when **Sullivan** considered the study of personality and mental disease within the framework of interpersonal and social systems. His ideas about the influence of anxiety in human relations shed a new light upon the ways of communication of sick people (242). **Wiener,** a mathematician, finally systematized the theory of communication engineering. His formulations of the notion of feedback and its application to social behavior gave us the theoretical foundations for the understanding of the maintenance of pathology and the correction of information (257).

The present-day emphasis on communication has been foreshadowed in the **psychiatric literature** of the past fifty years, which is full of explicit and implicit references to the physiology, psychology, sociology, and pathology of communication. The much-talked-about differences between the descriptive, psychodynamic, developmental, genetic, interpersonal, and group approaches to psychiatry (266) are not as striking when the respective contributions of these approaches to the field of communication are considered. The common denominator is the data-gathering procedure of the psychiatrist, which necessitates that regardless of the viewpoint held the process of communication be dealt with. Whatever is observed can be nothing else but some element of behavior expressed by the patient and perceived by the psychiatrist, and the only means of making these observations known to others is to communicate the findings in oral or written form. Furthermore, any psychiatrist must communicate with his patients if he wishes to achieve any effects. Therefore, it is not surprising that, de facto, the psychiatric literature and the activities of the psychiatrist are dependent upon and organized around the function of communication. Unfortunately, many explicit references to disturbed communication are buried in publications which have been conceived in a different theoretical frame; and in many instances the original observations, which by necessity can only refer to behavior expressed by the patient to the observer, are left entirely implicit. Most of the knowledge about disturbed communication which has been accumulated in the course of time has not been codified in terms of communication theory. Nonetheless, it exists and is transmitted by word of mouth from psychiatrist to psychiatrist. In order to complement this informal body of knowledge with information published in print, this chapter contains a condensed survey of the pertinent literature. Some annotations about the progressive changes which have led to the contemporary emphasis on communication pathology have been added.

DESCRIPTION OF ABNORMAL MENTAL PROCESSES

The majority of descriptions of behavioral pathology derive historically from the period of **classical psychopathology** associated with the names of Bleuler (35), Janet (124), Jaspers (126), Kraepelin (135), Kretschmer (138), Kronfeld (139), Schilder (226), and others. The prevailing scientific attitude at the beginning of the twentieth century was to observe behavior and break it down into small part functions without any consideration of how to put it together again. However, we are indebted to the psychiatrists of that period for accurate descriptions of behavior as seen by a nonparticipating observer. Today these observations (155) are as valid as they were earlier in this century, provided that no etiological or prognostic connotations are attached to them. They are particularly helpful in evaluating difficulties of communication which are due to structural defects of the central nervous system. Seen from a bird's-eye view, the field can be outlined as follows:

Considering first the contributions that were made to the understanding of **disturbances of input and perception,** we meet the neurologists' and the neurophysiologists' attempts to correlate these with lesions of the central nervous system, the cranial and peripheral nerves (260). Similarly the ophthalmologists gave us an understanding of the lesions affecting the eye, the otolaryngologists of those affecting the ear; and the psychologists enriched our knowledge of disturbed apperception and recently of social perception (7). Interdisciplinary teamwork contributed toward the utilization of this information in the rehabilitation of the blind (63, 64, 197, 228) and the deaf (17, 259). Study of sensory defects today is the basis from which our knowledge of the different modalities of experience derives.

Disturbances of output and movement have fascinated a much wider audience. While the behaviorists were more interested in the reactivity of the organism and means of expression (8, 227), the neurophysiologists and pathologists concerned themselves with problems such as paralysis, involuntary movements, and disturbances of coordination (111). Psychoanalysts in conjunction with medical men finally contributed to the understanding of autonomic functions and psychosomatic diseases such as ulcers (213), hypertension, asthma, or colitis (5). Studies of disturbed motility increased our knowledge about distortions of communication and compensatory expression (223).

Language and speech disturbances is a field where the interests of the linguist, the psychiatrist, and the neurologist meet (258). Today there exist four distinct areas of investigation: 1. disturbances of symbolic expression as they occur in aphasia, agnosia, apraxia (57, 103, 108, 176, 253), including disturbances of laterality (33) and reading and writing difficulties (26); 2. disturbances of articulation and phonation as they are observed in dysarthria, dyslalia, and dysphonia (248); 3. disturbances of rhythm in verbal expression as in stuttering (16); 4. disturbances of speech as an expression of psychopathology (250). These may be the result of over-all attitudes (220) such as mutism or logorrhea (23); they may appear in terms of voice pathology (150, 168), in terms of language deviation (151, 265), or in terms of functional distortion of the symbolic process (140).

Disturbances of retention, recall, and recognition, both functional and structural, which have been the domain of psychiatrists and psychologists alike, lend themselves particularly well for measurement (239). Since declining memory for recent events has been the cardinal symptom of senility and retrograde amnesia of concussion, disturbances of memory were in the past considered to be a sure sign of brain disease (48). But the introduction of Freud's concept of repression moved the functional aspects of disturbances of memory to the forefront of attention (188). Gradually the mechanistic consideration of memory functions gave way to a more dynamic viewpoint which was reinforced by various studies of memory under the influence of hypnosis (40). Today the clinical psychiatrist is alerted to the fact that he might meet memory disturbances not only in organic cases but also in hysterical personalities (225) who suffer from amnesia, pseudologia, or repressed traumatic memories.

Knowledge about **disturbances of thinking, judgment, and decision-making** is based upon the assumption that behavior is controlled from a center. Thus autism (34), blocking, negativism, dissociation, delusions, obsession, and lack of insight are all terms which implicitly refer to disordered thinking. But in contrast to modern theories of communication which also postulate the existence of a control center, the older views neglected to consider input and output as a unit and conceived of thinking as a self-generated process. Today we know that what looks like spontaneous thinking is merely a delayed response to earlier input or a reaction to organismic demands. Although the older and popular notion of thinking (189) is not eliminated altogether, communication experts today abstain from assuming a one-to-one correlation between thinking and overt behavior. As a matter of fact, they abstain from making any inferences about thinking and are more inclined to deal with decision-making and the management of contradictory information. Both of these processes can be assessed when input is compared to output, either of a person or of a social organization.

Disturbances of consciousness and confusional states are met primarily by physicians who deal with acute diseases and accidents. The term "consciousness" as it is used in this connection indicates levels of responsiveness to outside stimulation. Depending upon the reactions of the patient, his condition is labeled as coma, sopor, torpor, stupor, drowsiness, or somnolence (199). Milder degrees of impairment are accompanied by disorientation (121) in time and space and by inaccuracy and slowing down in performing intellectual tasks. Since the level of responsiveness is correlated with the oxygen uptake of the brain (99), studies of disturbed consciousness are of vital importance in aviation medicine and in geriatrics. To the student of communication, the problem of responsiveness and alertness which bears on the issue of irritability of living matter is basic because without it communication could not take place.

For a long time scientists have been aware that logical appraisal of **feelings and emotions** such as hunger, rage, or fear is impossible.

Faced with the limitation of scientific procedure, they have treated emotions as a subjective expression of the organism and left these "animalistic" aspects of existence to naturalists, psychiatrists, soothsayers, and artists. In an attempt to make this intriguing subject amenable to scientific inquiry, naturalists (65) and physicians (50) began to concentrate on the objective component of emotional expression—that is, on glandular secretions and contractions of the striped and the smooth muscles. Correlation of these manifestations with lesions of the brain (58) did not yield the expected results—with the exception, perhaps, that lability of emotions could be related to the existence of diffuse brain disease. Not until Freud (93) began to emphasize the totality of the emotional state and its relation to past and future action did the world obtain insight into the phenomena of anxiety, guilt, and depression.

In modern communication theory, the emotional state of an individual is conceived of as the sum-total evaluation of all events which occur inside the organism. These are perceived by the outsider as a kind of metalanguage which is helpful in the interpretation of messages. Emotions thus express the appraisal of existence from the inside out, while intellectual functions represent the view of the same events from the outside in. These two aspects of experience not only are complementary, but they also involve different principles of codification. Emotions are codified in analogic terms and central as well as peripheral structures are simultaneously involved. Intellectual and logical aspects of existence are codified in digital-verbal terms, involving central structures only (207). Correspondingly, the principal seat of digital-verbal codification is located in the forebrain while the mediation of analogic forms of codification occurs through the thalamic and hypothalamic region.

During the classical period of psychopathology, many of the detailed observations of disturbed behavior were classified into groups and integrated into a whole through the construction of **psychopathological types** (175). Addict (185), kleptomaniac, malingerer, impostor (24), fetishist, delinquent (47), homosexual, exhibitionist, hypochondriac, introvert (130), schizothyme (136), and anal character (74) are but a few of the terms still in use. In resorting to typologies, psychiatrists distorted the chronological sequence of events inasmuch as they assumed that an individual behaved in such and such a manner regardless of age, date, or situation. Although typologies have been largely abandoned, they nonetheless represent valuable statements of probability. An individual can be classified as being of a certain type if in a given situation he is likely to react in a predictable way. In terms of communication, the behavior patterns subsumed under the term "type" can be used within a given network for prediction of systematic distortions. However, the distortions will not be entirely a function of the individual's behavior inasmuch as other participants can compensate for, attenuate, or exaggerate the disturbance. Today, therefore, we have to recognize that the construction of typologies constitutes a valuable method in studies of prediction, provided that the social situation is defined and the typology of the other participants is known too.

Description of Abnormal Psychodynamic Processes

At the turn of the century, dissection of the personality into part functions prevented the development of a comprehensive theory of human behavior. Then came Freud, and his greatest contribution to psychiatry was, perhaps, to introduce a form of observation and interpretation which opened different vistas for the understanding of personality (91, 93). Instead of focusing upon isolated functions, Freud made the interrelationship of processes the center of his theory. The novelty of his approach was based on the fact that no single observation was considered satisfactory and that multiple observations in different areas at different times were thought to be necessary for the establishment of psychoanalytic facts. The replacement of raw data with **derivative data**—comparisons, relations, gradients, or ratios—is the outstanding feature of modern dynamic psychiatry. Although critics of the psychodynamic approach maintain that these complex data do not constitute facts but actually are interpretations which vary from observer to observer, it does not follow that the basic conception of psychodynamic data is false. It merely means that so far the most significant relationships have not been isolated.

In contradistinction to the interpersonal approach which emphasizes transactions and conflicts between people, **psychoanalytic psy-chiatry** emphasizes the internal conflicts of patients—the more or less autonomous phenomena which occur inside the individual which are repetitive, time-enduring, and somewhat independent of the social situation. Thus, regardless of the differences that may exist between various schools of psychiatry (264), there exists agreement that conflict is the source of frustration and that frustration may be handled in a variety of ways. Since the integration of antithetical forces both in symbolical and in actual terms is complicated by the impact of traces of past experience, frustration is frequently handled in a way which does not terminate but rather prolongs the existing contradictions. Conflict and its management thus become the focus of observation and theory construction in dynamic psychiatry (104, 118).

Not all dynamic psychiatrists—and this includes a number of experimental and clinical psychologists—emphasize the same con-stituent parts in the analysis of **conflicts.** The ingredients that make up conflicts are defined by those variables of personality that a particular psychiatrist chooses to adhere to. Among the motivational forces which are conceived of as the generators of be-havior are included instincts, drives, needs, desires, wishes, and the "id" (89). A second set of forces, which is supposed to counter-act the instinctual forces, bears upon the function of control: in-hibition, conscience, morality, values, sense of duty, or the "super-ego" (25). The anticipatory forces which are supposed to enable man to withstand frustration—aspiration, fantasy, hope, faith, be-lief, idea, the "ego ideal"—are included in a third group. A fourth set of forces is thought to implement whatever emerges from the clash of instinctual, controlling, and anticipatory forces; it includes such items as habits, traits, attitudes, defenses, the sensory-effector system, the "ego." Strangely enough, whatever forces exist outside of the individual are lumped together and are referred to as environ-ment (254).

Communication theory eliminates the necessity to assume the existence of a multitude of forces. This viewpoint is arrived at by considering that any force, when in action, must be **actually repre-sented;** thus the presence of other people is perceived through our sense organs and is centrally represented in terms of nervous impulses; so are memories, aspirations, and values. In other words, at any one time all forces within the organism and those that impinge from the outside are represented in terms of messages which are coded in specifiable ways. It is these messages that the communication expert deals with, either in terms of the codifications which he can observe or in terms of effects which he can experience. He thus can abstain from speculating about the origin of forces, interesting as this may be.

The psychoanalyst is not content with tracing behavior to its component forces; he also specifies which of the behavior patterns are used as defenses against frustration. The evidence of conflict is embodied in the phenomena of anger, rage, resentment (69); anxiety, apprehension (92, 112, 216); fear, phobia (86); shame, ridicule, disgust (79); guilt, self-destructiveness (21, 163); depression, grief, despair, hopelessness (80); loneliness (97, 263). All these phenomena are unpleasant and are thought to be managed by **mechanisms of defense** which are intended to diminish the feelings of frustration. The intrapsychic workings of the mechanisms of defense have been described under such terms as sublimation, projection, introjection, identification, reaction formation, denial, avoidance, isolation, repression, and conversion (81).

However, a difficulty arises at this point. Since any behavior pattern may be a mechanism of defense, it is almost impossible to decide what is or is not a defense; the term "mechanism of defense" hence becomes almost synonymous with behavior. It is perhaps this very difficulty which induced experimental psychologists and physiologists to study reactions and adaptations to stress (49, 261). Modern studies on the nature of stress (262) and the role of the environment (232) describe the disorganization of behavior which occurs when the capacities of the organism are taxed beyond their limits.

With the growing awareness of the weakness of instinct and superego theory and the questionable distinction between gratifying behavior and defense, psychoanalysts and psychologists began to emphasize **ego psychology** (70, 78, 230). This newer trend is of great interest to the student of communicative behavior. Although psychoanalytic formulations represent condensations of a variety of observations which occur over a period of time, they nonetheless reflect communicative behavior much better than did the earlier attempts to reduce behavior to its component forces. Under the term "ego psychology" much valuable information has been collected about the ways patients communicate and on the impact they have upon others, although the findings still are formulated in terms of mechanisms of defense, transference, and countertransference. Since the ego mediates whatever happens inside the organism, the scientific observer and therapist can only perceive whatever has been expressed. At this point, the views of psychoanalysis coincide with those of communication theory. One might even go so far as to say that the psychiatrist who is interested in communication takes up where the psychoanalyst begins to leave off.

DESCRIPTION OF ABNORMAL DEVELOPMENT AND GROWTH

A valuable source of information about disturbed communication is found in the study of the **life cycle** of biological organisms. A tissue, an organism, a group, and a society all undergo transformations in the course of time. These alterations may bring about conflict and tension inasmuch as the adaptive equilibrium with other structures which are characterized by different rates of change may be disturbed. Therefore, any individual has to undergo adaptive developments if he wishes to remain healthy and adjusted to his environment; but if his development is retarded or qualitatively different from the expected or optimal behavior for his age, then pathology is said to exist.

The study of **physical interference with growth** traditionally has been the domain of physicians. Studies of malformations or prenatal diseases which prevent growth (cerebral palsy, hydrocephalus, hermaphroditism, aplasia, dysplasia) have shed some light on the ways of communication of these patients (20). Studies of heredo-familial and degenerative diseases of the central nervous system which interfere with growth (muscular atrophy, sclerotic diseases) (13), although more concerned with physical invalidism, nonetheless contain references to abnormal communicative behavior. Conditions of infectious, toxic, metabolic, or traumatic origin which temporarily or permanently interfere with growth (goiter, infantile paralysis, dwarfism, obesity, blindness, deafness) (172) have given us insight into the compensations that an organism has at its disposal when one area of functioning is interfered with. Some of these conditions, both congenital and acquired, interfere with human relations by distorting physical appearance. Conditions such as squinting, loss of limb, hyperkeratosis, acromegaly, disfiguring scars, and polydactylism deprive the child of his natural appeal. Adults in return tend to pity the child, overprotect him, or reject him (17). Finally, studies of the behavior of the mentally deficient, which contain accurate descriptions of the ways of communication of oligophrenics, have informed us about the influence of intelligence on human interaction (141).

Social interference with growth perhaps has more serious consequences because character invalids—unlike physical invalids—often assume positions of responsibility. Aside from gross cases of physical abuse or neglect of children, social interference with growth is implemented by deviant communication. The phenomenology of keeping a newborn baby alive and the actions necessary to stimulate his further growth are at first indistinguishable from the phenomenology of communication. Only at a later age when symbolic communication has been developed can growth and communication be separated. Communication belongs to those human functions which are the hardest to master and take the longest to learn. Since each step is built upon the previous one and since decades of continuous practice are required before an individual becomes an effective communicator, any interference at an early stage leaves its indelible mark. Stimulation from the environment may be lacking, exaggerated, or ill-timed, and growth therefore may be retarded. Early experiences which constitute the basis for later development may be so inadequate that in spite of proper care in the later years the individual does not reach his full potentiality. The acquisition of skills may be indefinitely postponed if competent teachers are not available or if opportunities for practice are not provided. Thus child psychiatrists, child-development specialists, and biologists have made some of the most significant contributions to the understanding of communication pathology (44, 45, 100, 181).

Functional interference may result in a variety of clinical pictures. The most severe is a form of psychosis which resembles schizophrenia in adulthood (27, 133, 245). Less severe are the psychosomatic conditions such as asthma, convulsions, tics, or skin disorders associated with scratching (28, 244). Then there are the minor disturbances which may range from simple thumbsucking or enuresis to aggressive behavior toward children or adults (113, 247). Some twenty years ago, investigators hoped to correlate early behavior patterns with later clinical symptomatology. In this early phase of child studies, emphasis on social relations (123) led to studies of abandonment, emotional deprivation (83, 237), overprotection (149), delinquency (47), and rivalry or seduction (148). But soon doctors came to recognize that, although massive deprivation or overprotection leaves significant scars, the **what** of social action was perhaps not so important as the **how**. Inconsistency, discontinuity, and poor timing thus were recognized to be even more disturbing than particular kinds of action such as overprotection. Along the same line, Sullivan (242) stressed the disturbing effects of the parents' anxiety upon the child and Szurek (243) emphasized the general attitude of the parent. Ruesch (207, 215) pointed out the fact that nonverbal communication through interpersonal movements has to be mastered before verbal communication can be learned and that in psychotic children nonverbal exchange is extremely deficient.

A great many of the functional disturbances of growth are reported in the literature as **disturbances of learning and maturation.** The prominent role of psychophysiological infantilism, emotional immaturity, and disturbances of identity in the etiology of psychiatric disorders today has been generally accepted (74, 201, 224). However, not all experts would go so far as to subscribe completely to the psychoanalytic doctrine which, in adherence to the genetic principle (106) and the theory of fixation (94), explains psychoneurosis on the basis of repetition compulsion of earlier behavior patterns. The learning psychologists (70, 169), who deal with the same phenomena in terms of conditioning, problem-solving, and learning through imitation, took a somewhat different tack. By dealing with such entities as drives, implementations, cues, and rewards, they specified behavior patterns which are of interest to the student of communication. Particularly does the notion of cue as a problem-solving entity come close to the notions of communication theory.

While for the clinician psychoanalytic formulations prove perhaps more suitable, the experimentalist finds formulations in terms of learning theory more adapted to his needs. However, formulations of growth difficulties in terms of communication seem to satisfy both the clinician and the experimenter. For example, the ways of communication of immature persons can be characterized by lack of diversity of approaches, deficient feedback devices, and overspecialization in certain kinds of languages. Since continued actual participation of the patient in pathological networks seems to be the most significant factor for the continuation of his disturbance, no assumptions about fixation, repetition compulsion, or conditioning need be made. Actually the patient operates in networks in which his deviant ways of communication operate satisfactorily until biological maturity forces him to leave home and seek other communication systems. At such a time, the difficulties in communication begin to show.

Description of Abnormal Experience

Following the descriptive epoch of psychiatry there came in succession, and partly overlapping, the constitutional emphasis, the psychoanalytic era, and the period of studies in human development and growth (171). But no field remains stagnant, and new horizons are constantly opening up. With the growth of field theories and the abandonment of Aristotelian classifications, with the progressive relativism of science and the acceptance of the principles of complementarity and uncertainty, the behavioral sciences gave up many of their futile attempts at establishing causal connections and began to study patterns of interrelatedness. After the fundamentally new viewpoints of the Gestalt psychologists had become accepted (11), European philosophers and psychiatrists, under the influence of

Heidegger and Binswanger, likewise turned away from the dissection of psychic phenomena and their reduction into part functions in order to favor the study of **modes of experience** and the acceptance of that which exists in its totality (235). Within the past two decades, therefore, some psychiatrists slowly gave up the tendency to isolate progressively smaller segments of behavior and turned once more to the study of larger Gestalten and to what today is known as phenomenology (22).

The kindred spirit that governs psychiatrists, psychotherapists, and philosophers often puzzles the more biologically oriented medical men. Although on the surface their interests may appear to be divergent, the bond among them arises from the awareness of a common difficulty. **Language,** particularly written language, does not permit the consideration of all aspects of behavior at once. An individual who wishes to speak or write about an event must use language which by necessity refers to some selected aspect of that event. A listener is capable of understanding the event in its entirety only after having studied not one but a great many selected aspects. Because this procedure is very time-consuming and renders written reports rather bulky, short cuts frequently are taken and consequently many details are omitted. When fewer words are used and a lesser number of aspects are treated, the listener is inclined to pay too much attention to what is mentioned and disregard that which is omitted. This peculiarity of language and the resulting difficulties in the description of behavior have brought about certain verbal classifications which are not based upon the characteristics of pathology but rather upon those of the human reporter and the language he uses (255). Analytic dissections thus are frequently assigned substance and body as if they existed independently of the organism and had a life of their own. This is particularly true of theoretical constructs, be they of the order of final diagnoses or of the order of intervening variables. Terms such as schizophrenia and Oedipus complex do not refer to something the patient experiences or the onlooker can observe. Through abstraction, events which happened at different dates are telescoped and appear as one; gradually the psychiatrist forgets this inherent distortion and becomes a victim of **verbal unreality.**

In giving up the attempt at longitudinal integration, at establishing causes, and at making predictions about future events, the psychiatrist is free to observe and empathize with the patient's experiences of the moment. By making all that happens at any one period of time the focus of observation, by emphasizing the now rather than past or future, the psychiatrist arrives at a cross-sectional appraisal of experience. This attitude has of course a deep therapeutic effect. It helps the patient to live and experience in the present, and this mode is the only one that will help him to engage in meaningful action and participation with others.

The contributions of the existentially oriented therapists (122) have been concerned with such diversified phenomena as understanding (68); the experience of time and space (110); the experience of sexual perversion (38), of having delusions (30), of being afflicted by disease (31), and of being alienated from the self (240). For communication theory, the study of abnormal experience has been valuable in the clarification of selectivities of perception and emphases in evaluation. At the same time, the concern with the now has paved the way for a method of understanding which is devoid of value judgment or scientific dissection. This kind of understanding is a function of analogic thinking (207) which, for the appraisal of nonverbal behavior, is far superior to digital-verbal thinking. Furthermore, this kind of understanding is invariably communicated to the patient and influences his behavior favorably.

DESCRIPTION OF ABNORMAL INTERPERSONAL AND GROUP PROCESSES

Among the disciplines which accumulate knowledge about human beings and the world in which they live, the sciences occupy a specialized position. The scientific method is applicable when the observer can remain uninvolved; when his time, space, and mass scales are different from those of the observed; when he can neglect the identity of the particles he is studying; and when he can concern himself with the quantitative aspects of mass effects. But much information which bears upon the qualitative and unique aspects of identified individuals is lost through scientific procedure; at best, it yields a one-sided picture of human behavior (62).

Although physicians consider mass effects when they deal with bacteria, cells, or antibodies, they nonetheless are primarily concerned with a single, identifiable patient. Through communication, the doctor exerts an influence upon his patient and in turn is influenced by him. For the psychiatrist, the framework of communication or of interpersonal relations has particular significance because it enables him to abandon his relatively artificial position—or shall we say his pretense?—of being an uninvolved scientific observer. Communication theory thus puts the observer back into the network and makes him a **subjective participant** (241). The subjectivity which formerly was regarded as an undesirable by-product is now productively utilized. One of the most significant aids in this approach is the utilization of self as an instrument to gauge the effect the self has upon others and the impact others have upon the self. No longer is the doctor concerned with inferring motivations and intentions and behaving as if he were a supernatural observer; instead, he describes interpersonal processes in terms of the effects communication has upon the participants, including himself. The phenomenology of interpersonal communication (170) hence furnishes a framework in which the subtleties of two-person interaction can be understood. The phenomenology of group behavior furnishes a framework in which individual behavior and psychopathology can be tied to the communication system of still larger groups. Concern with communication of multiperson systems also has another interesting side effect. Information gained about interpersonal and group processes is complementary with information about individual psychopathology and intrapsychic processes. The more we are concerned with one the less we think about the other, never being able to focus on both intrapsychic and interpersonal processes at once.

Present-day explicit knowledge of communicative behavior falls into several areas. A great deal is known about **disturbances of adaptation to existing communication systems** (12, 53, 96), which phenomenon is frequently referred to as culture change (200, 202, 214). An individual's communications may be inappropriate to the social or physical situation and may be ill-matched to language (128), rules, roles, sex, or age of the other participants (217). This inappropriacy can be observed in displaced persons (161, 231, 249), foreigners, delinquent persons (4), liars, impostors (24), and with-drawn, logorrheic (23), mute, or aggressive persons (192).

But **pathology** also may be **induced by others.** In authoritarian, centralized networks, the pathology of the leaders may be trans-mitted to the audience by force of repetition and the use of modern propaganda methods (125). Likewise, anxiety of a mother may be transmitted to her child (243) and panic may spread rapidly in a disorganized group (82). Through contact with persons holding certain attitudes, a complementary type of pathology can be induced (204, 216), and through hypnosis abnormal behavior may be sug-gested (40). In psychotherapy, it is well known that patients dream the sort of dreams their therapists wish to hear. With Freudians, patients have Freudian dreams; with Jungians, they have Jungian dreams. The communicative phenomena referred to as transference elicit certain kinds of countertransference, and vice versa (206). Breakdown of communication can also occur when information transmitted contradicts or is inconsistent with social, biological, and physical reality—that is, the laws of nature. A mother who urges her child to undertake certain tasks prematurely is inviting fail-ure (193).

Disturbances of the **group as a whole** arise when the situation does not provide for help, assistance, security, exchange, opportu-nity, or development of the participants (174). As a result, intra-group tension in the form of splits between minority and majority groups (42) and disturbances in class and caste relations (252) may appear. Rebellion, strife, or disturbed morale, with all its repercus-sions upon the organization, may prevent the successful manage-ment of interpersonal or intrapersonal conflicts. Frequently internal strife may be masked and appear as intergroup tension; this at first may contribute toward a temporary intragroup integration, but later the internal dissension begins to show, leading eventually to disorganization (117).

In many instances, mental disease can be traced to disturbances of the group as a whole (56, 116). This applies particularly to diffi-culties within the family (46, 178). Usually one individual carries the symptoms and the breakdown of communication is blamed upon him, although the other participants and members of the family are usually as abnormal in terms of communication as the one who is labeled sick. Rehabilitation is here a function of changing the network as a whole (210).

Some disturbances of communication can be traced directly to **structural defects of the communication network.** For example, a network may not be capable of handling the load of messages and is taxed above its capacity. Or a network may be deficient in feedback circuits and corrective devices; its inflexibility then invites disaster. Or the language, codification, or interpretation schemes may not be shared by all participants; overspecialization, which in large groups is called nationalism, then prevents successful communication (67). Overpopulation of one area and underpopulation of another leads to inadequate distribution of facilities and lopsided communication. Thus mental disease has been related to ecological factors (71, 76, 77, 147) and, on a small scale, breakdown of communication in a mental hospital likewise has been traced to inadequate arrangement of the networks (238). But inasmuch as disturbed communication is the subject of this book, the reader will find more details in the following chapters.

GENERAL SOURCE MATERIAL ON HUMAN COMMUNICATION

Before proceeding to the discussion of communication pathology proper, and particularly because disturbances of communication are related to such a variety of other factors, a brief review of the general source material on human communication here seems to be in place. The list of references is by no means complete, but the books and articles in the list below may help the reader to understand disturbed communication within the wider network of human communication.

1. The history and development of the art and science of communication:

   CHERRY, E. C.: The communication of information. Amer. Scientist, 40: 640–664 (1952).

   HOGBEN, L.: *From Cave Painting to Comic Strip.* New York: Chanticleer Press, 1949.

2. Scientific philosophy and theory of communication:

   AYER, A. J., and Others: *Studies in Communication.* London: Secker & Warburg, 1955.

Conference on Cybernetics: *Circular Causal and Feedback Mechanisms in Biological and Social Systems.* Trans. 6th, 7th, 8th, 9th, and 10th Conferences. New York: Josiah Macy, Jr., Foundation, 1949–1953.

KORZYBSKI, A.: *Science and Sanity* (3rd ed.). Lakeville, Conn.: Int. Non-Aristotelian Lib. Publ. Co., 1948.

WIENER, N.: *Cybernetics, or Control and Communication in the Animal and the Machine.* New York: Wiley, 1948.

3. Information:

RAPOPORT, A., WEAVER, W., GERARD, R. W., SAMSON, E. W., and KIRK, J. R.: Information theory. ETC., 10: 241–320 (1953).

SHANNON, C. A., and WEAVER, W.: *The Mathematical Theory of Communication.* Urbana: University of Illinois Press, 1949.

4. Anatomical and physiological foundations of communication:

ASHBY, W. R.: *Design for a Brain.* New York: Wiley, 1952.

CANNON, W. B.: *Bodily Changes in Pain, Hunger, Fear, and Rage.* New York: Appleton, 1929.

McCULLOCH, W. S.: Why the mind is in the head. Pp. 42–57 in *Cerebral Mechanisms in Behavior* (The Hixon Symposium). (L. A. Jeffress, Editor.) New York: Wiley, 1951.

McCULLOCH, W. S., and PITTS, W.: The statistical organization of nervous activity. J. Amer. Statistical Assoc., 4: 91–99 (1948).

WALTER, W. G.: *The Living Brain.* New York: Norton, 1953.

5. Perception:

ALLPORT, F. H.: *Theories of Perception and the Concept of Structure.* New York: Wiley, 1955.

BEXTON, W. H., HERON, W., and SCOTT, T. H.: Effects of decreased variation in the sensory environment. Canad. J. Psychol., 8: 70–76 (1954).

6. Evaluation, decision-making, and memory:

CAMERON, D. E.: *Remembering.* New York: Nerv. & Ment. Dis. Monogr. No. 72, 1947.

PIAGET, J.: *Judgment and Reasoning in the Child.* New York: Harcourt, Brace, 1928.

SNYDER, R. C., BRUCK, H. W., and SAPIN, B.: *Decision-making as an Approach to the Study of International Politics.* Foreign Policy Analysis Project, Series No. 3. Princeton: Organizational Behavior Section, Princeton University, 1954.

7. Transmission and expression:

ALLPORT, G., and VERNON, P.: *Studies in Expressive Movement.* New York: Macmillan, 1933.

DARWIN, C.: *The Expression of the Emotions in Man and Animals* (1872). New York: Philosophical Library, 1955.

8. Digital, verbal, and linguistic aspects of communication:

HAYAKAWA, S. I.: *Language in Thought and Action* (1941) (2d ed.). New York: Harcourt, Brace, 1949.

OSGOOD, C. E., and SEBEOK, T. A. (Editors): *Psycholinguistics: A Survey of Theory and Research Problems.* Int. J. Amer. Linguist., Memoir 10 (Indiana University Publications in Anthropology and Linguistics), 1954.

PIAGET, J.: *The Child's Conception of Number.* London: Routledge & Paul, 1952.

9. Analogic and nonverbal aspects of communication:

BIRDWHISTELL, R. L.: *Introduction to Kinesics.* Louisville: University of Louisville, Department of Psychology and Social Anthropology, Research Manual, 1952.

CRITCHLEY, M.: *The Language of Gesture.* London: Arnold, 1939.

RUESCH, J.: Nonverbal language and therapy. Psychiatry, 18: 323–330 (1955).

RUESCH, J., and KEES, W.: *Nonverbal Communication.* Berkeley and Los Angeles: University of California Press, 1956.

10. Language:

MILLER, G. A.: *Language and Communication.* New York: McGraw-Hill, 1951.

MORRIS, C. W.: *Signs, Language, and Behavior.* New York: Prentice-Hall, 1946.

11. The conversational and literary aspects of communication:

LEE, I. J.: *The Language of Wisdom and Folly.* New York: Harper, 1949.

LEE, I. J.: *Customs and Crises in Communication.* New York: Harper, 1954.

MEERLOO, J. A. M.: *Conversation and Communication.* New York: International Universities Press, 1952.

12. Social situations, roles, rules, and the individual:

MEAD, G. H.: *Mind, Self, and Society.* Chicago: University of Chicago Press, 1934.

PIAGET, J.: *Play, Dreams, and Imitation in Childhood.* New York: Norton, 1952.

RUESCH, J., and PRESTWOOD, A. R.: Interaction processes and personal codification. J. Personality, 18: 391–430 (1950).

WARNER, W. L., MEEKER, M., and EELLS, K.: *Social Class in America.* Chicago: Science Res. Assoc., 1949.

13. Social interaction and interpersonal communication:

PARSONS, T., and BALES, R.: *The Family; Socialization and Interaction Process.* Glencoe, Ill.: The Free Press, 1955.

PIAGET, J.: *The Language and Thought of the Child* (2d ed.). London: Kegan Paul, Trench, Trubner, 1932.

RUESCH, J.: Social technique, social status, and social change in illness. Pp. 123–136 in *Personality in Nature, Society, and Culture* (2d ed.). (C. Kluckhohn, H. A. Murray, and D. M. Schneider, Editors.) New York: Knopf, 1953.

SULLIVAN, H. S.: *The Interpersonal Theory of Psychiatry.* New York: Norton, 1953.

14. Group processes:

CARTWRIGHT, D., and ZANDER, A. (Editors): *Group Dynamics.* Evanston, Ill.: Row, Peterson, 1953.

HARTLEY, E. L., and HARTLEY, R. E.: *Fundamentals of Social Psychology.* New York: Knopf, 1952.

REDFIELD, C. E.: *Communication in Management.* Chicago: University of Chicago Press, 1953.

15. Societal networks:

DEUTSCH, K. W.: *Nationalism and Social Communication.* New York and Cambridge: Wiley and Technology Press of M.I.T., 1953.

WIENER, N.: *The Human Use of Human Beings—Cybernetics and Society.* Boston: Houghton Mifflin, 1950.

16. Propaganda, communication, and public opinion:

LAZARSFELD, P. F.,and ROSENBERG, M. (Editors): *The Language of Social Research.* Glencoe, Ill.: The Free Press, 1955.

SMITH, B. L., LASSWELL, H. D., and CASEY, R. D.: *Propaganda, Communication, and Public Opinion.* Princeton: Princeton University Press, 1946.

17. Social and cultural factors in medicine:

CAUDILL, W.: Applied anthropology in medicine. Pp. 771–806 in *Anthropology Today.* (A. L. Kroeber, Editor.) Chicago: University of Chicago Press, 1952.

RUESCH, J.: Social factors in therapy. Pp. 59–93 in *Psychiatric Treatment* (ARNMD 31). Baltimore: Williams & Wilkins, 1953.

SIMMONS, L. W., and WOLFF, H. G.: *Social Science in Medicine.* New York: Russell Sage Foundation, 1954.

18. Communication and psychiatry:

HOCH, P. H., and ZUBIN, J. (Editors): *Psychopathology of Communication.* New York: Grune & Stratton. (In press.)

JOHNSON, W.: *People in Quandaries.* New York: Harper, 1946.

RUESCH, J.: Synopsis of the theory of human communication. Psychiatry, 16: 215–243 (1953).

RUESCH, J.: Psychiatry and the challenge of communication. Psychiatry, 17: 1–18 (1954).

RUESCH, J., and BATESON, G.: *Communication: The Social Matrix of Psychiatry.* New York: Norton, 1951.

19. Development and growth:

GESELL, A.: *The First Five Years of Life* (8th ed.). New York: Harper, 1940.

GESELL, A., and Ilg, F. L.: *The Child from Five to Ten.* New York: Harper, 1946.

HOCH, P. H., and ZUBIN, J. (Editors): *Psychopathology in Childhood.* New York: Grune & Stratton, 1955.

ISAACS, S.: *Social Development in Young Children.* London: Routledge, 1945.

20. Communication in the animal world:

Conference on Group Processes: *Group Processes.* Transactions of the first conference. New York: Josiah Macy, Jr., Foundation, 1955.

FRISCH, K. VON: *Bees.* Ithaca: Cornell University Press, 1950.

TINBERGEN, N.: *Social Behavior in Animals.* London: Methuen, 1953.

21. Automatic control:

BROWN, G. S., and CAMPBELL, D. P.: Control systems. Scientific American, 187: 56–64 (1952).

RIDENOUR, L. N.: The role of the computer. Scientific American, 187: 116–130 (1952).

Chapter Two

Gratifying and Frustrating
Communication

Statement and Response

THE SCIENTIFIC analysis of a communication process cannot encompass all aspects of the interchange at once. The human mind has to treat **successively** that which in nature happens **simultaneously**. Similarly, in ordinary daily-life communication a listener cannot respond to all the shadings of another person's statements at once; he must reply first to one part and later perhaps to another part, except that in practice he usually never gets around to replying to these other parts of the message because in the elapsed time a new and perhaps more exciting topic might have arisen. Thus, in replying a receiver will selectively shape his responses around certain parts or aspects of the message and neglect other parts and aspects which he deems to be irrelevant. His acknowledgment may be an interpretive response to the statement of the sender or, of course, it can also constitute a new message to which he expects the other person to reply.

The distinction between **initial statement and response** is tied to the recognition of the roles of sender and receiver, which in two-person situations are subject to rapid change. In larger groups, these roles are somewhat more stable in time. Although it must be granted that in a rapid exchange of messages the roles of sender and receiver cannot be clearly distinguished, there are in social life a great many situations in which these roles can be clearly observed and the initial statement can be isolated from the reply. The observing participant can easily distinguish the reply of parents who acknowledge the spontaneous expressions of their children—questions which are designed to gather information, actions which need guidance, and pleas for help and support. The man in the audience can separate the response of a lecturer from the questions of his students; and we all as recipients of a present usually acknowledge actual or pretended pleasure at the arrival of a gift and reply in words to the initial statement—the gift from the other person.

Responses or acknowledgments constitute **feedback patterns** which occur when a person selectively replies to one or more aspects of a message in preference to another. The patterns which result from various combinations of initial statements and replies are similar in both children and adults, with the distinction that in the case of a child a reply to his message has a considerably greater impact upon his character formation than in the case of the adult. In children, communicative exchange falls upon virgin soil and the child has no way of controlling or avoiding communication with certain adults upon whom he is dependent. An adult, either by selectively responding to the statements of the child or by exposing the child to statements of his own, imperceptibly directs and controls the communication system of the child. Selective feedback in parent-child communication is, therefore, of greatest interest in the study of personality development, particularly with regard to those repetitive patterns which govern the life of any family.

We know that to secure healthy development any person has to be supplied with the right kind of stimulus at the right time and in the right amount. This is particularly true of children. **Quantitatively inappropriate responses** of the parents to the infants' primitive messages such as "I am cold," "I am wet," "I am tired," or "I have had enough" establish deviant feedback circuits. Ill-timed or quantitatively inappropriate responses on the part of the adult tend to confuse the child; in such instances, the child's expressed desires either are not responded to sufficiently or are responded to too early, too late, or in such an overwhelming way that the child feels paralyzed. Even well-meant but premature steering of the infant on the part of the adult may reinforce, attenuate, or frequently alter his original expression and constitute an interference with his growth. Disturbances which arise out of quantitatively inappropriate responses are of greater importance in the younger child whose capacities for perception, evaluation, and transmission are exceedingly limited. Later on, as the child grows up and acquires the mastery of speech, locomotion, and social approaches, the quantitatively deviant reply is of lesser importance. By that time the discrimination of cues identifying various actions and objects is already well under way and the qualitatively inappropriate responses begin to do greater harm. In adult life, finally, quantitatively erroneous responses of others elicit reactions of frustration; but if the situation does not last too long and does not occur repeatedly usually no permanent harm results.

Qualitatively inappropriate responses can produce disturbances which are in no way different from those produced by the quantitatively inappropriate responses. To offer food when thirst is prominent, to offer fluids when excessive cold has to be managed, are self-explanatory examples. But most interaction does not take place on such a plane. The child's awareness of his own needs, the clarification of cues, the acceptance of reasonable limits, all these occur when adults reply to the child's messages in a clear and unequivocal way. If, however, the adults reply in ambiguous terms, if their reply does not clarify the statement of the child, or if their answers are inconsistent or inappropriate to the situation, then the child is frustrated and the foundations for disturbances of communication have been established.

The observation of patterns of communication prevailing in childhood does not suffice for accurate **prediction** of adult personality structure, social relations, and ways of communication. The ultimate adult patterns of communication will also depend upon a number of factors which often escape observation. The frequency of repetition of certain interchanges in later childhood, the absence or presence of patterns which might compensate for or attenuate the damaging effects of other messages, the social situations in which an individual might find himself are variants which cannot be foreseen. Thus there are some indeterminate factors which escape prediction; however, observations of adult patterns of communication—and especially of disturbances of communication—lend themselves to accurate prediction. People who use certain types of qualitatively devious acknowledgments not only get themselves into trouble, but since their patterns are fairly stabilized by the time they are grown up, their recurrent use of devious acknowledgment can be assumed to be certain.

SUCCESSFUL COMMUNICATION

Formal characteristics

Public opinion holds that gratifying communication is almost exclusively related to the receipt of pleasant and gratifying news. In this book, however, the proposition is maintained that gratifying communication is principally, although not exclusively, related to certain **formal characteristics of communication**. In emphasizing the ongoing process of communication rather than any specific content, the author advances the hypothesis that any change in content of a message is accompanied by a change in the form of communication. This change in form may consist of a shift in the neuronal network, a shift of the channels or symbolization systems used, or a change of action sequences, or it may involve a change in the wider social network. The relationship between the form and the content of a message is of importance because content, or the "what" of a message, is difficult if not impossible to assess scientifically. The forms of communication, in contrast, which include all those features embodied in the "how" of communication, lend themselves much better to clinical observation and scientific reporting.

Perhaps the foremost criterion of successful communication consists of the presence of **feedback circuits** which provide an opportunity to relay back to the original sender the effects that a statement has had upon other participants. Such feedback networks can be detected when a formal analysis of the pathways of communication reveals provisions for rectification of errors, consideration of the audience and its reaction, and the awareness that the steering of successful communication is based upon the cooperation of at least two if not more people. Clinically, a person who is participating in a well-functioning network is characterized by the presence of an operational attitude—curiosity, and eagerness to find out what the effects of a statement or an action may have been. Such a person usually considers other individuals and groups in terms of whether or not they will be able to cope with the effects of a projected statement or an anticipated action. Such a person incessantly works toward improvement of the facilities for feedback. He asks others for suggestions and incorporates these in his new plans.

Another criterion of successful communication is related to the successful mutual **fit of over-all patterns and constituent parts.** Such integration provides for specialization and diversification of functions without frustrating the participating members through over-specialization of their tasks. In such networks, operations are carried out without overload of one part and underload of another. No particular station is either overburdened with or completely relieved of work. To the casual observer, a well-functioning network or individual appears to operate without effort. Thus the attention of the onlooker is not directed toward any particular function; the whole appears as an integrated unit.

The **efficiency of operation** is a third criterion of successful communication. In effective functioning, the language used is representative of the technical operations and is simple and economical in its denotation. Instructions are clear, agreed upon, and understood by all. The participating members seem to be aware of the goal of their activities and the purpose of their communications. Messages are timed so that the receivers are capable of perceiving and interpreting them without undue haste.

A fourth criterion is related to the **flexibility** of network and procedures. Roles and rules are modifiable; people can substitute for each other; and flexibility is maintained in order to reorganize the network according to changing conditions. Usually there are safety devices present. In groups, these are special circuits for expediting unusual messages or actions—for example, the postal provisions for special delivery, the emergency networks of police and fire departments, or the right of chaplains to break through the established channels to call the commander's attention to unusual cases. In a flexible network, there always seems to exist a tendency toward growth, regardless of whether the system consists of a single individual, a small group, a large organization, or a society of people.

This growth is implemented by long-term planning, flexible revisions of the program, and an emphasis on taking the hurdles as they come. Such a procedure results in smoothness of operation, acceptance of errors and provisions for their correction, and ability to cope with little tensions as they arise.

~ If feedback, appropriacy, efficiency, and flexibility constitute the principal **criteria of successful communication,** there exist nonetheless a host of other indices which may appear in isolated cases only. In some instances, the absence of pathology may serve as a criterion of successful communication, although it must be granted that in certain situations pathology can lead to efficient communication, provided that all the participants share in certain specific ways in the disturbance. In other instances, creative production may be an index of successful communication, while again in other cases organizational skill may indicate an individual's communicative success.

The subjective reaction of pleasure

Scientific analysis of formal characteristics is not all there is to the assessment of communication. Another, and perhaps the most important, criterion of successful communication is the **gratification** that an exchange of messages provides for the participants. The release of tension experienced after a successful communication contrasts with the persistent production of unresolved tension after failure to communicate. To be understood is a pleasure; to reach an agreement is expedient and pleasant; to be understood and to reach agreements is deeply gratifying. If such gratification is repeated over and over again, the individual or group is likely to be well informed, adaptable, and capable of withstanding frustration. Apparently those who are participants in a successful network and function well themselves have all the advantages over those who are less fortunate. Scientifically, these facts are not yet fully understood. But empirically they have been well established.

For the sake of discussion, an exchange shall be considered in two sections: Person A's attempts to get an idea across and Person B's endeavor to **understand** what A is trying to say. These two parts should not be conceived of as single isolated sentences, although on occasion such may be the case. More often than not, such an exchange will involve a series of statements made by the two persons in question. Theoretically speaking, successful communication takes place when correspondence of information between the two persons has been established. In practice, however, nobody can verify whether such correspondence has been achieved and the observer can only infer from certain indices derived from the communicative behavior of the participants whether agreement has been reached. The most significant criterion of agreement is found in the acknowledgment of Person A's statement by B and the effect such acknowledgment has upon Person A. In the process of communication, therefore, four possibilities have to be distinguished:

1. **Acknowledgment** of receipt of statement **with understanding.** When Person B fully acknowledges the statements of Person A in terms which are qualitatively and quantitatively satisfactory to A, he indeed expresses in word, gesture, or action the following idea: I fully understand; I appreciate what you say; I get it.

Such positive acknowledgment indicates that a sensation of closure has occurred in Person B; in turn, he signals to A that he believes that correspondence of information has been established. When Person A perceives this acknowledgment, he compares in his mind Person B's behavior with the reaction he expected. If the acknowledgment of Person B matches the expectancies of A, and A signals to B that such is the case, acknowledgment of understanding has occurred. Person A's experience of being understood is related to his ability to have elicited in B a piece of information similar to the one held by himself. The success of this action produces in A a sensation of pleasure and satisfaction.

2. **Acknowledgment** of receipt of statement **without understanding.** Now a word about negative acknowledgment. When Person A makes a statement, he anticipates several possibilities: first, that he will be understood; second, that he will not be understood; third, that his statement will be distorted. As his attention is geared to the assessment of these possibilities, he attempts to determine whether or not Person B is disposed to perceive his intentions. Regardless of whether the statement has been understood or not, Person B's readiness to explore the intentions of A, to listen to what he has

to say, and to grasp the way he feels is reflected in an attitude which is easily perceived. To find readiness to be understood is gratifying, irrespective of whether or not understanding can be achieved or agreement can be reached. Therefore, negative acknowledgment, implying lack of understanding but readiness to listen further, can be as gratifying as positive acknowledgment to the effect that the statement has been understood. In this latter case, Person B may express in word, gesture, or action the following idea: I do not understand; I do not get it; Say it differently; Elaborate further.

3. Acknowledgment of **mutual agreement.** Acknowledgment of agreement existing between Person A and Person B in terms which are qualitatively and quantitatively satisfactory to both involves reciprocal statements expressing the idea: We got together; We made a deal; I am of the same opinion as you are; We have the same interests.

Whenever people attempt to reach agreements, they limit the universe of discourse. Agreement thus is reached at the price of neglecting the areas of disagreement. Since the needs of individuals and groups change as time passes on, complete agreement on all subjects is never maintained over a long period of time. It seems inherent in the processes of living that agreements are limited in time and as to subject matter. If there were complete and permanent agreement, man's chance for survival would be reduced by elimination of alternative ways of thinking and acting.

The pleasure experienced in reaching an agreement is somewhat different from the pleasure experienced in being understood. Understanding requires the benevolent attitude of another individual, while agreement in no way implies such an attitude. Thus it is easier to reach a limited agreement than it is to be fully understood. Many agreements are reached between people in one area without the participants' testing agreement or disagreement in other areas. But if agreement is accompanied by rather complete mutual understanding, then the pleasure experienced is extremely gratifying.

4. Acknowledgment of **mutual disagreement.** Disagreement existing between Person A and Person B may be acknowledged in a variety of ways:

—By the absence of any acknowledgment, which indicates lack of both understanding and agreement—for example, somebody's walking out of a conference in protest.

—By hostile responses without previous warning that this would be the form of interaction—for example, initiation of hostilities without declaration of war.

—By phony mutual assurances of the existence of agreement without preceding clarification in view of a past record of disagreement—for example, political opponents' shaking hands and proclaiming brotherhood on the occasion of a patriotic gathering.

—By the overt declaration that no agreement can be reached, leaving the future course of events open—for example, negotiations of two business firms for merger that did not materialize.

—By the overt declaration that no agreement can be reached and that from now on hostilities will take the place of conferences—for example, the formal declaration of war.

The reactions of pleasure and frustration in the face of disagreement are variable. Some people delight at the outbreak of hostilities, being relieved of the task of seeking compromises and feeling more related to the opponent in battle than at the conference table. Others may feel depressed when they see that they are not understood and that no agreement can be reached. On the whole, the stronger the ego boundaries of an individual the better he can tolerate disagreement without ill effects. But an individual who is dependent upon others for proper functioning and whose abilities and limitations are not clearly delineated will react with frustration to any kind of disagreement. It is well to point out, however, that many overt disagreements are based upon the mutual **agreement to disagree.** For example, any debate, boxing bout, or argument is based upon agreements about how to disagree. The fight is then carried on according to certain rules, and only when these are broken—for example, when a fighter hits below the belt—does real disagreement come into being.

Understanding and nonunderstanding, agreement and disagreement, thus are phases which occur in the process of healthy, normal, and potentially successful communication. But if misunderstanding and disagreement become goals in themselves, then we deal with a pathological process of communication.

DISTURBED COMMUNICATION

Formal characteristics

In the past, many of the phenomena described under the heading of psychopathology were considered as emergent events. Their sudden appearance was regarded as a step rather than as a **continuous function**, and the healthy person was thought of as lacking the features which characterized the insane. But more detailed studies soon revealed that the so-called normal person is not radically different from the mentally ill person. For example, it was discovered that every person has a breaking point and that people differ only with regard to the point at which the break occurs (10). Basically so far, no significant structural differences have been found to exist between normal behavior, on the one hand, and the psychoneuroses, personality disturbances, and functional psychoses, on the other. In modern considerations of pathology, therefore, the distinction between normal and abnormal, sane and insane, neurotic and psychotic, has become blurred. And what was formerly thought of in the psychoses associated with brain disease as a simple one-to-one relation between brain lesions and psychological dysfunction has in recent times turned out to be a much more complex relationship. Frequently the clinical picture is more significantly related to the premorbid personality structure of the patient than to the localization of the lesion in the brain (109).

Stimulated by the above-mentioned developments, the search for a **universal function** which characterizes healthy and ill people alike resulted in a progressively more intensive study of human communication. Every person is equipped with the potentialities of communicating with others, with the exception, perhaps, of babies with severe brain lesions. Disturbances of behavior—and this includes psychopathology—are accompanied and probably steered by the functions of communication. In focusing on the processes of communication, therefore, a way has been found to describe normal and abnormal behavior on a continuum and to discard the theory of the emergent and discontinuous nature of mental pathology.

The distinction between sick and healthy people, therefore, can be based upon quantitative differences of communicative behavior. But the quantitative definition does not take into account an entirely different set of disturbances: those that result from applying a form of communication at the **wrong time** or at the **wrong place**. A statement made by Person A may be a perfectly acceptable one. The counterstatement made by Person B also may be perfectly acceptable. But when the two statements are considered together, the combination of the first statement with the second may give the whole exchange the flavor of the abnormal. Nobody who says in a friendly voice "Good morning" considers "Kamala, an East Indian tree" a normal response. Timing, spacing, fit, and probability of occurrence thus are important considerations which may crisscross or overlap the purely quantitative aspects of disturbances of communication.

Disturbances of communication thus are characterized by two aspects: the quantitative deviation and the inappropriate pattern. Both contribute to communicative pathology, the **definition** of which can be remembered by the following verse:

> Too much,
> Too little,
> Too early,
> Too late,
> At the wrong place,
> Is the disturbed message's fate.

In considering pathology of communication, a distinction has to be made between disturbances which affect children and those which involve adults. In **childhood**, communication with the parents serves a dual purpose. It transmits information and it teaches communicative skills. The acquisition of a body of knowledge and of communicative skill are prerequisites for the development of autonomy. Parents and teachers exercise their prerogative in selecting the value systems to which they wish to expose children. But selectivity means control. Deviations in personality development occur when early in life controls are administered too intensively or too long, or when they are missing altogether. Where early and strict selectivity is imposed upon the child, the proper balance between anticipatory behavior and realistic action becomes disturbed. Premature specialization requires skills which the child is not prepared to master. It produces in the youngster a sense of helplessness and inferiority. As a result, the child must continuously rely upon the help of others, and this interferes with the development of autonomy. If in addition every minute of the child's time is occupied and scheduled, even his fantasy may falter. Under such circumstances, his courage for experimentation is curtailed and the child tends superficially and indiscriminately to imitate the adult, who in turn feels flattered at having become an apparent idol to the child. There where parental control prevents the development of autonomy or where the parent-child relationship is limited to particular topics, specialized channels, unusual skills, specific verbalizations, or gestures, one function tends to be overvalued while equally important functions remain undeveloped.

In cases in which the parents do not exert any control, the child is faced with another kind of difficulty; he is exposed to so many choices that he is not able to coordinate the various components of experience. The integration of unconscious motivation, conscious thought, effective implementation, and modification of environment through action is a long and complicated process. The child may achieve this unity only when the motivation is appropriately matched to the implementation, when the effects achieved have been correctly anticipated, and when the rewards specifically satisfy the needs. When selectivity on the part of the parents is missing, the do's and the don't's are not clearly defined and repressions essential for further growth cannot be solidly established. The child who is left to himself may on his own establish some contact with outsiders. However, such casual relations usually do not last long enough to teach the child more consistent ways of communication.

In **adulthood**, the exercise or practice of communication does not materially change the methods of communication of an individual. After a person has reached the age of twenty or thirty, his ways of communication are set. This does not imply that a therapist skilled in the management of disturbances of communication could not influence or change such practices; as a matter of fact, this occurs all the time, but the effort, exercise, and time involved are great. Furthermore, at this age life situations have been found which fit the existing patterns of communication, and the material or emotional investment in marriage, profession, or business may be too great to allow an easy change.

The characteristics which enable an **observer** to recognize disturbances of communication frequently emerge only after prolonged contact with a person or group. When an outside observer is introduced into a group, it will take him some time to get acquainted with the members, to learn their particular language, to detect who talks to whom and about what. After the observer has become thoroughly familiar with the characteristics of the network, he eventually is able to detect those aspects of the system which are not functioning satisfactorily. Foremost among the formal criteria is the observation that interference with the free flow of messages must lead to a disturbance of communication. Similar to a broken power line which can black out a whole village, a small disturbance of communication in one part of the human network can interfere with the functioning of the whole network.

Interference with the free flow of messages manifests itself in several ways: messages do not get through; letters, presents, or telephone messages are not delivered; oral communiqués either are not relayed or are mutilated. Appropriate replies cannot be obtained, and correction through feedback does not function. Although there is evidence that initial communiqués reach their destination, no reply is received in due time. Petitions and applications are acknowledged but not acted upon; desired explanations are not given, and the receivers do not seem to react to the information contained in the initial communiqués.

A second criterion is the **inappropriacy of the reply.** Either it does not fit the circumstances or it is irrelevant and is not matched to the initial statement. The reply may be exaggerated, as in the case of the person who explodes or is visibly upset when asked a polite question; or it may be overwhelming, as it is to a child who asks for a utensil and is immediately given a whole battery of implements.

Inefficiency of communication manifests itself in the use of clumsy language and circumstantiality. Inability to read or write or to use modern communication machinery such as telephone, typewriter, or recording machines seriously interferes with successful communication. Bombardment with messages or complete silence; continuous, tiresome chatter; insistence; or repetitiousness all lead either to redundancy or to loss of information. The absence of enlightening remarks and of statements which might guide a person in the right direction are equally disturbing. In this case, warnings which tell the other person what he does wrong or comments on how successful he has been cannot be relied upon to steer behavior.

Lack of flexibility in the communication network manifests itself in exaggerated control. Every message is checked and counterchecked; every action is prescribed, as in security setups in wartime or as in the case of mothers who are overprotective of their daughters. Extreme redundancy and loss of information are characteristic of these conditions. In exaggerated permissiveness, everybody can say and do anything he wishes; rules are disregarded and some of the exchange resembles chaos. Information is thus inefficiently disseminated.

The subjective reaction of frustration

While the above symptoms do not exhaust the list of indices of disturbed communication, they may illustrate the nature of the criteria. They are based on people's experience that a balance has to be found between adequacy of reply and introduction of new topics, between self-expression and adaptation to the situation, between repetition and new formulation, and between flexibility and rigidity. This balance, which is geared to the human being's tolerance for social stimulation and his need for expression and action, is frequently upset. The resulting **frustration** becomes the foremost **criterion of disturbed communication.** When a person cannot think clearly or cannot reach a somewhat unambiguous feeling state, signs of frustration appear. Then the individual feels tense, restless, irritable, or wound up. Communication within himself apparently has broken down. When a person cannot talk reasonably with another person, when understanding and agreement cannot be reached, the same signs of frustration make their appearance. Here, apparently, interpersonal communication has broken down. When a person is excluded from a group, either because of social prejudice or because sanctions have been invoked by the group against that individual, signs of frustration likewise appear. In this case, communication with the other members and with the group as a whole has ceased to exist. Finally, when a person cannot accept certain cultural values, even though the events which indicate the existence of such values do not affect him directly—for example, a lynching in another state —he also becomes frustrated. In this case, the individual feels separated from the other citizens because he does not share the same assumptions about life, which fact leads to or is the result of a breakdown of communication.

From the evidence gained in clinical practice, we seem justified in assuming that the individual becomes frustrated when his habitual connections with others are interrupted or severely curtailed. And if we wish to be old-fashioned, we can postulate the existence of an inherent need in the individual—the **need to communicate.** Apparently communication with self and with others and participation in small groups or larger bodies of people are imperative if the individual wishes to survive and is to remain healthy. Furthermore, we have to conclude that the foremost subjective criterion of disturbed communication is the appearance of signs of frustration. In adulthood, of course, the impact of disturbances of communication is less intense than in childhood, since the adult possesses a number of compensating devices.

The empirically derived postulate of a human need to communicate can be supported by a number of systematic observations. From the history of persons who have been incarcerated in dungeons or condemned to long-term solitary confinement, or of persons who have been in prisons and concentration camps, we know that isolation produces suffering beyond description (37). From animal experiments it has been learned that newlyborns tend to die when separated from the mother, in spite of being properly fed, and that licking by the mother animal is essential for the proper functioning of the intestinal tract of the newborn (194). The experiences gained in orphanages, the information we possess about marasmus infantum and hospitalism, and observations made in the field of child development indicate that in infants the communicative connectedness with the mother is rather specific and that loss of the person with whom communication has been established as well as the absence of tactile stimulation can lead to serious consequences—even death (236).

Chapter Three

The Genesis of
Disturbed Communication

SOME POTENTIALLY DISTURBING PROCESSES

A CAUSE can be defined as a piece of information which describes the conditions under which certain events take place. In medicine, causes usually refer to conditions which have been isolated because of their pragmatic value; either they can be prevented from arising or they can be changed once they have arisen. In the following pages, certain **conditions** have been listed which in combination with other factors are known to contribute toward disturbances of communication. This does not mean that in each and every case the presence of such a condition indicates pathology. Instead, such a condition should be conceived of as an element which in the presence of other aggravating elements will lead to disturbances of communication. Thus, we might label the phenomena described in subsequent pages as potentially disturbing; the actual presence of a disturbance depends on a host of other factors.

Overload and underload

Every communication network is characterized by its capacity to handle signals in transit. When the load is too heavy, the machinery breaks down; when the load is too small, the machinery may deteriorate for lack of use. This principle applies to man as well as to machine, to small networks as well as to large.

Overload for the individual means functioning in excess of his capacity. Every person has limits in terms of his tolerance for stimulation, his ability to cope with ideas and to make decisions, and his energy to perform action. These tolerance limits are largely a function of age. In the first few months of life, when the infant is asleep most of the time, the majority of stimuli tend to be too intense. At this age, the infant has to be protected by the mother from overexposure (123). As the child gets older, he develops a variety of "buffer systems"; he learns delay of gratification and his frustration tolerance increases, reaching its maximum in middle age. In old age, overstimulation is less of a problem than is exhaustion as a result of excessive exercise. But in all age groups stimulation in excess of the tolerance limits leads first to alarm, then to anxiety, and finally to disorganization and breakdown (216).

Children who are exposed to a more or less continuous barrage of demands and expectations tend to develop characteristic disturbances of communication. The parents seem to remain oblivious to the child's limited capacity to absorb such stimulation. To satisfy the parents, the child may react by responding with superficial gestures or words, or he may protect himself by withdrawal; pseudoresponsiveness and obtuseness are ways of reducing the disruptive influence of the parents.

Underload, particularly in the form of emotional deprivation, results in absence of pleasurable affect. In infancy, lack of opportunity to form an attachment to a mother figure, deprivation for a period of at least three to six months, or changes from one mother figure to another seem to be causally related to the development of the affectionless and psychopathic character (39). Adults who do not respond in an appropriate way and deprive the infant of tactile stimulation may precipitate the clinical picture of marasmus infantum. This condition is characterized by the wasting away and occasional death of the child in the absence of any tangible physical findings. It occurs more frequently in homes with rigorous hygienic standards than under conditions of manifestly inappropriate care. Because of their precarious condition, these marantic infants frequently are hospitalized; but medical care alone does not check the progressive course of the disease. Continuous and personalized contact with one and the same nurse seems to be a prerequisite for the babies' favorable response to medical management (195).

Adults who are shut off from the rest of the world usually become introspective. They lose much of their communicative skill and frequently show signs of **apathy** and generally exhibit a lack of zip and zest. Adults who lose a beloved person and are suddenly deprived of their partners tend to develop grief reactions (80). People who have to relinquish certain ideals and abandon well-established standards tend to become depressed. From the standpoint of communication, the **depression** has a reparatory function. When input deriving from another person is suddenly removed, this loss is compensated for by an increased internal input. As the depression deepens, restriction of thought, slowdown of movements, and disregard for external input become lifesaving devices. The individual then simply hibernates and has time to readjust to the changed internal or external conditions (98).

Excessive output, like overwork, when kept up for prolonged periods of time results in fatigue. Movements become slower, coordination suffers, and the efficiency of action is greatly reduced. Under these conditions, the individual's lessened alertness and his lack of distinctiveness in expression seriously interferes with communication. To protect himself, the individual seeks rest, shies away from others, and avoids taking on additional tasks.

Output below par is equally disruptive. Lack of exercise prevents the individual from building up reserve power; his physical fitness suffers; he usually lacks the confidence necessary to tackle physical and mental tasks with any success. Communication with others is seriously impaired when motor disorders affecting speech, facial and gestural expression, and action interfere mechanically with the output functions. Both excessive output and output below par have been extensively studied by the military (10). Every field commander knows the devastating effects that fatigue or inactivity may have upon the morale of the troops. Civilian and military aviation experts are well aware of the problems of operational fatigue; they have entrusted flight surgeons with the supervision of crews in order to adapt activity to the capacities of the individual.

But overload and underload do not afflict the individual alone; they affect all **social networks.** The postal service may break down if too many packages are mailed at once; death may take a heavy toll when people stampede to the exits of a burning assembly hall.

Officials responsible for the safety of the population develop safeguards to ensure maximum efficiency. In emergencies, priority ratings are established; services are rationed; use of facilities and machines is restricted. Government agencies are quite aware that as long as the communication networks in group and society can be kept working without breakdown the health of the nation is assured.

Incorrect timing

Almost all life processes run off in cyclical rhythms and recur after specifiable intervals. Among the biological cycles, the rhythms of sleep and wakefulness, hunger and satiation, exercise and rest, and the menstrual cycle are but a few examples. But biological cycles do not exhaust the instances of periodicity in human life. There are, for example, seasonal cycles: automobile accident rates have their peak in December and their low in June (173); suicides and first admissions to mental hospitals have their highs in June and their lows in December (179). Also there are the periodicities of greater magnitude such as the forty-one-month cycle in business activity or the eighteen-year cycle in building; and finally there are the secular trends in climate and culture which beg an explanation (119).

If we accept for a moment the statistically established facts of rhythm and periodicity, then it matters at what point of the cycle an activity is undertaken. If we try to talk to somebody who is very tired or if we attempt to make a decision when we are hungry, we are likely to meet with failure. Acrobats performing on the high trapeze have to time their signals with split-second precision if they wish to avoid disgrace or death. To be effective, remarks made in a conversation or in a public debate have to be properly timed. One of the basic causes of disturbed communication thus is found in improper timing of messages—improper here referring to "out of season" with regard to short- and long-term biological and social cycles.

Improper timing of signals, statements, and messages has its most devastating effects in early childhood. Not only has every child his own feeding and sleeping rhythms, but most children also have their own gradients of growth which change with advancing age. A sensitive mother will adjust her demands, proffer help, set limitations, and provide for the physical necessities according to the development of the child. And her perception of the infant's readiness is, of course, dependent upon proper scanning of a series of cycles. Obtuseness in perception or compulsiveness in action may induce a mother to time her messages badly. **Ill-timed messages** on the part of parents have to be delivered with greater intensity and have **to be repeated** more often than well-timed ones. In turn, children may react in a variety of ways; one child may try to comply by making a maximum effort, and an ordinary task then becomes a stress situation. For example, a four-year-old child who is fed when tired may eat so slowly that all food becomes cold and unpalatable. In the same situation, another child may have a temper tantrum and refuse to eat at all, while a third one may passively submit and become apathetic. The parent's reaction of exasperation, anger, or withdrawal of affection will further aggravate the situation.

In adulthood, improper timing frequently takes the form of **inappropriate preparation** of the other person for coming events. If a new idea is to be understood, its introduction has to be properly timed. Asking prematurely for a favorable decision when a problem is not fully understood frequently results in failure. For example, when a board of trustees has to pass on a new building plan they must have time to familiarize themselves with the project. Eventually, when enough information has been supplied and enough time has passed, a vote can be called for. But premature action may lead to a refusal of the board to accept the proposal.

Ill-timing may lead to a breakdown in communication when actions or **statements are improperly separated** in terms of time. Nobody can understand anything when at a meeting several people talk at once. Conversely, if a discussant comments on a topic that was brought up earlier, the audience may fail to connect the two events and may dismiss the speaker's comments as irrelevant.

The subject of time relationships in communication has been substantially clarified by experimental psychologists. Both the experimentalist and the communication expert deal with the problem of how most effectively to connect the statement of one individual with the statement of another. In the field of conditioning (239), this sequence is referred to as the relation of conditioned to unconditioned response; in the field of human learning (169), it is referred to as stimulus and response. In communication, this sequence would be referred to as **statement and reply.** To be effective, the statement of Person A and the reply of Person B obviously have to be separated in time. But once a time interval separates the two statements, the coherence or integration into a pattern is facilitated the more closely the statements are connected in time. Thus severe disturbances of communication may occur if this time interval is either too short or too long.

Statements inappropriate to the situation

The number of possible choices is always greater than the number of choices actually made. The understanding of a statement or action depends upon proper assessment of the things that could have been done or said in comparison to those that were actually done or said. To understand the route chosen by an expedition, the career a man has selected, or the topic he elaborated upon in a public speech requires knowledge of the alternatives that existed at a given moment. When a person talks or acts, the bystanders can understand his actions and words only if they can compare the actual choice against a background of available choices. This is possible if they are familiar with the situation or if the speaker takes the trouble to inform the audience explicitly of the **context** that prevailed at the time of the original action and the context that exists at present. Many comic and tragic situations have arisen because people misinterpreted the context of a situation; and many jokes have been constructed on the principle of first misguiding the listener as to the possible choices and then "exploding the bomb" to catch him by surprise.

The formal and informal education of an individual is aimed at transmitting information about the range of possibilities to be expected in any situation. The recognition of the context of an action or statement is the mark of the person who is healthy and successful in human relations. In daily life, therefore, the experienced person constantly compares his action with the context of the situation. For example, if a person is invited to a party the host of which is unknown to him, he may arrive when everything is in full swing and discover that all wear formal dress while he himself is dressed in street clothes. Since he knows that the guests whom he was to meet tend to dress informally, he becomes aware of the fact that he might have come to the wrong house. Upon renewed check, he finally discovers his correct destination.

But for a child who does not receive appropriate instructions, this sense of fit or style may be difficult to acquire. If the mother consistently makes statements that are inappropriate to the situation, the child does not learn to scan the available possibilities correctly. And should they occur to him, he learns to disregard them. For example, a mother who consistently dresses her little son in girlish clothes creates an embarrassing situation at school. The boy eventually may adapt by becoming "insensitive" to wearing the right clothes for the occasion. As he grows older his inappropriate attire may affect others as being odd, peculiar, or displaced, and he thus primes other people in a confusing way. As a result, he has difficulty in establishing communicative contact with other people, and his statements will be received with suspicion.

Difficulties of communication arise either when the individual **misconstrues the context** of a situation or when in the course of an exchange he cannot make clear to others in what capacity he is acting or in what frame of reference he is talking. Among the patients that do not perceive the contexts of situations appropriately we find persons with psychosomatic illnesses, infantile personalities, certain types of psychopaths, many homosexuals, and a large number of ambulatory schizophrenics. Self-centered, narcissistic, and autistic personalities frequently perceive context but neglect to inform others of the context in which they are operating. Acutely psychotic patients not only misconstrue the perceived context but also tend to omit references which might aid the doctor in the interpretation of their verbalized or acted-out fantasies or delusions. Thus, when the doctor attempts to understand certain schizophrenic patients, he may grasp the details of their statements without knowing in what context they are to be interpreted. In many patients with organic psychoses, the perception of the context is disturbed while the expression of what they are talking about is quite comprehensible. Thus, an aged person may misinterpret a situation and mistake the morning toilet for a preparation for an operation; although the situation is misperceived, the action within such a mistaken framework may be quite appropriate.

Devious acknowledgment

Every person who makes a statement expects a response. This reply guides the speaker or writer and steers his subsequent actions. If the response implies understanding on the part of the other persons, the speaker feels that he can proceed on the course he has taken. Appropriate response therefore is one of the most important factors for psychological growth. The child connects his desires, implementations, and gratifications with the responses of the adults. An appropriate response clarifies; it welds desire, implementation, and gratification into a unit. Unsatisfactory acknowledgment, in contrast, has devastating effects: it fuses elements that should be kept separate.

To secure the child's healthy development, his messages have to be replied to with appropriate intensity at the right moment. This is particularly true in the first few years of life, which are characterized by the child's limited ability for delay of gratification and limited tolerance of excessive stimulation. Before the infant is in a position to learn much about language and symbolization systems, communicative exchange is mediated almost exclusively through variations in timing and intensity of stimuli and in changes of context. A sudden and intense noise, an abrupt drop in temperature, a sudden increase in the pressure exerted by mother's hand are the signals to which the infant's organism reacts almost automatically. As the child grows up, qualitatively inappropriate replies become more important than quantitative variations.

In adulthood, quantitatively inappropriate response to statements of others is the mark of the sick. From complete lack of response to excessive response there exists a sliding scale: Lack of response is observed in catatonic and depressive conditions, in trances and dreamlike states, during sleep or in reveries, under anesthesia, in coma, or in excitement or delirium. Minimal response is observed in people who are drowsy, sleepy, or intoxicated. Exaggerated responses are given by persons suffering from diseases such as hyperthyroidism, hypoparathyroidism, tetanus, rabies, alcoholic intoxication, meningitis, and encephalitis, and by anxious, fearful, and panicky persons. The intensity of the reactions is regulated in part by the ductless glands such as the thyroid, parathyroid, adrenal, and pituitary, and in part by the central nervous system. Removal of the inhibitory function of the cortex initially increases the responsiveness to stimuli. With progressive clouding of the sensorium and loss of consciousness (199), exaggerated response to social or physical stimulation diminishes and gives way to paralysis and lack of response. The various stages observed in anesthesia may here serve as a classic example.

Acknowledgment is a particular form of response. It involves recognition of the fact that a statement has content. Acknowledgment thus not only is a response to something that was done or said but also constitutes a specific reply to the referential property of the statement. Exaggerated acknowledgment is observed in those who "lay it on thick," in persons who dramatize, and in those who wish to flatter or win others. Exaggerated acknowledgment is disconcerting to the average person inasmuch as it overstimulates, frustrates, and often embarrasses him.

A variation of the exaggerated acknowledgment is the **poorly timed acknowledgment.** Premature acknowledgment cuts the pleasure of mastery and often prevents completion of an action. Knowing that human beings crave acknowledgment, some people withhold acknowledgment as a means of frustrating or tormenting others. A step-by-step description of this sadistic technique is difficult; clearcut, however, is the effect it produces upon the victim. Similarly, acknowledgment delayed for too long is not sufficiently connected with the initial statement, and in effect it resembles the situation in which a message receives minimal or no acknowledgment.

But quantitative variations do not exhaust the varieties of frustrating replies. **Qualitatively deviant acknowledgment** of a statement constitutes a response which in many instances is extremely damaging. By replying to an incidental aspect of a statement, the receiver disregards the intent of the sender. This the author has called a tangential reply. An example may serve as an illustration. Johnny comes running toward his mother joyously shouting, "Look, I caught a worm!" Mother looks at Johnny and, in a dry, pleasure-killing voice remarks, "Go and wash your dirty hands." The child, entirely deflated, disappointed, and confused, enters the house. By directly initiating a new message—the order to wash hands—when she saw the mud-covered fingers of her youngster, she in fact disregarded his intentional statement. Had the mother said, "Yes, this is a lovely worm," and paused, she then could have initiated a new message: "and now you go and wash your dirty hands."

In executing a **tangential reply**, the receiver takes cognizance of the sender's intention to communicate but disregards the content of the statement. By countering with a side remark, he confuses the sender, who does not understand the connection between statement and reply. The counterstatement of the receiver may bear upon any aspect of the initial statement; it may emphasize the type of language used, pick up one of the qualifications, comment on the emotions of the sender, or illuminate another facet of the same topic. In replying tangentially, the receiver deprives the sender of the pleasure of being understood; at the same time, he makes a bid for control by launching another statement which he expects to be acknowledged in turn. The tangential reply is used by conversation sharks who need to demonstrate their alleged superiority. They bank upon the fact that others will take the trouble to reply to the new topic which they introduce and assume that others will not reply in a tangential way. The tangential reply has particularly devastating effects when the first person is unaware of the shift that has taken place. Thus, any manipulatively gifted person can "make a monkey" out of the other individual. But if the shift has been perceived and the first person is verbally and manipulatively gifted—as small children are not—then this form of reply may backfire on the one who uses it. Finally, if in a conversation both people engage in tangential replies, the exchange becomes disconjunctive and eventually breaks down. This sort of communication is sometimes observed in conversations between schizophrenic patients.

The following scheme (page 56) may re-emphasize the difference between a gratifying reply and a tangential one:

Gratifying reply: Initial statement of Person A
                    Acknowledgment of Person B
                    Full stop
                    New statement of Person B
Tangential reply: Statement of Person A
                    Counterstatement of Person B (with shift of topic)

Threatening content

When in the course of an exchange of messages content impinges upon the anticipatory behavior of the communicators, a number of emotional reactions, varying from pleasure to discomfort, may be elicited. If the individual is capable of managing these reactions, the process of communication will continue uninterrupted; if, however, the content elicits apprehension, anxiety, fear, shame, guilt, or depression, the individual will feel threatened and become defensive, which reaction is likely to interfere with communication.

The content may threaten the security of the individual in several ways:

Messages containing **threats to** the **personal safety** and integrity of the individual may undermine his unconscious beliefs in his own immortality (158). Dangers may be presented in the form of a sentence such as "I shall kill you"; they may appear as a written or oral announcement of loss of employment; or they may appear as disease, imprisonment, or reminders of advancing age.

Messages containing **threats to** existing **human relations** may greatly disturb the individual. Such a message may refer to disease afflicting the children, death of a family member, expulsion from a group, or reduction in status.

Messages **threatening** the successful conclusion of **actions in progress** indicate future frustration. All individuals and animals once set upon a task do not like to be interrupted. Apparently the anticipatory behavior is so strong that anticipated interference is treated as if it were interference itself. The dog that anticipates being robbed of his bone, the child who anticipates having to leave the playground, the lover who anticipates being apprehended by the father of the girl are examples that apply.

Messages **which** when checked upon **do not correspond to reality** are highly disturbing. When a person discovers that he has been the target of lies, unfulfilled promises, or misrepresentations, he usually reacts with anger and mistrust, and he frequently severs relations with the one who has betrayed him. Lies are not threatening in themselves; they are threatening, however, because they raise doubts as to the validity of words; if verbal symbols are not to be trusted to stand for real events, communication and the means of relatedness to others are undermined.

Messages which destroy faith and hope have a paralyzing effect. Operationally, hope can be defined as a belief in a possibility which, although improbable, has a slight chance of occurrence. For example, a wife can expect a husband who is a prisoner of war to return upon cessation of hostilities. If he does not return, she still might hope for some years to come. But if she has been informed of his death by reliable sources and she still hopes, then her hope has become a delusion. The anticipation of pleasure inherent in all hopes helps the individual to tolerate existing frustration. When hope is gone, the existing frustration becomes unbearable.

Messages which interfere with magic thinking are depressing. All people seem to need an area in which thinking is unchecked by rational propositions. As long as magic thinking is shared with others and not contradicted by fact, it is not a sign of psychological disturbance. In society, religion has been entrusted with the organization of this aspect of human behavior. But when people extend their magic thinking to subjects that can be verified and checked or when others do not share their beliefs, then they are considered abnormal. But whether or not pathology exists, any information which threatens, undermines, attacks, or denies the existence of magic beliefs creates anxiety. Countless are the religious wars and innumerable the lawsuits which have been conducted to defend one belief or to attack another; and therapists are familiar with the anxiety which arises in patients when evidence is brought to demonstrate the delusional nature of a belief.

Messages which impinge on pre-set, mandatory responses may be highly disturbing. Obligatory responses may be the result of training— for example, the honor code of warriors requires that insults be dealt with in an almost ritualistic way; or a highly developed sense of responsibility will force a person to take on certain tasks which he cannot refuse when called upon. People are aware of their mandatory reactions and they frequently dread messages which may remind them of their obligations, particularly when these interfere with their freedom.

The emergence of threatening content may create disturbances of communication because under such circumstances ordinary feedback circuits and correction procedures cease to function. The individual then tends to react like a conditioned animal. To overcome the **reflex-like response,** regardless of whether it is inborn or acquired, the individual has to have an unusual frustration tolerance; he must be capable of "keeping his head," and must be able to choose the best of the available solutions rather than to react according to the "built-in" reflex-like safety reactions. Such rational behavior is observed in selected people who have received special training: aircraft pilots, ship captains, statesmen, surgeons, or, in brief, individuals equipped to face emergencies. But most people fall short of this goal, and this includes the majority of patients with the exception of one group. There are ambulatory schizophrenics in whom childhood experiences, training, and indoctrination in conformity have left few traces so that learned automatic responses were faintly established and inborn reflex-like responses were not reinforced. These patients still can scan and choose the most appropriate reaction, provided it can be "figured out." Countless experiences during the war attest to the rational responses of such individuals at the time of stress.

Compensatory and Aggravating Factors

It is difficult to specify the causes of disturbed communication because a single condition rarely is responsible for pathology and one feature may attenuate or aggravate another. Therefore, it is preferable to talk of constellations or patterns which have a certain probability of producing pathology. This probability changes with the age of the individual. Interference with a function that is being learned is more disturbing than interference with a function that already has been mastered. And interference with a function that is salient in a person's pride mechanisms or basic to his interpersonal relations is more disturbing than interference with more peripheral functions. If a girl has been a ballerina and paralysis permanently prevents her from dancing, the disease has interfered not only with her favorite mode of expression but with most of her human relations as well. Her subsequent adjustment will largely depend not upon the severity of the paralysis itself but rather upon other skills and modes of expression which can compensate for her disability. The assessment of pathology of communication thus is intimately tied to the understanding not only of the disturbance itself but also of the various compensating and aggravating factors which stabilize or change the existing pathology.

Aging and predilection age

Age is the most significant single factor in the etiology of communication pathology. In patients of a given age group, etiologically and structurally differing disturbances of communication assume a common flavor. In early childhood, the pathology of communication is primarily related to organic or functional interference with perception and locomotion. Diseases, accidents, or malformations may disable sensory organs or the motor system. In young children, expression is almost entirely nonverbal and the widest use of all muscles is necessary. If disease or trauma affect the eyes or the ears, scanning and observation are not learned. When children are afflicted with infectious diseases, their alertness suffers and drowsiness and even delirium are rather frequent. Functional interference with perception and locomotion has a similarly devastating effect. Children who are not taught to observe and those who are prevented from exercising show the results of this restriction in later difficulties of perception and expression. While interference with interpersonal communication has the most serious consequences in infancy, interference with group communication and decision-making is the crucial factor in adolescence and adulthood. In later years, interference with decision-making and memory are more disturbing than in younger years when few decisions and little recall are expected.

Communication is learned in the course of several decades. Its gradual evolution is largely a function of **biological maturation** with the implied necessity that one step be completed before the next one can be taken. Nonverbal communication exists before verbal communication is practiced, and interpersonal situations have to be managed before group situations can be tackled. If one step is omitted, the individual may still progress, but when he meets a situation which requires a particular form of communication that he has missed he will become disturbed. An only child, for example, who did not participate in extracurricular activities in school and who did not frequent the playgrounds, may progress up to a certain point without knowledge of group relations. But when as an adult he is faced with the problem of getting a job or working in an office, his inexperience with group process may result in anxiety with all its deleterious effects upon communication. Learning to predict and to make decisions requires a long apprenticeship. Therefore, society dares to entrust vital decisions in matters which affect the group only to individuals who are in their forties and fifties. Most executives are found in the age range of fifty to eighty, not only because of seniority but also because of their skill in prediction and decision-making, which is far superior to that of younger men.

Predilection age for various disease groups reflects the fact that people encounter different kinds of difficulties with communication at different stages of development. First **admissions to state hospitals** express the relationship between communicative process and predilection age most clearly (156). In the youngest age groups, admissions for dementia praecox and behavior disorders predominate. This incidence reflects the self-protective response of the child to frustrating interference or lack of parental interest, resulting either in withdrawal or in heightened interaction with the use of action language. In the young adult group, dementia praecox is first among admissions, reflecting the fact that people at that age withdraw from group and interpersonal contact after they have discovered that their communication system does not function in extrafamilial situations. In the middle-aged group, alcoholic psychoses in the male and manic-depressive or involutional psychoses in the female predominate. Alcoholism is the result of strained communication which is characterized by intolerance for differences and disagreement and by sensitivity to personal acceptance or rejection. Drinking, of course, smoothes over these rough spots. Depression results from a high level of aspiration and failure to reach these pre-set goals. This idealism, combined with an exacting conscience, interferes with the correction of information, and communication may become precarious. The person then can no longer be held together by promise of the future. In old-age groups, arteriosclerotic and senile psychoses predominate, indicating that at this age level the organs of communication cannot keep up with the functional demands.

Disease, trauma, and functional interference have the most catastrophic results at that age level at which a function is being developed. Interference with functions that are not being learned has a less disturbing effect. Therefore, one might state that the effect of interference is dependent upon the age at which it occurs. These facts can be embodied in **three principles:** first, the principle of evolution, which requires that simpler functions be mastered before complex ones can be tackled; second, the principle of learning through imitation, which requires that the youngster be in contact with his human tutor; and third, the principle of communicative elaboration, which constitutes a safety valve which is put into operation whenever the youngster meets with frustration. A brief review of the salient features of development and the nature of possible age-specific interferences is reproduced in Table I (pages 62–63).

Coincidence and spacing of traumatic events

If only one condition has to be met, a superb machine usually can be built to fit the purpose. But as more conditions are added, the machine becomes less suitable. So far, no machine has been built which is equally efficient in the air, on land, and in or under the water. Nor do we know of an animal which is equally adept at flying, running, walking, and swimming. In functional adaptation, the same principle applies; **adaptation to one set of conditions** is relatively easy; but as more conditions have to be met, stress increases until a point is reached where a person breaks down or his behavior ceases to be adaptive.

In communication, adaptation to one person's way of communication—for example, his tendency to be redundant—is easy. But to adapt to a system in which there are fast and slow, redundant and succinct, "what-oriented" and "how-oriented" people is more difficult. Adaptation to ten people is more difficult when they are assembled together in one room than when they can be seen one after another in two-person situations. It is easier to accept one piece of bad news than several. Surgeons are well aware that news of the death of a relative should be kept from a patient who has just come out of shock. Likewise, a mother may tolerate the news of the death of her newborn child but may break down upon hearing that her husband has been killed as well. The crucial factors in the adaptation to new circumstances, the learning of different ways of communication, or the acceptance of traumatic information is the spacing and timing of these events.

TABLE I

PATHOLOGY OF COMMUNICATION AND PREDILECTION AGE

Age Level	Salient Features of Development	Age-specific Interference with Communicative Behavior
Intra-uterine period: (40 weeks)	Organism responds to thermal, mechanical, and chemical stimuli.	Toxic, infectious, vascular, hormonal, and mechanical interference with communication apparatus of foetus.
Neonatal period: (1st 12 wks)	Infant learns to respond to tactile, auditory, and visual stimuli.	Stimulation exceeding the tolerance limits of the baby, including neglect and erroneous timing.
Infancy: (3 to 24 months)	Mastery of head, eye, and hand movements (second quarter); trunk and fingers (third quarter); legs and feet (fourth quarter); speech (second year).	Interference with muscular system and locomotion. Premature training, insufficient exercise; absence of nonverbal exchange, particularly in terms of action, may prevent the establishment of feedback processes.
Early childhood: (2 to 5 years)	Interpersonal communication with one person at a time (mother, father, sibling, or other relative or friend).	Interference with speech and social action; selective and tangential responses; separation from mother; and interference with perception.
Later childhood: (6 to 12 years)	Group communication with several persons at a time. Learning communication with children of the same age, with emphasis on members of the same sex.	Interference with group behavior; broken families, nonparticipation in school; separation from father; erroneous setting of limitations; lack of transmission of skills at home; lack of responsiveness of parents in verbal terms.
Adolescence: (12 to 18 years)	Interpersonal communication with members of opposite sex resumed; growing attempts to communicate with members of outgroups.	Interference with participation in autonomous groups, with premating behavior, with attempts to make decisions and to be independent; inadequate provisions for athletic activities and the acquisition of information.
Young adulthood: (19 to late 20's approx.)	Mastery of the complexity and heterogeneity of adult communication and the multiplicity of roles and diversity of rules. Communication with age superiors. The young adult is occupationally placed in a position of subservience; observes and follows orders.	Interference with mating behavior, with the acquisition of skills and the learning of multiple roles. Change-over from family system of communication to other systems may be interfered with by relatives; nonconformance to group practices may jeopardize support from the group.

TABLE I (*continued*)

PATHOLOGY OF COMMUNICATION AND PREDILECTION AGE

Age Level	Salient Features of Development	Age-specific Interference with Communicative Behavior
Middle adulthood: (30 to middle 40's approx.)	Peak of communication with age inferiors and children. Switch from role of perceiver and transmitter to position of greater responsibility.	**Interference with communication vis-à-vis youngsters.** Position between two generations is delicate and ill-defined when pull from either side is too strong.
Later adulthood: (45 to 65, approx.)	Intake of information and learning now displaced in favor of output of information, teaching, governing and ruling. Participation in decision-making groups.	**Interference with independence and decision-making.** Realization of failure to implement self-chosen ideals; collapse of wishful thinking; interference with identification with younger generation.
Age of retirement: (65 to 80, approx.)	Preparation for relinquishment of power and gradual retirement from decision-making. Philosophical considerations after completion of life cycle. Symbolic and global treatment of events.	**Inactivity.** Sudden withdrawal from participation in communication networks. Lack of stimulation.
Old age: (80 +)	Life in retrospect, with emphasis on early memories.	**Interference with equilibrium.** Tolerance limits for over- and understimulation and over- and underactivity quickly reached.

During the formative years, adaptation of the human organism is directed toward two sides—toward the requirements of the organism and toward the demands of the environment. The child has to meet the restrictions and the necessities of functioning imposed upon him by the growth of organs and organ systems at the same time that he has to meet the expectations of other people. Therefore, in periods of intensive growth—for example, during teething, the learning of walking, or the spurt of physical growth at puberty—the child is less able to respond to external demands. Then all of his resources are subservient to coping with his inner growth, and during these periods the adults are wise to minimize their demands. Thus, a mother with common sense will avoid forcing toilet training upon a child who has to cope with an infectious disease or the arrival of a newborn sibling. "One thing at a time" is the slogan of healthy growth; "several things at a time" is that of pathology. Multiple, simultaneous influences require multiple adaptations. Such situations are more difficult to master but can be managed if there exists a unifying influence through communication. But disturbances of communication arise when such multiple adaptations are accompanied by equally manifold ways of communication—in terms of both content and form. If, however, discrepant experiences can be elaborated in a unifying, interpersonal situation over time, many of the contradictions can be resolved. For example, when at the time of his mastery of the basic vocabulary a child is exposed to **two language systems**—say French spoken at home and English spoken at school —the impact may be serious enough to retard his language development. If, however, the languages are learned in succession, no such ill effects can be observed. The practical solution of this problem is to send the child to a French-language school first, and later, perhaps at the age of ten, to an English-speaking school; or the parents could speak English at home and postpone the speaking of French until the child has mastered elementary English.

In the absence of a unifying influence, conflicting means of communication may be handled in a variety of ways. A youngster may refuse to cope with the contradictory events altogether—for example, a child who is exposed to different languages may refuse to learn to talk. Another child may compartmentalize functions which really are not separate; he may link matters of body care and emotions with one language and matters of play with another. Other children may give up the attempt at establishing any kind of orderly system and may learn to speak a mixture of languages such as those observed in culture contact areas. Sham adaptation to contradictory circumstances constitutes another solution; in such a case, the child concentrates on entirely different functions which are not involved in the conflict—for instance, learning to play a musical instrument— and only superficially meets the language problem.

Corrective experiences

Parents may unwittingly interfere with the self-corrective tendencies of their children by restricting autonomy and observation, interfering with expression and conversation with outsiders, preventing problem-solving and experimentation, or insisting that children should have blind faith in their elders. Parents who emphasize words and neglect action block nonverbal corrective feedback, and those who neglect words limit the child in his ability to acquire information and to reach agreements. But if an individual has thus acquired deviant techniques of communication, later life experiences can serve to modify, improve, or aggravate his disturbance. When a difficulty is confined to one kind of relationship, it can be attenuated or compensated for by successful communication in another kind of relationship; the child whose mother gives tangential replies may have a father who gives satisfactory acknowledgments and provides for successful communication. If one avenue of expression is blocked, another may be developed to perfection; the person who cannot speak in public because of blushing and stuttering may compensate for his difficulties by becoming a fine writer.

Compensatory experiences are brought about by many different circumstances. Sometimes the addition of more people to a family or group dilutes and disperses the noxious influence of one person. In other instances, a person may establish a new relationship which gratifies a heretofore unsatisfied need, and all his other relationships improve. Sometimes it is a matter of letting grass grow over traumatic events, thus giving the individual a chance to adapt. Or it may be a question of leadership whereby contact with a significant person may put an end to vacillation and doubt, as in the case of a medical student who, after hearing a visiting professor describe a field of activity, resumes his neglected studies with new vigor. The effectiveness of the compensatory or corrective experiences thus is related not only to the choice of the strategic moment but also to the nature of the therapeutic agent. The introduction of a new element of communication—for example, provision for feedback and acknowledgment—into a system where such a process was not known before will exert a beneficial effect. Here something is supplied which is essential for the functioning of any system. The beneficial experience also may be related to the introduction of a factor which compensates for previous hardships, and it is not surprising that an orphan raised in an institution may need special attention and help in establishing two-person relationships when taken into a family.

In **therapy,** much use is made of the principle of corrective experience (6). Because the individual afflicted with disturbances of communication is unable to correct—in part or as a whole—his inappropriate attitudes, beliefs, thoughts, feelings, and actions, an attempt is made to teach him those methods and techniques which will enable him to correct his information and performance. Implicitly through action and explicitly through word, the patient is influenced in such a way that he learns to derive pleasure from his own growth rather than from the reapplication of the old and inefficient methods.

Corrective experience in ordinary life situations and in therapy is based on combinations of the following processes:

Checking of old information with newly made firsthand observations

Checking of old information against observations made by others

Checking of newly acquired information against observations made by others

Checking of old and new information with the general cumulative body of knowledge in the field ›

Trying out skill and correcting erroneous performance

Trying out skill and having performance corrected by others

STABILITY AND FLUIDITY OF COMMUNICATION PATHOLOGY

Duration, rigidity, and reversibility are criteria which help the therapist to decide whether or not the pathology will be amenable to change. In order to get a clear picture of the driving forces which keep pathology active, the therapist has to understand the vicious circles which to the untrained observer may appear as static conditions. Essential to his understanding is the determination of the **extent of the feedback circuit:** does it involve one person alone?

does it include other people and involve groups? is it related to cultural values? A forty-year-old man with a marked washing compulsion may attend to his activity regardless of the presence of other people. The feedback circuit here involves only one person; although the frequent washing may be irritating to others and may interfere with continuous conversation, therapy will be aimed at changes to be brought about in the patient himself. Quite different is the situation in problems involving interpersonal pathology. For example, a man of fifty and a girl of eighteen who are ill-matched in terms of sex, vitality, interests, and ways of communication may make each other angry and unhappy, but after separation each may function successfully. Here, the feedback circuit involves two people and the pathology is reversible in so far as it ceases to exist after the separation. Therapy in such a case has to be directed at a lessening of the mutual interference which prevents either partner from seeking appropriate gratifications.

Feedback and the vicious circle

To clarify further the difference between intrapersonal and interpersonal pathology, a word ought to be said about the nature of feedback (257). When information about an ongoing action is incorporated into subsequent actions, a feedback of perceived effects has occurred.

Within the organism, the adjustment of the nervous system to a world of continuous variation and the conservation of its level of activity are achieved by adapting input to output and output to input (153). This adaptation is achieved by means of negative and positive feedback, which thus becomes a steering device. Negative feedback opposes what a system is doing; it stabilizes position, speed, or direction; when a person is set on a wrong course, negative feedback stabilizes his pathology. Positive feedback intensifies what a system is doing; it alters position, it increases or decreases speed, or it changes direction, and hence also changes pathology. The ways in which information is fed back are not bound to any one system of codification as some recent experiments indicate (251). Apparently when in selected cases the frequency of certain cerebral action potentials is fed back to the organism through flicker of a light source, this rhythmical stimulation can provoke crises in behavior and result in a convulsion.

Feedback is not only a process upon which learning and the correction of errors are based but it is also responsible for the continuation of faulty perception and action. In therapy, the psychiatrist is faced with the problem of changing negative feedback, which stabilizes pathology, into positive feedback, which mobilizes pathology. In practice, the difficulty of therapy consists of introducing the kind of positive feedback which will decrease rather than increase pathology.

In the past, and particularly under the influence of psychoanalysis, psychiatrists believed that positive feedback could be introduced by studying how pathology had been established in the first place. The unconscious material, when made conscious, was supposed to bring about a change for the better. However, this theory can be accepted only with restrictions. The situation which originally leads to the establishment of psychopathology involves a complicated interpersonal and group network within the family. As the individual gets older, an internalization process takes place whereby content and manner of the exchange later will be reflected in the mind of the person. With progressive maturation, the original interpersonal and group relations may be abandoned, but by now the patient's behavior is stabilized through negative feedback within himself. The therapeutic process therefore must involve another person with whom new interpersonal feedback circuits are established, which in turn will be internalized and superimposed on the older intrapersonal feedback mechanisms.

An example may illustrate the case. An anxious mother and father induced a boy to wash his hands constantly. The family lived in a tropical climate and believed that the febrile diseases afflicting people in the neighborhood and a member of the family resulted from infections transmitted by interpersonal contact and touch of polluted objects. The disease had a high death rate. The boy experienced stability of family relations, reward, and peacefulness after washing; he experienced reprimand when he did not wash. Since the admonitions were kept up for several years, to wash meant to be safe.

In later life, then, whenever he experienced anxiety he went about washing himself. In the course of time, the intervals between cleansing sessions became progressively shorter. Inasmuch as the patient could not live very well without touching objects, he had to return to the washroom time and time again. The belief that objects and people were contaminated was firmly entrenched in his mind; he had studied bacteriology and collected evidence of the presence of bacteria on his hands. The stabilization of pathology in this case was due to the fact that anxiety of the father and mother, transmitted in an interpersonal context, was associated with a dangerous situation. The ritual of washing was thought to be a lifesaving device and was associated with an optimal emotional state and freedom from anxiety; hence the boy learned to handle all anxiety-producing situations by washing. But inasmuch as he could not exclude bacteria from his life, each contact with an object or person became a stimulus for further washing.

In many cases, the vicious circle involves several persons, and **individual pathology may be triggered by the actions of others.** For example, a couple, aged thirty-eight and forty, consulted the psychiatrist because of marital incompatibility. The husband spent much time away from home in the company of his mistress. His wife had a phobic character. She did not object to his philandering provided he returned home in the evenings—the time of day at which she experienced her greatest fears. The conflict became marked when his mistress likewise claimed his evening hours. When he attempted to solve this conflict by seeking a divorce, he began to feel guilty, which feeling made him return to his wife. When he made an effort to give up his mistress, he became angry and irritable with his wife; and after a few weeks of home life he soon returned to his mistress. When one mistress left him, he promptly took another. When his wife decided to leave him, she became depressed and he became irritable and unbearable with his mistress. The steady state here involved a triangular situation in which there were: the husband in the role of strong man—compensating for a physical handicap; his wife in the role of a psychological invalid, dependent upon his presence for the alleviation of fear; the succession of mistresses— usually young girls who were in need of a father figure.

The vicious circle thus worked as follows: the man treated his wife as he did his mother, who also had a fearful character; he treated his young mistresses like his younger sister, who had died. One of the mistresses considered him as a father she had never had; she even wanted to be on good terms with his wife, to the extent of suggesting that she move into their home. She had searched all her life for a family and had no particular desire for sexual activities, although in her immature way she appreciated touch, caress, and affection. The wife, finally, treated her husband like a child, just as her own overprotective mother had done with her. She was not interested in sexual intercourse, but needed the man as a source of income and as protection against her fears. Of the trio, each member had his own pathology and each fed into the abnormalities of the others; communication was disturbed because all three operated with wrong premises and unrealistic roles. When one person wanted to break away, the others played into the pathology by provoking guilt in one, fear in the other, and loneliness in the third. All felt somewhat caught; all knew of the existence of distortions. Eventually therapy, at first with one psychiatrist and later with three different ones, led to a successful reorganization of the life of each of the participants.

Regressive and progressive reorganization

The more highly specialized a feedback pattern becomes, the more difficult it is to alter. The more vested interests people have, the more fixed their ways of communication become. The more specialized pathology becomes, the less it is likely to change. In cases with highly organized pathology, compensatory adjustment is extremely difficult and breakdown, regression, and psychosis are frequently the only solution. In an **acute psychosis**, regardless of its etiology, a patient is for practical purposes incommunicado. While in toxic, infectious, degenerative, and neoplastic diseases of the brain the organs of communication are affected directly, in the functional psychoses and in acute anxiety states a similar communication barrier exists without apparent brain damage. In both organic and functional psychoses, the existing communication network is maintained as long as the exchange of messages is somewhat successful and therefore gratifying. But if the exchange does not have any gratifying results, then disorganization sets in. The organism apparently attempts to shunt those parts of the network that do not seem to operate satisfactorily; this may involve the repression and isolation of certain memory experiences or the abandonment of certain control functions within the own organism. When a patient "regresses," he relinquishes something that did not work in the first place; and what appears as disorganization is an attempt at reorganization in a different way. In other words, a psychosis is a self-healing process.

Regressive reorganization is a necessary transition between highly specialized pathology and readjustment, because specialized pathology means that the patient cannot try anything new but has to repeat the same pattern over and over again. Thus the obsessive becomes more obsessive and the fearful more fearful. The communication system of such a person becomes progressively smaller and more restricted. When further limitation is no longer possible, the only change to be expected is disorganization. The introduction of randomness creates a new basis on which organization can occur. Regressive behavior thus can be considered a step toward improvement. In many instances, the patient cannot undertake this reorganization alone; he needs the help of others.

Progressive reorganization starts from random or somewhat organized behavior. The communication network then is progressively expanded. This growth is not based upon changes of existing pathology but upon development of processes and functions which have heretofore been neglected and underdeveloped. As such growth takes place, pathology in other areas of the personality recedes. In therapy, the psychiatrist has to decide whether the patient suffers from a form of pathology which is the end product of a development or whether he deals with an undeveloped person who can, through further growth, be improved. The situation is almost analogous to the process of evolution, where an overspecialized species becomes extinct because it cannot adapt to changing conditions while an underspecialized species has not developed further because the conditions are not conducive to such a development.

Conscious inspection and discordant events

On many occasions, human beings perceive events without being aware of the traces these events have left inside of them. Frequently people smell, taste, hear, and see things which they only later become aware of having perceived. This fact can be demonstrated either by means of recall from memory or when in the presence of similar events people recognize having been exposed to such stimuli before. In general, conscious awareness of what is going on occurs when we encounter failure (256). When a situation cannot be mastered, the organism reroutes information in such a way that various aspects can be analyzed through conscious inspection. The information so derived is applied to future similar situations. However, the field of consciousness is limited and only a few aspects can be scrutinized at any one time. Therefore, any piece of information which appears in **consciousness** represents but an infinitesimal part of the information the organism possesses as a whole. Consciousness thus can be conceived of as a special feedback device (66) in which information deriving from memory or from exteroception is put through special scrutiny either because immediate understanding was impossible or because failure was encountered in action.

In rotating pieces of information through consciousness, we are primarily aware of that particular piece of information upon which we are concentrating. But we also are in some vague way aware of the existence of things we are not focusing upon. When we greet a person, for example, we are dimly aware of many circumstances that surround our encounter. This **background information** permeates our field of awareness but remains less distinct than the picture of the person we are talking to. Furthermore, the action which we perceive is rapidly scanned against the memory of other actions which could have occurred but did not. For example, when one sees a person eat a hot dog, one knows that at that moment he might be eating a hamburger, a steak, or a sandwich, and with some effort one could list in succession all the things he might be eating. Thus, when a piece of information is viewed in consciousness it is run off, as it were, against this somewhat less conscious background of possibilities. The more complete this background information is, the better the understanding of the event in question.

There exist many memory traces which do not rise to consciousness. This inhibition may be the result of several circumstances: first, the experience may have occurred a long time ago, so that the particular memory trace has been condensed and fused with later memories; secondly, the experience may have occurred recently and may not have been properly coordinated with the corresponding previous impressions; thirdly, the cognitive aspects of an experience may have been discordant with the emotional aspects. It has been Freud's great contribution (91, 93) to clarify the function of the unconscious in the development of neuroses and psychoses. He postulated that **repression** is the principal mechanism in the production of neurotic symptoms while the upsurge of unconscious forces occurs primarily in psychotic conditions. Today we can add that inadequate interpersonal feedback characterizes both insufficient and excessive repression.

The phenomenon of **isolation** represents another method of coping with intense, threatening, or discordant experiences. Instead of being inhibited—as in repression—such memories or fantasies are elaborated in complete isolation from all other memories. The two bodies of information are treated as if they belonged to two separate persons. It appears that moderately contradictory pieces of information can be clarified by inspection in the mind of one individual, but highly contradictory pieces of information or memories of frustrating events have to be handled with the help of another person. Apparently when a person cannot repeat an experience in action and when the affective component of the experience is discordant with its intellectual counterpart, he needs elaboration of such an experience in an interpersonal context. With another person, he may obtain meaningful replies which help him to organize these discordant memories. Interpersonal elaboration can be compared to a slow-motion study; it rolls up certain events slowly and safely while other events are ignored. Through this process, the individual acquires the ability to relegate irrelevant material to the background and the other person helps him in connecting emotional concomitants with intellectual content.

The **unconscious** is made up of a number of part functions:

—A pool of analogically coded information which remains in the background

—A system of cataloging events stored in the pool for ready reference

—A feedback circuit which enables us to select and view in magnification and detail any part of the information which is stored in the pool

—A system of transferring the anologically coded items such as feelings, fantasies, and sensations into language so that memories can be elaborated in an interpersonal context

Disturbances of communication arise when any or all of these "safety valves" do not operate properly. Without a diversified pool, understanding of any but the most commonplace events becomes difficult. People thus travel "to broaden their outlook"; doctors attempt to see a wide variety of patients; and psychiatrists usually have had contact with several value systems and cultures (202). But patients who have lived a restricted life, isolated from outside contacts, lack diversified approaches for meeting human relations successfully. When events are not properly placed, catalogued, and filed against a background of similar experiences, their ready availability is endangered. When the emotional input of events is frustrating and discordant with their intellectual impact, one of the two has to be repressed, isolated, or distorted. When the machinery for conscious inspection, the ability to concentrate and to think logically, is missing, rational behavior and accurate prediction of events become difficult. And finally, when inner events are not translatable into terms which make them accessible to others, the individual cannot share, exchange, modify, or elaborate his experiences.

Value judgment as disruptive reply

In popular speech, terms such as good or bad, cheap or expensive, acceptable or unacceptable, desirable or undesirable, denote the use of a value concept. This is closely linked with two notions: that value can be ascribed to any object or action and that value is a quantity that makes comparative evaluation possible. Value thus is a device which facilitates the comparison of action with action,

action with object, and object with object. For example, by assigning a value to a rosebush, an individual can compare this plant to a necktie. Value is also a device by which closely similar things can be differentiated. An original painting that looks very much like its copy may be differentiated from it by its price. Values, therefore, fulfill a useful function; in placing heterogeneous events on a continuous scale, they pave the way for future decisions (210).

But if value judgments are given as replies to statements of other people, more likely than not they will have a disruptive effect. If Johnny, age five, comes to his father and asks, "Daddy, what does 'bitch' mean?" and father replies, "That is a bad word; don't use it," the child still does not know what the word means. The father, instead of replying meaningfully to the question, compares the child's statement to the standards of acceptance, pins the universal value of "bad" upon it, and then announces the result of his deliberations. The child is puzzled at the reply because the father did not verbalize his standards and did not explain the complicated process that is involved in the transfiguration of a particularized statement into generalized value terms. The effect a value reply has upon participants can be compared to a court procedure. When the judge or the jury announces the verdict, communication between the defense and the prosecution stops and the trial has come to an end. And when unsolicited value judgments are employed in a conversation, they serve in the function of terminal statements which close the ongoing exchange.

If Person A makes a statement and Person B replies with a value judgment, more likely than not A is going to get angry. The anger is a response to B's judging and weighting the statement of A, a procedure which A did not ask for. In this case, B assigns himself the higher status of a judge and relegates A to the lower status of the accused. But not only does B increase his status, he also gives a tangential reply which is frustrating to A. By not giving his personal reaction but by introducing instead an impersonal standard which is backed up by the church, the law, the majority, or any other authority, he threatens A, whose anger in all probability also will affect B. Similar to the officials of a court who hide behind the cloak of office when they are exposed to the scorn of a condemned prisoner, B becomes more pompous and righteous as he sees A's anger, perhaps because he realizes that he has not dealt with A's statement in a direct and specific way.

If one person introduces a value judgment as a reply to a statement which did not call for such a response, or when two people respond to each other by using value judgments, communication becomes strained. Under such circumstances, denotative statements are omitted, information ceases to be exchanged, and correction cannot occur; and unless one person yields and submits to the values of the other, the relationship breaks down. This, however, in no way refers to the situation in which both persons have agreed to **search for values** and to pass judgment—for example, on the merit of certain taxes on tobacco. In this case, value judgment is not used as a reply; instead, all the participants have agreed to compare one issue—in this case, taxes on tobacco—with another issue—perhaps an increase of the retail sales tax. The perniciousness of the value judgment in ordinary conversation and interaction is bound to its unsolicited introduction, which takes the other person by surprise and erects, as it were, an artificial barrier between the participants.

Communication in terms of value statements frequently occurs when nations, political parties, or pressure groups clash at a parley. Such communication is in itself an index that the participants have **not understood** each other. The same can be observed in the family circle when parents condemn a child's statement because they did not understand his intentions; or in a psychiatric hospital when a nurse berates a patient for using vile language. Resorting to value statements helps neither the speaker nor the listener to introduce meaningful action for the solution of the problem that is being discussed.

Chapter Four

Interpersonal Pathology:
Disturbances of Communication
in Childhood

PATHOLOGY of communication arising in two-person situations is studied best at its source—namely, in infancy. Any child is born of a mother, and unless this mother or an appropriate substitute cares for the infant, he will die. Participation in a **two-person communication** system is absolutely necessary if the child is to survive. The child must therefore attempt to adapt himself to the communication system into which he is born, whether it is normal or abnormal.

The newborn infant is not a fully developed human being. From twelve to fifteen additional years are needed before full biological maturity is reached. Though potentialities for growth are predetermined, certain physical and social conditions must exist if postnatal development is to take place. Among these conditions, one of the most significant is the opportunity to participate in successfully functioning systems of communication. The way the infant's early expressions are acknowledged will to a great extent determine his future ways of communication. This genetic principle is generally accepted. It means that if children adopt certain reactions in emotionally important, usually familial, situations, they are later on likely to adopt similar reactions in structurally analogous situations. In each phase of postnatal growth, the infant needs specific care so that those functions which he is attempting to master receive proper guidance, control, and stimulation. But if appropriate stimulation in terms of threshold and timing constitute the first specific requirement, feedback is the second. Information about the effects of the infant's statements and actions must be relayed back to him so that he can learn from his errors.

Content and form of such **feedback** steer the development of both successful and disturbed communication. Much of what is called personality development is dependent upon communicative exchanges which bear upon the following matters:

Identity:	I am (not)	You are (not)
Relationship:	I am (not) to you	You are (not) to me
Action:	I do (not)	You do (not)
Impact:	I do (not) to you	You do (not) to me
Cooperation:	I do (not) with you	You do (not) with me
Feeling:	I (do not) feel	You (do not) feel
Interpersonal feeling:	I (do not) feel about you	You (do not) feel about me
Thinking:	I (do not) think	You (do not) think
Interpersonal thinking:	I (do not) think of you	You (do not) think of me
Expectation:	I (do not) expect	You (do not) expect
Interpersonal expectation:	I (do not) expect of you	You (do not) expect of me
Value:	I am (not) good I am (not) bad	You are (not) good You are (not) bad

Disturbances of communication arise when the child does not receive a satisfactory acknowledgment in any of these matters. This may consist of a distorted answer, undue weighting of one aspect in neglect of another, poorly timed replies, or replies which exceed the tolerance limits. Since quantitative disturbances have been discussed in Chapter Three, the discussion here shall be confined to qualitative deviations of communication.

Selective Reinforcement

In responding to one aspect of behavior rather than to another, the parent exercises his prerogative of steering the child in a desired direction. **Selectivity in reply,** therefore, is not to be confused with pathology. Almost all families profess some specialized interest in one area or another. Through repeated exposure to particular topics or approaches, a child gradually acquires information and techniques which prepare him for particular fields of endeavor: scholastic achievement, art, music, crafts, technical pursuits, sports, trade, or homemaking. The child also learns such general skills as play, social know-how, value principles, citizenship, and all those subtle features which distinguish between boys and girls.

Under certain conditions, selectivity leads to the development of **pathology:**

—If the adult's response is too discriminating or if it is not discriminating enough in relation to the developmental state of the child.

—If the adult's response overstimulates one function and neglects another. This selectivity is particularly harmful when functions which are about to be learned or which have not been fully mastered are neglected.

—If selectivity is so one-sided that what the child learns at home does not prepare him for what he will encounter outside the home.

—If selective reinforcement steers the child in a direction that does not coincide with his innate abilities.

—If the selectivity interferes with the correction of information so that the child is uninformed or possesses a distorted view of the world.

Selective reinforcement frequently is implemented by means of tangential responses. Since this form of reply constitutes one of the most frustrating forms of communication, the selectivities thus imposed upon the child cannot be mastered without anxiety and its damaging implications for communication.

Codification and language

In the course of maturation, three types of language are learned in succession (201). In the first few months of life, the statements of the infant are mediated primarily through the autonomic nervous system. Intestinal and cardiovascular manifestations are the result of contraction of the smooth muscles, which at that age constitute the principal effector organs of communication. This can be called **somatic language.** With the development of hand-mouth coordination and locomotion, statements begin to be mediated primarily through the central nervous system; the striped muscles become the principal effector organs, and action is used to call attention, to please, or to retaliate. This can be called **action language.** With the development of speech and the learning of reading and writing, expression is entrusted to special muscle groups; words and gestures which are exclusively reserved for discursive communication are referred to as **verbal language.**

Selective acknowledgment of one type of language in preference to another has its most significant consequence in childhood. In order to communicate with children, parents must adapt their language to the developmental stage of their offspring. Parents exert leverage by acknowledging the child's statements in terms that are understandable and satisfying to him; without having experienced such acknowledgment for each type of language, the child will not be able to learn it. For example, if a three-year-old receives satisfactory acknowledgment of his action language but not of his verbal language, that child will tend to use action language even as an adult. This does not mean that such a child cannot speak; it merely means that he experiences the pleasure of communication only in terms of action language. In adult life, when most people have mastered all three types of codification, the language spectrum used will depend upon the occasion. For love-making, organ and action language are most suitable; in war, action language; at the conference table, verbal language. However, not all participants will use the form of codification that is called for. Some—the psychopathic personalities —are most skilled in the use of action language; others—the psychosomatic patients—prefer somatic language. These selectivities largely determine the choice of interpersonal relations in that such persons seek others who know how to "speak their language."

Denotation and connotation

Denotation and connotation are two different ways of signifying. The denotative, or extensional, meaning of words refers to the external world, to objects and actions that have verifiable characteristics to which the majority of observers can agree; the connotative, or intensional, meaning involves associations and feelings arising in the human organism at the time such words are used or perceived. Most expressions have, of course, both denotative and connotative characteristics (107). In the course of interpersonal communication, selective reinforcement tends to emphasize either the denotative or the connotative component. In maximizing the denotative aspects, a person expresses an objective, verifiable view of an event in so far as it can be reconstructed in words. In maximizing the connotative aspects, a person relies upon his own as well as the other person's associations and feelings to fill in that which words have left unsaid. Obviously the two views stand in a complementary relationship to each other. Connotative statements have to be connotatively elaborated; denotative statements have to be denotatively interpreted. Some parents are not aware of this distinction and tend to respond connotatively to the denotative statements of their children.

An example of how **distortions** are introduced when denotative and connotative interpretations do not work hand in hand is given below. A patient reports: "I sat at the swimming pool and lunch was served. Another woman, whom I had just met, said, 'Doesn't this grapefruit juice taste stale? I bet you it's canned.' Thereupon I replied, 'Grapefruits grow all around us. Why should they use canned juice when fresh fruit is available?' 'Oh, well,' said the other woman, 'I guess I just don't care for juice today.'"

The patient interpreted the "stale" literally and reacted to the idea of canned versus noncanned fruit. She overlooked the fact that the other woman wanted to say something like "I don't like grapefruit juice" or "The food is not very good here" or "Why do they serve this sort of thing?" or perhaps she simply wanted to make conversation. As a rule, this patient has a tendency to seize the literal and denotative meaning and to overlook the connotative aspects of the spoken word.

Perception and evaluation

Almost every person has **preferred channels of perception**. One individual has to see things in order to understand them; another has to touch them; a third has to hear them. In the course of interpersonal communication, a participant will respond to the other person's statement more appropriately when he can receive it through his preferred channel of perception. This applies particularly to various modes of verbal denotation. One person may be sensitive to the spoken word—and therefore may easily absorb information from lectures; another person may prefer to read rather than to listen; and a third person may be rather insensitive to both spoken and written words and will need illustrations in order to understand. Children are taught to use their sensory modalities in certain specific ways and to observe the modes of perception of others. Comments of parents which point up perception may take the following forms: "Do you smell gas?"; "Watch how that dog sniffs the tracks of his master"; "Look how gently he touches her hair"; "Do you hear the jays chattering?" Musical parents train their children to hear tones; gourmets cultivate discriminating taste; dancers emphasize the perception of movement. But in the course of selective reinforcement, a number of things can happen which may lead to pathology.

Biological growth implies a progressive shift of observation from nearby objects to those farther away. The child-rearing practices in our culture support this trend of relegating to secondary position the sensations of smell, taste, touch, temperature, and equilibrium as the development of the distance receivers progresses. All higher forms of symbolization are contingent upon this **shift** in perceptual emphasis from the **proximity to the distance receivers,** and it is not accidental that more words refer to visual and auditory impressions than to touch, smell, or taste. For the growth of the child, it is important that the experiences with the distance receptors be paralleled by speech development so that they can be elaborated through appropriate contact with an adult. Lack of physical contact with others and immobilization may force the premature use of the distance receptors at a time when language development has not yet progressed sufficiently to label various experiences. Conversely, blindness or deafness may force the child to use the proximity receivers where the use of the distance receivers might be indicated. While healthy development enables the individual to use all sense modalities according to the requirements of the situation, the functionally or organically disabled person may have to avoid certain modalities and overcompensate for the deficiency in other spheres.

The most effective way of **steering perception** toward healthy growth is to respond to the initial statement of the child by using the same modality. If the child touches, touch on the part of the parent is an effective reply. But if the reply is given in another modality, it must be matched in content to escape being tangential. This applies particularly to verbal replies given in response to action statements of the child. Replies that are ill-matched in terms of modality may lead to the development of pathology. For example:

Child's statement	*Parent's reply*
Sniffing at flower	Sniffing likewise (matched reply, same sensory modality, action language)
	I know it smells good (matched reply, verbal language)
	Let's read a story about flowers (elaboration, acknowledging specific action, but introducing new action)
	What are you doing? (tangential reply, acknowledging action in general but not action of sniffing at flower)
	Let's go inside (completely unrelated reply)

All people's responses by necessity are selective. Among the selectivities that operate in social situations, the **perception of having been perceived** has the greatest impact upon subsequent communication. It marks the moment when interpersonal communication begins (210). The acknowledgment of this perception characterizes the socially alert person. For example, there is nothing more frustrating for a patient than to wait in a waiting room to keep his appointment with a doctor who is supposed to be in but who does not show up. Lack of explanation for the waiting leaves the patient bewildered, and he does not know whether to wait a while longer or to leave. Doctors often miss this strategic moment and fail to acknowledge the arrival of the patient. The relatively undisturbed patient, in return, may behave as if no social situation had been established at all, while the autistic and narcissistic patient may behave as if he had been perceived but purposefully ignored.

The announcement of a change in an interpersonal situation is likewise marked by the individual's perception that he is being, or is no longer being, perceived. Parents teach their children to observe such changes; they may comment: "You cannot hide any longer; they have seen you," or "Mrs. X has seen you; go and say hello to her." But those parents who do not train their children in this respect handicap the youngster in learning gracious social behavior.

Selectivity is even more pronounced in the process of **evaluation.** The functions included under this heading comprise: interpolation, extrapolation, and prediction; reconstruction and memory; decision-making; and imposing decisions upon others (control) or accepting the decisions of others (adaptation). Pathology arises under the following conditions:

—When one of the part functions is not properly developed
—When one of the part functions is delegated to or usurped by another person
—When premade judgments (prejudices) or built-in, automatic reactions take the place of flexible evaluation
—When the scanning mechanism is poor or standards for comparison are erroneous
—When memories become repressed, forgotten, or isolated
—When the input is filtered and information is distorted or incomplete so that decisions are based upon fictitious material

Parents influence their children by making decisions for them; they also let children watch adults make decisions so that the youngsters can learn by imitation. The most powerful tool in producing defective evaluation is the **tangential response;** and perhaps the most frequent form of interference is to provide the child with the elements of choice and then to prejudice the outcome. For example, the parent says, "Which of these guns would you like?" The child makes his choice and is told that the chosen gun is too expensive. Finally, the child has to accept the gun that mother had chosen in the first place. Had she said at the beginning, "This is the only one we can afford," she could have avoided the later tangential response. If the child is exposed repeatedly to these tangential influences, he does not learn to weigh information in its totality but will tend to let one factor prejudice the outcome.

Another form of disturbance arises when parents do not teach their children to **reduce the number of possibilities** to two. When a person is confronted with multiple choices, the number of the possibilities has to be reduced. For example, if a man is faced with a choice of five neckties, he will not group two versus three but he will group one against four in succession and ask the question, "Do I want this one or not?" In this type of slicing, one item is chosen for possible selection against all the other items for possible exclusion. In almost all situations, choices are ultimately based upon "yes" or "no" responses whereby the "yes" is a small slice and the "no" is a big slice. However, there are people who are incapable of such simple arrangement. Some compare too many items; some cannot let the unchosen heap go. But the most ineffective way of choosing consists of emphasizing the general as opposed to the differentiating characteristics. If one necktie is to be chosen and the mother raves about the good quality of silk which characterizes all five neckties, she does not help her son to choose one; and if she repeats her performance, she systematically impairs her son's ability to decide.

Action and expression

The infant's crying right after birth constitutes his first communicative statement, and the adult's response to this crying is instrumental in the baby's survival. The first step in establishing relatedness, therefore, is the adult's reaction to the nonverbal expressions of the infant; the second step consists of having the infant respond to nonverbal expressions of the adult. But all along, the adult's responses have to be geared in modality, quantity, and timing to the child's biological and psychological maturity. The parent has to realize that early in life motor responses are mediated primarily by the smooth muscles and the autonomic nervous system. Gradually responses get more complex and the striped muscles and the central nervous system assume more importance. In the second year, speech development enters the picture, but several more years have to pass before words represent a first approximation of the thoughts and feelings of the child. At first, words are used and practiced for their own sake; later, words and sentences are casually and erratically juxtaposed with action; still later, action and word are coordinated; and finally verbal expression may substitute for action altogether. Misunderstandings frequently occur when adults interpret the loosely used words of children as having communicative significance, while the child is actually rehearsing the pronunciation and usage of verbal responses. At this stage, the principal content is still mediated through action and other nonverbal means, and the child is well into his teens before parallelism gives way to complete synchronization of action, thought, and feeling with words.

Disturbances of communication arise when parents do not provide **appropriate stimulation** of the function that is being exercised. In the case of expression, this would mean not to provide the opportunity for interpersonal action; riding piggyback, exchanging presents, playing tag or catch, wrestling—all these are activities which cannot be carried out alone. A similar effect is produced when parents respond above or below the level of integration at which the child operates. To repeat an activity which the child has mastered or to introduce an activity for which the child is not prepared retards his development.

When parents do not respond at all or reply tangentially to one element rather than to another, this selective response tends to slice the "togetherness" of action with thought, feeling, and word and thus exerts a disintegrating effect. The motive-oriented parents selectively respond to the child's intentions, needs, desires, and display of effort. Implementation-oriented parents tend to emphasize technical skills and the manipulation of people; or they may encourage the child to go through the gestures of action without paying attention to whether or not such action is really effective. Effect-oriented parents selectively emphasize success, accomplishment, or failure.

The selective, systematic **acknowledgment of motivation** can in many instances be documented by the kind of verbal comments made. "What made him do that?" is a question that expresses a concern with need. "You look as if you'd love to get on that horse" is a comment emphasizing desire. Some people acknowledge needs and desires in nonverbal terms. They read in the faces of others what they might aspire to and spend a great deal of time in satisfying or frustrating such wishes.

Acknowledgment of effort represents a particular kind of emphasis on motivation. Such parents are satisfied with an external token of inner forces and are content to acknowledge the intention. "He tried hard, and that is all that matters" is a comment in which effort is valued and effect is neglected. "You have shown your good will; now it's up to him" is a commentary on a person's intention and attitude. In other families, it is customary to acknowledge effort in nonverbal terms. Here the emphasis is on good will, and to have tried, irrespective of the effects achieved, therefore becomes the measure of success. For example, a twelve-year-old boy who helps his father sand down a chair that needs to be repainted makes a few movements with the sandpaper, whereupon his mother pats him on the back. This action becomes a signal for the boy to quit his work and to go and have a drink of water. Later, the mother exclaims, "Haven't we an efficient helper!"

While the acknowledgment of motivation emphasizes the motor that drives action, **selective acknowledgment of implementation** emphasizes the nature of the action. A comment such as "I like the way you did it" or "You handled this situation in a superb manner" verbally points out skill. There are persons who, irrespective of motivations, tend to analyze in great detail the technique used to achieve results. This is particularly true of sports enthusiasts; and the post-mortems following tennis tournaments or yacht races are characterized by analysis of what happened. The emphasis upon procedure frequently includes those features which bear upon the ability to influence others; some people emphasize manipulation, salesmanship, and the mastery of social techniques. There is a gleam in the eye of the father when he hears that his son has been elected class president, and he already envisions him as the future director of a large corporation. The acknowledgment of social manipulation is seen particularly in families where the parents delight when the children succeed in manipulating them. For example, a boy of eleven suddenly starts to perform all the chores his mother asks him to do; he brings his father the newspaper; he engages in conversation about father's favorite sport—in brief, he is a model child. Then he pops the question: "May I go to the circus?" The father is so proud of his son's performance as well as of his efforts to please that he takes him immediately to the circus. The next day Johnny is his old self again and stops being a model child.

Frequently a social technique amounts to carrying out a symbolic action. Sending greetings to a sick person, congratulating some casual acquaintance on the occasion of his birthday, calling upon people who are not at home, apologizing after having seriously hurt another person—all are symbolic actions. In social life, the interpretation of such symbolic actions is distinguished from that of actions which have a practical impact. **Selective acknowledgment of symbolic actions** is detrimental to children if the symbolic action contradicts the physical action. If parents allow their children to be destructive and accept apology as a form of reparation, the child may be encouraged to continue on his destructive path—provided he expresses his regret. In adult life, the performance of a symbolic action is often a convenient way of coping with a situation which cannot be improved through real action.

Selective **acknowledgment of effect** achieved may be expressed in such a sentence as "You passed the exam; isn't that wonderful!" or "You can be proud of yourself; you were invited to supper by one of the most distinguished matrons of this city." In the acknowledgment of results and accomplishments, arbitrary points on a sliding scale are emphasized. Parents who selectively acknowledge effects induce their children to "make the grade," to pass examinations, to get elected, and to close a sale; but they do not emphasize the pleasure derived from the skills which lead to success, nor do they help the children to enjoy the success once it has been achieved. Such people tend to acknowledge statements only when the "goods are delivered"; everything else is regarded as unessential routine. For example, a fourteen-year-old boy comes home and tells how he earned fifty cents by mowing the lawn of the neighbors. Father praises him for his success and disregards the fact that the boy pressured the neighbors into having their lawn mowed by telling them a sob story that he wouldn't be able to go to the rodeo otherwise. "The result is what counts," father says. "Never mind how you get it."

Some people are selective in acknowledging either long-term or short-term success. Persons who demand immediate results cannot tolerate a delay of days or weeks, and they neglect long-term goals. Their children are rewarded for any performance which yields results in a matter of minutes or hours. Teen-agers growing up in such families are encouraged to accept any job if it pays a few cents more than another, regardless of the skill that is learned. Continuity of education from day to day or from year to year is interrupted by the principle of the immediate "pay-off."

In some families, popularity and **acknowledgment of status** are the cornerstones of existence. Parents who are social climbers are skilled in picking out and selectively acknowledging all those actions and statements which are presumed to carry prestige or which are thought to be implemental to future improvement in status. Such a parent will cheer when his son tells of having been invited to the "house on the hill," but he will neglect to acknowledge the account of the boy's visit to "the wrong side of the tracks."

Selective **acknowledgment of destructive action**—the emphasis upon the "do not's"—is found predominately in families who have children with behavior problems. Such parents tend to reply primarily to irritating expressions of their children, and the children learn that critical and sarcastic remarks usually initiate a significant communicative exchange. Here, the children learn that destructiveness, antagonism, and interference produce the much longed-for reactions in the parents, while ordinary behavior will not bring about any particular acknowledgment. "Don't bite your fingernails," "Don't scratch," "Don't touch my things," are comments which block the child's development because they do not indicate in which way actions can be carried out satisfactorily. "No's" and "don't's" block and inhibit, whereas a friendly "Here, not there," "Now, not later," point the way in the desired direction.

In the world of grownups, the police and the military are trained to acknowledge destructive actions and to ignore constructive actions. The same applies to certain critics, reviewers, and news analysts who make a living by acknowledging in sarcastic or ironic terms the sometimes searching and experimental expressions of others. Through sarcasm, these experts indicate that a particular subject matter has attracted their attention, and so ingrained is their destructive practice that the public takes it for granted that a subject either is attacked and ridiculed or is not mentioned at all.

In acknowledgment, selectivity can focus upon the ability to provide for **redemption** and to make restitution for damages produced. In families where such an emphasis predominates, the character of the children is shaped in the direction of "making it up" regardless of whether or not the redemption fits the situation. It is appropriate for a mother to insist that her boy clean up water colors spilled on the floor; but if he is required to pay a five-cent fine and the maid wipes up the spilled paint, the boy learns not to correct his mistakes but to redeem himself instead.

Emotional response

It must be assumed that the human being experiences sensations of **pleasure** when physiological functions operate satisfactorily; thus the baby relaxes and goes to sleep when he has been fed. But in infancy, hunger can be gratified only when adults supply the right kind of food at the right temperature, in the right amount, and at the proper time. This necessitates close contact and handling by the adult, and the infant learns to associate pleasure with being touched, carried, bathed, and played with. Withdrawal of or mere interference with these social pleasures may produce discomfort, rage, panic, or apathy. The emotional reaction of the child to physiological and social stimuli guides the adult, in turn; when the child cries, the mother gets alarmed; when the baby smiles, the mother feels contented (237). Based upon nonverbal communication, these interpersonal gratifications are safety mechanisms which enable the child to endure displeasure in physiological functioning. When a child falls and hurts himself, the emotional response of the mother is comforting and the hurt can be overcome. But children who do not have the cushion of interpersonal support often cannot manage frustrating situations, and as a result they protect themselves against exposure or they develop tension. If children are not exposed to interpersonal stimulation, they become emotionally retarded, apathetic, depressed, and unresponsive, and they do not learn to delay response to frustration. If they are exposed to excessive interpersonal stimulation without the appropriate emotional help of an adult, they become tense and tend to develop temper tantrums or tension diseases. Excessive stimulation then is handled either in the form of an emotional outburst which involves the whole organism or in the form of a tension syndrome which affects selectively the respiratory, intestinal, or vascular system.

In many families, however, the emotional response of adults is quite satisfactory when the child is small. The mother recognizes the needs of her baby and her responses on a nonverbal level supply the infant with the necessary support. But difficulties may arise when verbal communication develops and the parents are given an opportunity to show progressively greater selectivity. Then unconditional emotional response is converted into a conditional means of achieving leverage. By selectively lifting out of context one reaction and by disregarding another, the parents exert a powerful influence upon character formation. **The emotional response** becomes **a reward or a punishment.** The parent can with his own emotions selectively acknowledge or ignore the emotions of the child. In saying "You look pleased, and so am I," the parent indicates that to be pleased is important. A sentence such as "You look as if you were going to blow your top and I am going to get mad" emphasizes the danger of anger. "You look awful. I should put you to bed" selectively points toward anxiety and the succorant reaction of the parent. "You are scared and I am scared for you" or "I am ashamed of you; you are bashful" reinforces with the parent's emotion the fear or shame of the child. The advantages of this kind of acknowledgment lie in the ease with which the child understands the expressions of the parent. The potential damage can be seen in the conditional association of the child's emotional response with the emotional response of the parent. This situation interferes with freedom of expression.

The **acknowledgment of pleasure and frustration** sets the scene and determines to what degree pleasure can be experienced, in what subject matter, when, and where. If parents acknowledge the child's signals of satiation and pleasure, he learns to rely upon his intra-organismic signals of gratification and frustration. With equal ease, however, parents can attenuate or alter such intraorganismic signals. As a matter of principle, a mother may induce her son to eat what is on his plate, thus teaching him to disregard the feeling of satiation. Or the mother may indulge the wishes of her child, granting special foods, toys, and privileges and, through oversatiation, produce dis-interest. The same pertains to the acknowledgment of frustration. Some fathers believe it will make men out of their sons if they ex-pose them to physical frustrations and reward them for having suffered deprivation; thus a child may be rewarded for standing cold, rain, or hunger, although there is no stringent reason for doing so.

An individual's emotional state customarily is acknowledged through changes in the other person's nonverbal ways of expres-sion. Usually an individual's gross deviations from ordinary emo-tional states are acknowledged immediately. For example, it is customary in Western civilization to lower the voice, to assume a serious expression, and to avoid pleasantries when expressing sym-pathy to a person in grief. The verbal statements of a highly excited person, of one who is intoxicated or in pain, or of an obviously de-pressed person are not taken literally, and another scheme of inter-pretation is applied. In such situations, the receiver disregards the overt content of any message and reacts primarily to the affective elements of expression. The acuity of reaction to such emotional expression varies: the psychiatrist is prepared to perceive the slight-est changes; the military man is usually trained to disregard minor reactions but is ready to cope with the pressing emotional needs of his men.

Selective reply to emotional expressions of others is contingent upon the age of the participants. Nonverbal reply to the infant's expressions is the only possible response; and when this is inappro-priate, repetition lays the foundations for later disturbances of com-munication. In adulthood, there are several possible ways of replying to emotional expressions. These assume a particularly prominent position when agreement on a given subject cannot be reached. If at such a moment an affective bridge can be established, the exchange is likely to continue. In many disputes, the expression of anger, disappointment, or hope has saved the situation. But if a person is incapable of responding to another's emotional expression or when he gains pleasure from willfully withholding acknowledgment, communication is likely to be interrupted.

Identity

Used in the psychological sense, the term "identity" subsumes all those processes which clarify an individual's awareness of his functions vis-à-vis others and of what he has to expect from himself. The elements which contribute to what is called identity do not change much with time and circumstance. Attitudes toward law, sex, public service, men, women, and children or traits such as honesty, fidelity, and tolerance remain relatively stable throughout a lifetime. The assumption of role, in contrast, subsumes a flexible attitude which, dependent upon the situation, defines the mutual relationship with other persons.

The child's **foundations of identity** are laid when adult behavior is imitated. As time passes, imitation of other children's behavior and own experiences are added to round out the block of information that defines the child's knowledge of himself, including the recognition of his abilities, skills, potentialities, limitations, and defects. A consistent and continuous relationship with one and the same person from birth through the formative years is essential for the establishment of identity (74). When the child reaches school age, multiplicity of social contact and inconsistent behavior in one person can be tolerated if a solid beginning of identity has been established. This sequence in development is very much akin to the learning of a new skill; at first, instruction must be simple, consistent, and without exceptions; later, complexities and irregularities can be learned. While the acquisition of identity is tied to early interpersonal experiences, the mastery of role is a function of group experiences which by necessity occur later in life.

Identity is felt as a permanent, somewhat unalterable part of the self; role is felt as a temporary function which is assumed. The

awareness of identity and role determines to a large degree the acknowledgment received from others. Thus, awareness of **identity
and role** is a prerequisite for successful communication. In all expressions of the individual, this awareness is transmitted to the receiver; it primes him with regard to the interpretation of messages
and in a subtle way defines form, timing, and content of the statement. Pathology of communication may arise when an individual's
identity is ill-defined or when a person feels that he does not possess
an identity at all. Disturbances also occur when an individual cannot or will not function in a certain role and when such inability
or refusal is not openly stated.

Inasmuch as children do not have a fully developed sense of identity, roles and functions within the fold of the family have to be
clearly defined; otherwise confusion will result. When a mother
wishes to comment upon her five-year-old girl's tendency to make
grimaces, she can proceed in one of several ways. If she acknowledges the grimacing and indicates that this is not the right time but
explains that making faces is quite appropriate when imitating animals, the child's awareness of identity and role will be strengthened
in spite of the fact that her activity has been criticized. If, however,
the mother indicates that faces must not be made and that a child
who makes faces cannot claim to be her daughter, then she disturbs
the child's sense of identity. The daughter can handle the situation
in either of two ways: she can repress the tendency to make faces
and forego the pleasure of learning how to impersonate or she can
make faces behind her mother's back and lose faith in her mother's
common sense. Either solution, if repeated in other similar situations, will handicap her awareness of identity.

Fantasy

Fantasy enables people to imagine, to extrapolate and interpolate,
to reconstruct the past, to anticipate the future, and to distort perceived events if necessary. In early childhood, before the limits of
what is possible have been tested, fantasy elaboration of traumatic
experiences is carried out frequently in the form of play. Dolls and
toy animals, for example, enable a child to separate action from person: the threatening activities of a stern father may be reassigned to
the less threatening figure of a Teddy bear. Fantasy and play act

as a buffer system; they make rumination possible; they help the child to tolerate frustration, and they implement delay in gratification. They help to bridge the unavoidable disruptions in interpersonal relations; a child can tolerate being put to bed in a separate room when he assigns the role of mother to a big blue elephant which he hugs tightly while falling asleep.

Pathology can develop when selective acknowledgment emphasizes one or the other of these experimental and defensive activities. A mother who induces her daughter to draw charming and fantastic figures at an age when she should begin to sketch more realistically, or a mother who does not check the imaginative but embellished stories of her son, selectively emphasizes the fantastic to the detriment of realistic approaches. Unless time and place for the use of fantasy are specified, either selective encouragement or suppression serves to distort the child's view of the world and undermines the foundations of healthy communication.

PREMATURE AND BELATED RESPONSES

The parent's responses must be matched to the child's state of development, not only in terms of their intensity but also in terms of timing. Intuitive parents seem to know when the moment has come to lift restrictions and to supply opportunities for testing out and exercising functions that are being developed. Rigid, disorganized, or insensitive parents tend to miss such strategic moments and tend either to force premature development or to retard the child's growth.

Forcing premature development

Premature insistence on learning leads to **apparent mastery** which induces the child to perform certain gestures to the satisfaction of the adult without having full command of the newly acquired function. Without corresponding biological or psychological readiness, the learning of such tasks forces the child to memorize some relevant clues; to stick rigidly to rules; and, because of the precariousness of the task, to forego experimentation through trial and error. Premature achievement is possible only if the parents spend an undue amount of time with the child and appeal to his magic belief in extraordinary attainment. The body of information pertaining to such premature functioning frequently remains an unintegrated island. It cannot be assimilated because its complexity does not correspond to other experiences of the child; thus it eludes any correction necessitated by changes of internal or external conditions and keeps the child dependent upon guidance from adults.

If the child is pushed beyond his limits, **development may well be arrested.** When exposed to analogous situations in adolescence and adulthood, an individual realizes that he cannot spontaneously master the task at hand, and he reacts with anxiety. Advice and guidance which carried such a person through the original situation are sought anew because of the realization of his state of helplessness. The disturbances which arise from this type of upbringing are rather characteristic. Rigid perception, evaluation, and action take the place of flexible behavior. By leaning upon others, the individual ignores his inherent potentialities and fails to develop different approaches. Observance of obsolete rules or adherence to antiquated principles of evaluation will prevent him from correcting information through personal experiences. Such is the case when parents become impatient with the child's nonverbal forms of communication. Instead of responding by doing things with the child, calling attention to observations of interest, or demonstrating action in slow motion, these parents tend to use words which the child does not understand and cannot apply. Premature verbalization and apparent skill with numbers take the place of much-needed experience in the process of interaction.

Special difficulties are encountered by so-called **child prodigies.** These children, regardless of whether they are musicians, acrobats, chess players, or actors, are pushed to the limits of their capabilities. Their premature specialization becomes possible because external stimulation plays into innate talent. The child learns to excel in one area of endeavor, but this excellence is usually achieved at the cost of arrested development in one or more of the other areas. At a later age, the then grown-up "child prodigy" discovers that compared to that of other masters his own skill leaves much to be desired.

When a child is sick, his mental speed decreases, his fatigue level is reached sooner, he tends to lower his level of aspiration, and he resorts to simple play and earlier forms of emotional expression. The adult has to play along with these changes because this is the best the child can do under the circumstances. To insist on high-level performances means unduly to frustrate the child, who needs all his resources to combat the disease. Many behavior disturbances begin after an illness during which the demands of the adults exceeded the capacities of the child. But even at times of good health, if adults insist upon consistency and tenacity when the child's fatigue level is reached, such inappropriate insistence spoils the child's readiness to learn and produces a breakdown in communication.

Parents are alarmed when in the course of development the child apparently reverts to already abandoned forms of behavior. For example, parents complain about the awkwardness of the seven-year-old which contrasts with the smooth and graceful movements of the five-year-old. This **apparent regression** is due to the fact that when movements are paired with purposeful—and particularly with aggressive—behavior, the synchronization between emotion and movement can be achieved only at the expense of smoothness. As a matter of fact, those adults who have retained the flexibility and smoothness of motion of the young child, as professional dancers have, may pay for their perfection with emotional immaturity and other character disturbances.

Delaying psychological growth

With the acquisition of coordination, the accumulation of knowledge, and the sharpening of perception, the child's patterns of communication have constantly to be altered, and obsolete patterns have to be replaced by new ones. Instead of encouraging development, some parents are delighted to keep their child a baby. Some mothers feel threatened by the progressive independence of their children; others can only communicate through somatic and action language and attempt to retain nonverbal ways of communication even when the child reaches the age of verbal discourse. Sometimes physical disease or lack of social intercourse will retard the development of the child. But, regardless of the reason, imposition of ways of communication characteristic of younger years prevents the child from acquiring new approaches, retards the refinement of observation and expression, and results in a diminished pleasure received from the process of communication. Mothers who reward their adolescent children with tidbits of food, who tuck in their teen-age children, or who remind their adult sons to put on a sweater in order not to catch cold are attempting to reinforce patterns which the individual struggles to leave behind.

When parents have a particular stake in **maintaining a function which is obsolete** for the child, attempts at reinforcing such a function block new growth. An extreme case of this sort was reported in the San Francisco *Chronicle* of June 27, 1955: A man, aged fifty-one, whose mother had recently died, was delivered to a hospital in Reading (England) for examination. The man had been a complete invalid since the age of eight; at that time, an attack of measles had left him frail and with impaired sight. Thereafter his mother had treated him as if he were completely blind and paralyzed. The examination at the hospital revealed no structural abnormality. Now, after forty-three years of invalidism, the patient is being rehabilitated. At first unable to hold a feeding cup, the patient is learning to walk and to carry on conversations, and he is being trained as a carpenter.

Interference with tempo and rhythm

The experience of **elapsed time** varies with different cultural and age groups. Children slice time according to units of experience which are separated by disruptions. The most basic of these disruptions is sleep, which structures the child's day into discrete entities. Tomorrow may mean "after my nap," "when I get up," or "sometime next week," without a clear reference to chronological time. Difficulties arise for the child when the adults impose chronological time too early. They then disregard the child's attempt to structure time in terms of his biological experiences—for example, in terms of "when I wake up," "when I can swim across the river," or "when I am as tall as my sister" (113).

The testing out of new tasks is frequently done discontinuously. The child will strike a few keys on the piano in the morning, some more in the afternoon, and the day thereafter. When fatigue sets in, the child stops and may turn his attention to another subject, only to take up his previous activity a little while later. Some parents are impatient and do not permit the discontinuous learning that expresses the child's attempt to slice the universe into time segments which he is able to tolerate. The span of attention of a child increases with the years, and only during adolescence has he reached a tenacity and vigility comparable to that of the adult. If parents insist that young children display the same consistency and the same span of attention that they themselves possess, they tend to disrupt the natural process of maturation.

In a culture like ours, where "time is money," there is little regard for **biological time.** Not much is known about the factors which induce some people to age slowly and others to age rapidly and why already at birth human beings differ in rate of activity. The fact is well established that some babies cry a lot, some little; that some are strong and make a lot of movements while others move less; that some are slow to learn a task while others are quick; that some need time to wake up in the morning and others are wide awake immediately. These facts lead one to believe that parents would be wise to accept the endogenously determined time and speed factors in their children. In this case, they would arrange things in such a way that the social surroundings would not interfere with the innate biological "clock" of the child. This also implies that parents have to adapt to the uneven rate of growth of their children. At each maturational level, one particular system undergoes a spurt of growth and then relinquishes its lead to another system. Thus, sucking, biting, grasping, holding, sphincter control, locomotion, speech, balance of the body, jumping, swimming, all are learned not simultaneously but in succession. Bodily movements become progressively faster and more accurate until the individual reaches the early twenties, at which time maturity of the motor system is reached.

To be effective, parents have to **respect** these **constitutionally determined time characteristics.** Stimuli have to reach the organism when it is ready for a particular action. If rhythm, maturational state, and speed of learning are disregarded or if strong and persistent stimulation reaches the child in a dormant or refractory period, disturbances of communication are likely to develop. Some children show undue persistence in their attempt to manage such interference; others withdraw from human contact; and still others develop rage or anxiety. To these responses of their children, the parents react in a variety of ways. If the child attempts to master the situation, the parent usually tends to become protective; if the child withdraws, this seeming lack of responsiveness may enrage the parent; if the child gets mad, the parent usually becomes punitive. The parents' anxiety in turn is fed back to the child and this disruptive influence makes the child progressively less capable of dealing with the interference.

Interference with the timing and **rhythm** of infants occurs when babies attempt to establish their own feeding schedules and bladder or bowel rhythm and adults attempt to change this biological rhythm. If babies are forced to go to the toilet according to the clock rather than according to the state of their bladder and rectum, they learn to disregard stimuli arising in themselves. Instead, they become dependent upon external admonitions, frequently at the price of developing severe gastrointestinal or urinary disturbances. Actually, such disturbances are the result of failure in nonverbal communication; had the mother understood the implicitly expressed rhythm of the child and had she respected his autonomy, in all likelihood she would have reacted in the proper way. In older children, the same sort of interference can be observed in the sphere of verbal communication. Some children talk a lot, some little; some answer after a pause, some immediately; some think fast, some slow. If parents begin to correct and criticize these innate features, disturbances of communication are likely to result. Interference with timing and rhythm is largely, although not entirely, responsible for speech disturbances such as stuttering and stammering.

CLEAR-CUT, DISRUPTIVE INTERFERENCE

The clear-cut "no" and the clear-cut "yes" express a certain finality which removes all possible ambiguity. However, certain "noes" and "yeses" may leave wounds, particularly when they involve an area of activity which is essential for the growth of the child. A "no" which consistently prevents a child from playing with his contemporaries may lead to isolation and severe disturbances of communication. A "yes" which consistently induces a child to indulge excessively in alcoholic beverages leaves its unalterable traces. Knowledge of when to say "yes" and when to say "no" is part of the cultural heritage of any group. How and when to say "yes" and "no" depend on the intuition and skill of the individual person.

Excessive prohibitions and control

In the exertion of direct power, the **command** is the statement of choice. It is implemented through gestures and words and is obeyed usually because the leader is able to reinforce it. Thus in the military situation disobedience vis-à-vis a superior officer leads to court-martial and perhaps even to death; the command of a judge is re-inforced by police; and the command of the collector of internal revenue is reinforced by the federal and local agencies to the point of confiscation of property and restriction of liberty. People know that such agencies can exert power if necessary, and they regard their simple requests as commands. Thus the tax collector collects money, the general commands troops, the policeman directs traffic, the fire chief restricts all people in and around a fire, the pilot com-mands crew and passengers of an aircraft, and the surgeon super-vises whoever is in an operating room. All these situations are limited and circumscribed and can be backed up by force; if not obeyed, appropriate sanctions are invoked.

A command is usually given in a tone of voice or worded in a way that implicitly states, "This is a command." In daily-life communica-tion, the cues which characterize command are well understood by all and accepted by most. Some people challenge a command be-cause they may believe that the one who gives it may not be en-titled to do so. Children have to learn to understand what is a command; they also have to learn how to give commands. A little boy who had tried in vain to make his big collie obey him once asked the help of his father by saying, "Tell Rolf in your mean voice to sit down." This boy had not yet learned to give commands.

Disturbances arise when commands are given in situations that do not warrant such a form of communication. The father who commands his son to sit down at a picnic to eat his sandwich misses the spirit of the picnic. The mother who commands her son to shake hands with a rival who has just beaten him up is interfering with the boy's way of managing a grudge. Command is frequently abused by parents who cannot distinguish between teamwork necessitating control and enlightenment involving the transfer of knowledge.

However, not all people control by giving commands. Some achieve **control** through manipulation of external circumstances. Instead of telling the child, "We will go and see Dr. Jones," parents may arrange to have Dr. Jones drop in when the child is around. Matchmaking and committee work are instances where control is exerted through arrangement of external circumstances. A known administrator once said, "If you want to get an unpopular measure through a committee, discuss something that the members will disagree upon for the whole session and then in the last five minutes, when everybody wants to adjourn, is hungry and thirsty, you bring up the unpopular measure and it will be approved." The same is true in a family where the mother may forbid the son to go to a movie, but the prohibition is lifted if he helps wash the dishes. The effect of such **manipulative attitudes** is that the child does not treat any message as a sincere expression on the part of the other person but always looks for some ulterior motive. The disregard of the overt content and the search for the implied control brings about difficulties in expression and inability to share emotions. Even more intricate than the direct manipulation of people are the arrangements of the material environment (215). Designed to control children or adults, the arrangement of chairs and tables, the timing of invitations, and the channeling of traffic can be employed to separate or unite people and to have them do certain things.

Overprotection is a kinder word than control but it refers to the same process. In overprotection, the mother functions as a filter, screening the communicative input and steering the output of the child. Thus, when such a dependent child is suddenly exposed to unfiltered messages, he is unable to scan, select, weight, and make decisions. And if there is nobody around who attenuates, reinforces, or encourages, he remains in a state of complete ineffectiveness. In this type of interpersonal approach, the child is reduced to the state of an effector or sensory organ while the parent acts as information center and decision-maker. The experience of being acknowledged is unknown to the child who is controlled, and therefore he ceases to grow. In these families recognition is not given for the child's sake but for making him carry out a desired operation.

Restrictions which delineate the universe of discourse, which limit movement in accordance with the skills of the child, and which prevent exposure to irreversible trauma are necessary and healthy tools of education. However, restrictions which interfere with problem-solving, with the acquisition of knowledge, and with testing out acquired skills have a destructive impact. Excessive prohibition leads essentially to the formation of an exacting conscience, and when the child engages in spontaneous activity he experiences guilt. Such guilt extends even to the communication process. The pleasure experienced in fluid interchange makes the child feel guilty. Such an individual is condemned to partial communication because were he to be successful his overbearing conscience would clamp down and induce him to interfere with or break off the successful exchange.

Control and **power** can be exerted **overtly or covertly,** and since in our Western civilization we have abolished slavery, absolute monarchies, dictatorships, and, for the moment, the patriarchal family structure, the exertion of control becomes more and more covert. In authoritarian groups, control is the method of choice; in democratic groups, control has gone underground. Conformity becomes the tyrant, and children are admonished to heed popular opinion. "Nobody in your class would dare to do such a thing" might be taken as an example of a statement of a mother who hides behind the anonymity of people at large. A child may see fit to rebel against personalized authority, but to rebel against public opinion makes him an outcast. Not to share with others the same values eventually leads to complete breakdown in communication.

Excessive aspirations and lack of limitations

The **expectancies** of the child are set in part by the experience of past growth and in part by the demands of the social surroundings. In the first year of life, both psychological growth and physical growth are very rapid, and as a result of this experience the child anticipates further growth. If one were to plot growth, one would find a steep rise of the curve in the first few years of life, a flattening in late adolescence, and a reversal of the curve in later years. The curve of expectancy, in contrast, seems to approximate a straight line, in which the child extrapolates from the experience of early growth without anticipating the flattening or the reversal. Together with the slowing down of early growth in general, one can observe that emotional, intellectual, and physical functions develop at different rates. Physical maturity is reached first, intellectual maturity is second, and emotional maturity is achieved last.

When a child extrapolates and expects his growth to keep up with the formerly established rate, he becomes overwhelmed by the anticipation of further growth and the acquisition of power. In order to counterbalance the expectation of omnipotence, the child needs exposure to corrective influences by significant adults. These corrections serve the purpose of molding the child's expectations in such a way that they will follow a path similar to that of the actual growth curve. If correction does not occur and expectation outdistances actual growth, anticipations become unrealistic. Under such circumstances, the individual is exposed to recurrent disappointments because none of his expectations come true. If, on the other hand, the expectations fall short of actual growth, the child suffers from feelings of inferiority. The setting of limits on the part of the parents thus reinforces or countermands the already existing distortions on the part of the child.

Parental expectations are usually not the result of conscious and precisely timed deliberations adapted to the child's growth. On the contrary, the parents' expectations are largely determined by their own—often unconscious—wishful thinking. Parents may consider children extensions of themselves, and then the child's growth is welcomed and promoted as long as it contributes to their own pride. If parents consider children as complements of themselves, the children's growth may threaten their notions of size, stature, and prestige. Frequently, therefore, parents will set limits for the child which implement their own irrational needs and which only secondarily help the child to match his level of aspiration with his abilities.

Absence of parental limitations frequently is observed in families in which children are left to their own devices. When the neglectful parents finally come home, they feel guilty. As a consequence, they may purchase toys, take the kids to the movies, let them smoke, or invite them to places of entertainment for grownups. Unspecified bedtime, too much pocket money, or absence of checks into the whereabouts of the child may strengthen his belief that he is more grown up than he actually is. All these guilt-determined actions on the part of the parents serve to stimulate the wishful thinking of the children. When such a child attempts to adjust his behavior and his communications to the implicit assumptions made by the parents, he is surprised to find that he gets into conflict. Contemporaries treat him as a freak, a phony, or an eccentric, and reacting to this mystifying treatment the child tends to increase the pitch of his aspirations. This procedure, which proved successful with the parents, is followed by more failure. Society may catch up with such a person because of his delinquent behavior, or he may join the make-believers—full of expectations but never ready to produce—who are found in the bohemian quarters and amidst the café society of any city.

The child's acceptance or rejection of parental limitations is largely a function of emotional reward received in the course of communication. If contact with parents is pleasant, children tend to accept limitations, although sometimes with resentment. If, however, communication is not gratifying, any kind of limitation may be totally rejected.

Exclusion

In some homes, the children are fed early and thus are excluded from the family dinner table. Some parents do not engage in any family enterprise. They have the nurse take the children to the park, and they don't take them along on picnics or trips. The same parents may relegate the children to another room for play while they occupy the living room. Instead of observing the maxim, "To each his own, but in a common task," such parents believe in "To each his own—let's all have different tasks." These families might as well not live under one roof. Such exclusion gives the children the feeling of a barrier which they have no way of crossing. If exclusion is practiced, the adults cannot serve as efficient models for the children's learning through imitation, and the growth of the children is delayed.

Exclusion is the fate of many children from prominent or **well-to-do families.** The parents are so busy attending to social and other obligations that they turn over the care of the children to hired hands. The children may be exposed to one nurse after another, and the effects of exclusion from their parents' lives is frequently reflected in their oppositional behavior. They become playboys or socialites and do not perpetuate the traditions or carry on the occupation, position, and interests of their parents. These children learned the ways of communication of their nurses, if any at all, and hence they seek the company of people they can talk to and have fun with. The conflicting influence of parents and hired help is reflected in their character structure and their inability to be personally satisfied and successful.

But there exists an even more subtle form of exclusion. When a mother dresses her daughter in outlandish clothes so that her playmates at school will tease her, or when she says, "I shall have a hot dog but I suppose you will not want one," she draws a subtle **line of demarcation.** The child unconsciously has to assert herself if she wishes to be included, and on many occasions the path of least resistance will be to do nothing and to remain excluded. Such children tend to become lonely and isolated unless experiences of being included attenuate these earlier impressions.

Ambiguous and Confusing Influences

Of his own volition and not necessarily stimulated by the child, the adult may make statements which bear upon his personal problems. These expressions of the adult can be understood by the child if they are distinct and unambiguous and if they are formulated in a simple manner. If, however, the messages of the adult are contradictory or are phrased in language which the child does not understand, confusion is the result. More often than not, the psychological methods which the child has to use to master this confusing situation will involve distortion, repression, or isolation, which processes form the basis of a great many disturbances of communication.

Inconsistent and contradictory behavior

The introduction of order into the randomness of perceived events is brought about by exposing the child to consistent behavior of others. When stimuli recur at regular intervals in similar situations, the conditions for learning and growth are favorable. If, however, the time intervals are irregular and the nature of the stimuli and the situation changes, learning is more difficult. Under **irregular conditions**, the child will spontaneously cling to something that remains stationary or similar; the mother, a Teddy bear, a bedcover, or a piece of clothing. This clinging to a consistent object is a sign of the child's intolerance for discrepancies. In the learning stage, this intolerance takes the form of a rigidly expressed need for order and exclusiveness. Later, when the function which was being learned is well established, it loses its initial rigidity and the former orderliness becomes an unnecessary crutch which then can be discarded.

As the child abandons behavioral rigidities, he begins to adhere to more abstract consistencies which might be called **attitudes**. Thus the child recognizes that life is an ongoing process in which variability of patterns is acceptable. If it is permissible to eat steak today and fish tomorrow, the abstract consistency might be the place and time of the dinner or the implements used. If it is permissible to get mad today and to be conciliatory tomorrow, the consistency might be the expression of emotions. The process of abstraction serves to reconcile contradictions. The attentive parent helps the child to find the level at which such consistencies can be found. And in those families where the contradictions are the greatest, the children tend to think more abstractly and have a vocabulary which contains more abstract terms; it may well be that the abstract tendency of schizophrenics is due to the presence of such contradictions.

There are people who on the surface display **contradictory personality features**. Those who live with them, however, sooner or later arrive at an understanding at a level of abstraction which eliminates these contradictions. Also, there are people who on the surface behave consistently but who underneath are inconsistent and confused. Pertinent examples are: the man who carefully writes a check for his daughter but fails to sign it; the father who sits at his desk at home under the pretext of working but instead regularly falls asleep; or the father who instead of telling the children that mother is sick admonishes them to heed her paranoid suggestions. All these contradictions contribute toward an ambiguous character structure in the children.

A similar effect is produced when a child has to face situations where **words do not correspond to facts** or where one action does not match another action. For example, a child may be told that he is now a big man and that he can steer the automobile; in this make-believe situation, he is put in front of the steering wheel, but when he starts acting as if he really wanted to drive the car he is cut to size with the reminder that he is a little fellow who cannot do such a thing.

In institutionalized children, disturbances may arise not so much because of inconsistent responses but because their **contact with adults is departmentalized.** If one nurse attends to feeding, another to dressing, and a third puts the child to bed, the impact of these adults cannot be coordinated. Such departmentalized, discontinuous, institutional care leads to the development of personalities which are either rigid or completely disorganized. Apparently the ability to transfer information gained from one experience to another similar experience is possible for the child only if the carry-over is mediated through continuous contact with one and the same person. In instances where children enter institutions after the foundations of their personalities have been laid and a sense of identity has been developed, departmentalization may result in introspection. In search for a continuous experience in the presence of inconsistent and discontinuous human relations, such children resort to withdrawal into fantasy life.

The child's detection of **inconsistencies** is a rather complex process. If a mother's feeling vacillates as to whether or not she likes the child, this will be perceived as an inconsistency. If the father permits the son to stay up late on one occasion, this will not be noted as an inconsistency if the privilege is a recognized exception. On Christmas and on birthdays, and perhaps on the Fourth of July, children may stay up longer, and they also understand that this practice is not extended indefinitely. But if they are permitted to go to bed at eight o'clock on one day and at eleven o'clock the next without any apparent rhyme or reason, this will confuse the child. Consistency, therefore, is a function of a larger pattern rather than being determined by repeated, isolated performances. If the child understands the pattern, certain apparently inconsistent events may be regarded as consistent. In this process, the child learns to integrate part functions into a whole. Such integration can only be acquired if the learning process proceeds in an atmosphere of optimal rather than minimal or maximal gratification. Repeated and consistent reward for unified action patterns, including awareness of motive, mastery of implementation, and observation of effects, contributes toward integrated personality patterns. This condition is met when the adults refrain from being inconsistent, from selectively rewarding isolated functions, or from giving quantitatively inappropriate rewards.

Anxious and disorganized behavior

The transmission of alarm signals occurs both in the animal kingdom and in the human world. Both the intensity and the strangeness of a stimulus, as well as its reference to known dangers, contribute to the alarm of an individual (216). Once an individual is alarmed, his condition of excitation may act as a stimulus for the alarm of other people. When a mother is disturbed, her anxiety is immediately transmitted to the children. The more anxious a person becomes or the more people are anxious, the more convincing the alarm becomes for those who have not been infected as yet. This feedback process quickly may lead to panic and disorganization (204).

In therapy, an attempt is made to have the patient express his anxiety, while it is hoped that during this time the therapist can remain relatively unaffected. Because of the therapist's nonanxious attitude, he is able, through negative feedback, to reduce the anxiety of the patient. The same process takes place in the relation of **adults and children.** If a mother picks up a crying child with reassurance, her strength and calmness help the child to recover his composure. However, anxious parents have a limited capacity to console their children. The crying of the child frightens the mother;

her anxiety is fed back to the child who, because of the mother's excitement, believes that his anxiety is well founded: "If it can frighten mother, then there must be something to it; I have a reason to be anxious." An anxious mother is alarmed not only when the child cries but also on many other occasions. Her anxiousness is betrayed by high pitch, tremulousness, and varying intensity of her voice. When she touches the child, she perspires and even smells anxious; she may grip the child's arm too tightly or too loosely; she may yank him out of his chair and throw him down abruptly. All these and many others are the signals which disturb the child.

Any message accompanied by anxiety is ambiguous. This **ambiguity** can be attenuated when the anxiety is verbally acknowledged. Through open acknowledgment, the two contradictory statements— that which is said and that which is done—are reconciled. To paraphrase the reaction of the parent in situations loaded with anxiety, one might say:

Help—"I understand your condition, but it does not affect me."

Delineation—"I understand your condition but it is your problem; I cannot be drawn into it."

Denial—"I ignore your condition."

Sympathy—"Your condition affects me too."

Infection—"Your condition affects me more than it does you."

Reaction formation—"Your condition affects me just the other way."

In situations where the mother denies her anxiety, its effects may be potentiated. Mother may say, "Darling, there is nothing to be afraid of," while her teeth chatter and she shakes all over. In the face of such ambiguity, the child has several alternatives. If he is old enough, he can blockade himself against the anxiety of the mother by means of withdrawal; or he can react to the anxiety and disregard the verbal assurance; or he can disregard and deny the anxiety and react to the verbal content. Any one of these solutions may lead to distortion, repression, or isolation of feeling, or, in brief, to a selective response which ignores part of the message.

Affective behavior discordant with other events

When action, thought, feeling, and word are integrated into a unit, the resulting behavior engenders a feeling of solidity and security. If one element, however, is split off, the receiver may become aware of the incompleteness of the statement. Most disturbing is the **splitting off of the affective component.** When the content of the statement expresses congratulations and the speaker's voice indicates sadness or when a mother assures her child of her love but leaves him, affect is incongruous with action. The perniciousness of discordant affect is due to the fact that the emotional aspects of a statement convey a meaning even when the intellectual aspects have failed to do so; but if emotions are incongruous, they confuse rather than clarify the statement. In multiperson situations, emotions serve as in interspecies and intergroup language; they are intuitively understood when all other methods of communication have failed. Thus, when contradictions arise in the use of words or action, recourse can be had by understanding the other person's emotional attitude. Or when in a dispute someone gets mad and discourse is disrupted, agreement is established on an emotional plane (215). But when emotions are not concordant with thought or action, they cannot be used for purposes of establishing communication. And children are particularly apt to rely upon emotions to relate to people whose words or actions they do not understand.

A particular disruption of communication occurs when **emotions are projected** onto others. They may say "You are nasty" when they mean "I am mad," or they may say "You depress me" when they mean "I am sad." Mothers who use this form of reply establish a causal relationship between the child and their own feelings and hence stimulate his omnipotent and magic thinking. A similarly disruptive effect is achieved when the emotions of the child are not permitted to be expressed at all. This occurs when mothers punish their children for expressions of shame, fear, and rage. By labeling the existence of emotions as an undesirable feature, they lay the foundations upon which feelings of guilt begin to arise in the child in connection with emotional expression. The result is repression with all its detrimental effects upon communication.

Emphasis on possibilities rather than facts

Emphasis upon things that do not exist, review of events that might have happened but did not, speculation about the unknown rather than the known, and consideration of potentialities rather than achievement introduce another form of pathology. If such techniques are used extensively with youngsters, they are reminded of their shortcomings, they learn to sit in judgment rather than to solve problems, or they begin to excuse themselves by pointing to their unrealized potentialities and tend to stay forever in the category of promising young people. Any solution chosen for a given problem can easily be criticized because usually there exist other alternatives. Thus it is easy to make people feel inferior by emphasizing what they did not do rather than to comment on what they did. An example might illustrate the case. A seventeen-year-old, at the time of high school graduation, brings home his report card full of A's with the exception of one B. Mother takes him to task and reproaches him for not having all A's and for graduating second in his class rather than first. The boy leaves the room and slams the door. But such momentary frustration is not the important feature. What matters is that within himself the boy begins to assess his deficiencies rather than his skills, thus laying the foundations for later feelings of inferiority. Before an enterprise is undertaken, the emphasis upon potentialities is constructive; afterwards, it is rather destructive. At that moment an operational analysis of the events that happened will be more profitable than the usual post-mortem discussions and accusations.

Chapter Five

Individual Psychopathology:
Disturbances of Communication
in Adulthood

In the nineteenth century, the concept of psychopathology was based upon the consideration of the individual as a unit separate from his surroundings; and if one had to indicate the location of psychopathology, one would have placed it within the organism. Today, we no longer hold such exclusively **intraorganismic views** and operational assessment of processes occurring within and between individuals, groups, and cultures has replaced the concept of psychopathological types. Today, we know that the individual and his social and physical surroundings constitute a functional unit and that disturbances which appear to affect the single person are in many ways tied to events which involve much larger systems. Although the older psychopathologists were not unaware of the existence of suprapersonal factors in the etiology of psychiatric disturbances, they did not possess a satisfactory theory to unify psychological, physical, and social events into one system. But it is amazing to discover that, in spite of this fact, the authors of classical psychopathology (35, 126, 135, 138, 155) paved the way for present studies of human communication by intuitively focusing upon disturbed communication. The phenomenological descriptions of such symptoms as hallucinations, illusions, delusions, and obsessions were based upon the observation of communicative disturbances of perception and evaluation. Description of compulsive, impulsive, catatonic, or cataleptic behavior was based upon observations of disturbances of expression and transmission. The recognition that individual disturbances of perception, evaluation, and transmission could be theoretically connected with events that involve multi-person or societal systems and that these in turn affect the individual's behavior was left to modern psychiatry.

In diseases which affect the human organs of communication, and therefore the functions of perception, evaluation, and transmission, classical psychopathology is as valid today as it was fifty or eighty years ago. Conditions associated with **brain disease** may be responsible for disturbances of perception, evaluation, memory, motility, and expression. Constitutional deviations in intelligence as they occur in the mentally deficient may be responsible for defective evaluation. Diseases of or injury to the sense organs may interfere with perception, as in the case of the blind or the deaf. Diseases or injuries affecting the muscles and bones interfere with action and expression; amputees, fracture cases, arthritics, and patients with muscular dystrophy or multiple sclerosis may here be mentioned as examples. Endocrine disorders such as hyperthyroidism or myxedema may produce some general effects which influence psycho-motor speed.

In the **schizophrenic and affective reactions,** the phenomenology of classical psychopathology is valid only with serious restrictions. Phenomena such as hallucinations, illusions, and delusions which affect the perceptive and evaluative functions of individuals have been described long ago; however, modern theories concerning the behavior of schizophrenics have come to recognize that these are symptoms of disturbances which may affect a whole group. A schizophrenic patient may begin to hallucinate the day his mother comes to visit, but can function without sensory disturbances on days when his participation in the group and on the ward is undisturbed. This does not mean that an individual—and particularly a sick person—does not possess a certain degree of autonomy, but it means that his symptoms reflect, among other things, disturbances of the supra-ordinate system.

In the psychoneuroses and the **personality disorders,** classical psychopathology is outmoded. Owing to the influence of Freud (91, 93), we have come to recognize that the significant pathology in this group of conditions lies not in the phenomenology of unusual behavior but in the repetitiveness of ordinary behavior patterns which are characterized by the fact that they do not ensure proper gratification and that they prevent the psychological growth of the patient.

In describing the psychopathology of adulthood, therefore, it is necessary to extend the considerations beyond the individual and to include **group and culture** as well. This is achieved by considering the group networks in which an individual participates. But in the analysis of a given network, difficulties arise. Psychiatric patients usually are not examined and treated in their natural habitat. When the patient is not together with his family, his adaptation to the ways of communication prevailing in his family will not be apparent, and therefore the doctor is inclined to focus upon his character; if the doctor were to see him in action within the fold of the family, he probably would focus upon the exchange taking place in that family group. Furthermore, difficulties arise when written language is used to describe disturbances of communication. In writing, it is impossible to encompass the whole network at once, and therefore the disturbances of communication presented in subsequent pages may appear as if they were disturbances of an individual nature.

In subsequent paragraphs, a number of communication networks have been described in terms of their effect upon one individual. The reader is cautioned to be mindful of that part of the system which has not been reported; similarly, the doctor has to keep in mind relatives of a patient who are not present in order to complete the picture of the family network.

The Infantile Person

Most authors agree that patients afflicted with chronic diseases of obscure origin have some features in common. According to Alexander (5), the majority of patients with psychosomatic disorders suffer from a vegetative neurosis which is not an attempt to express an emotion but is a physiological response to constant or to periodically recurring emotional stimulation. Other authors (2, 18) believe that persons with psychosomatic diseases suffer from generalized constitutional inferiority or from biological inferiority of organs and tissues. From the viewpoint of emotional maturity and communicative behavior, these patients have in common certain characteristics which I shall describe under the heading of "infantile personality" (201, 212, 218). This kind of individual is characterized by the use of somatic language, the employment of symptoms for purposes of social control, and certain deficiencies in correcting information and performance.

In clinical medicine, the infantile person appears most frequently as a patient who complains of **tension** symptoms. Over fifty per cent of the cases hospitalized on medical wards and probably close to seventy-five per cent of the patients appearing in doctors' offices suffer from tension symptoms. Among these, persons afflicted with chronic disease and psychological invalidism (212) are of particular concern to the physician. There are those who take pride in physical health and try to suppress somatic symptoms; their tension symptoms then appear in the mental field. Those who pride themselves upon mental health are more inclined to have somatic disturbances because physical disease constitutes a culturally and socially acceptable disability. As an example, we find the social climbers who tend to overadapt to external circumstances and who are unable to cope with the resulting stress. In their immaturity, they find it difficult to limit their activities until ill-health forces them to do so (200).

The infantile person with tension symptoms loves to live in groups; to talk about ailments and to exhibit the disability; to spend time in hospitals, rehabilitation centers, and health resorts. Human relations are casual and social status matters more than interpersonal relations. If the infantile person becomes involved in social conflicts, these are usually the result of certain assumptions and beliefs which are valid for intrapersonal functioning but are not applicable to multiperson situations.

Infantile persons thus tend to distort social events. In the process of perception, undue weight is placed upon proprioceptive stimuli, while certain exteroceptive stimuli are neglected. Information derived from perception through the chemical and mechanical sensory endorgans is given more weight than information derived from perception through the distance receivers. Apparently the shift from the **proximity** to the more complex distance **receivers**, which usually occurs in the course of progressive maturation, is absent or delayed. That which happens in the body, inside of people, or inside of an organization is more understandable to such a person than that which happens outside of his organism or outside of his organization. The poor or distorted perception of social cues is compensated for by stereotyped value judgments. "It is good to do this" and "It is bad to do that" are the traditional reactions of an infantile person who has to use prefabricated rather than flexible methods of appraisal. Inasmuch as the patients possess **unsatisfactory** means of **self-expression,** transmission likewise is disturbed. The infantile person's preference for proximity receivers leads to an overemphasis upon somatic signs and signals and a neglect of verbal or gestural signs and signals. This preference for somatic language seriously curtails discursive communication, and the exchange tends to remain on the level of ostensive communication. "Let a thing speak for itself" is the motto. The thing, in this case, is the body. Thus blushing, blanching, burping, salivation, scratching, and cold hands are used for the purpose of expressing significant inner events. Some patients even use these somatic manifestations to evoke or provoke emotional reactions in others. A whole family may be subdued and its life organized around the tyranny of a disabled individual who holds his illness like a club over the heads of the other family members. The consequences of a violation of diets, attacks of asthma, skin rashes, or pain are threats which the relatives cannot disregard easily.

The higher **symbolic functions** are underdeveloped. The vocabulary range tends to be limited; fantasy elaborations in such tests as the Rorschach and thematic apperception tests are primitive, unimaginative, and stereotyped. The infantile person seems to watch the behavior of others principally with body functions in mind. He does not assess the action itself but concentrates upon the organ that carries it out; and when engaged in action himself, he seems to pay more attention to his bodily sensations than to the impact he has upon others.

Evidence would indicate that the **internal codification** system of the infantile person involves rather extended pathways. In immature people, as in children, internal codification does not consist of purely cerebral representation. The elimination of unnecessary functions, including the elimination of peripheral concomitants of central representation, is incomplete. While the schizophrenic concerns himself primarily with symbolic matters and hence employs in his internal codifications networks that do not involve the effector system, the infantile person seems to stand at the opposite end of the scale. Infantile people use touch and action as means of signifying; figuratively speaking, they think with their bodies, feel with their bodies, and talk with their bodies. Practically all of their cerebral activities, both intellectual and affective, find repercussions in the periphery. When they try to think out a problem, they become tense, and what they call a feeling is a sensation localized in the stomach, in the heart region, or in the extremities.

In the process of maturation, the infantile person is prevented from replacing dependency upon the protective actions of others with reliance upon the exchange of information and cooperative interaction. The delineation of the physical, psychological, and social **boundaries** of the self is incomplete and arbitrary. Hence these patients have the naïve and magic belief that the other person's physical and mental state is identical with their own. Therefore, they treat messages as if they were transmitted within one and the same matrix or neural network, and they do not know that interpersonal messages have to be repeatedly recodified and translated. They do not utilize the perceived effect of their own actions upon others, and therefore they are unable to correct the image they possess of themselves. Everybody with whom they have voluntary contact is treated as an insider, and whenever they are forced to deal with strangers, members of outgroups, or other cultures they feel uneasy.

The lack of awareness of ego boundaries forces them to confine the content of messages to subjects of universal interest. References to eating, sleeping, elimination, sex, and other body functions make up the content of most messages. Infantile persons have **difficulties in acknowledging** the other person's statements directly; rarely do they decipher the other person's intent; nor are they able to make their own intent known to others. Because of their inability to deal with abstract matters, infantile persons are not skilled in predicting events to come. Their social actions and techniques, therefore, tend to be unsophisticated and primitive. Their mechanical actions are frequently much more complex. It is perhaps more than coincidental that many highly skilled mechanical workers suffer from psychosomatic conditions. Infantile persons tend to overadapt and do not know when and where to control. And if they exert social control, they simply impose those conditions upon others which have proved beneficial to themselves. For them, compromise is difficult if not impossible. They cannot predict accurately, and they also cannot say no. They have difficulties in initiating action, in the first instance because their information is incomplete and in the second because they believe that it is the task of others to initiate and carry out actions. To act upon information would mean to assert themselves, and to assert themselves would mean to become unpopular.

Among the **childhood events** which lead to the development of the infantile personality are lack of continuity and consistency in interpersonal relations; the impact of marital discord between the parents and broken homes are frequently mentioned as traumatic experiences. If the lack of consistency in human relations is not expressed in isolated traumatic events, it appears in the form of improper balance of parental functions; one parent may have been punitive and the other rewarding, or one may have been a dominating, central figure and the other a peripheral nonentity. In some instances, the parental attitudes toward the child changed with the arrival of younger siblings. If this change of attitude occurs at a time when nonverbal means of communication still prevail, the child cannot free himself from the ensuing tension by means of talking and frequently resorts again to the organ language of babyhood.

Various processes contribute toward **arrested development**. Usually skin stimulation and affection are provided by the parents and body care becomes a significant communal activity. When the child grows older, the parents of infantile persons continue to offer food, clothing, criticism, or advice pertaining to body maintenance. These procedures frequently are the only means of social contact, and the parental care is not adapted to the growth of the child. These well-meant body-care mechanisms frequently are so coercive that the reward obtained contains hidden threats; to the child, the parents are not acceptable as ideal models, primarily because they are anxious; when the child discovers that parental anxiety can be managed by letting father and mother care for and overprotect him, he pays the price of retardation in personality development.

THE PERSON OF ACTION

Traditionally in psychopathology, the person who expresses himself in action has been listed under such labels as "psychopathic personality" (131), "constitutional psychopathic inferiority," "defect reaction," "criminality," "instinct-ridden character," or "pathergasia" (164). In these descriptions, emphasis is laid upon overt behavior or the outer organization, although many comments refer to the lack of a moral superstructure, of warmth, and of feeling.

The action personality is found in many walks of life. One finds in the highly active organizer, the militant revolutionary, and the **adventurer** and explorer people of great accomplishment. But persons of action also are notorious for organizing gangs, for engaging in rackets, and for committing crimes. In the past, society provided better outlets for action personalities than it does today. In North America, such persons could go west, fight Indians, and colonize; elsewhere they could join the French Foreign Legion, migrate to the colonies, or roam the seven seas. Today there is little use for the adventurer, and the persons who became dashing cavalrymen during the Civil War hardly would make effective bomber pilots. Today the impulsive personalities find themselves more and more out of place, and their notorious unreliability makes them unsuited for modern technical jobs.

The person of action prefers to be with people because he cannot tolerate to be alone. If by force of circumstance he should find himself alone he becomes bored because his scant fantasy, his inability to feel, to imagine, and to think make introverted pursuits unrewarding and anxiety-producing. When in groups, the person of action does not make the same assumptions that other people do. A mature individual who knows how to communicate assumes that any other individual has a distinctly separate personality and also has wishes, desires, hopes, needs, values, and implementations which may differ considerably from his own. The person of action, in contrast, is incapable of making such assumptions and assumes that the other person is really an **extension of himself.** He uses others for all sorts of purposes and treats them as leg-men, as body extensions, as waste products, or as things. He assumes that all communicative exchange takes place in a continuous and homogeneous network in which communication proceeds with a minimum loss of information. He functions well with others when he can handle the group as a homogeneous entity; he submits readily to an authoritarian leader, or he may be willing to function as an extension of an authoritarian person.

The action personality is skilled in the **perception** of the needs and intentions of the other person. Quick and alert, he appropriately perceives those cues which help him in the assessment of the other person. He is quick to grasp the advantages which will give him a momentary superiority and opportunity to control the situation. Evaluation of perceived events is usually accurate and fast; however, his grasp of secondhand information derived from other people leaves much to be desired, and here his inability to cope with verbal symbols begins to show.

The action person's greatest **deviation** is met in the area of **expression.** Action is undertaken with the intent of making a statement to others rather than of implementing his own wishes. This procedure has peculiar implications. Inasmuch as learning is concerned with the gradual elimination of unnecessary functions, the really skilled person, the virtuoso, performs with the greatest of ease and the least amount of unnecessary motion. The elimination of unnecessary movements frequently makes the performance of a master not particularly dramatic. If, in contrast, an action is undertaken for the sake of impressing onlookers, a number of movements will be added which will make the performance less skillful but more impressive to the audience. This is one of the reasons why the action personality seldom acquires top-notch skills and frequently becomes the victim of accidents.

The person of action derives no satisfaction from **verbal exchange.** The psychopath really has no way of representing feelings or thoughts in word or gesture; and if he wants to express an inner event he has to resort to complicated physical actions which frequently entail the exchange of goods, physical contact, or the creation of a disturbance. The person of action cannot say "I dislike you"; instead, he may break a window or slug another person. Nor can he say "I like you"; instead, he may shower the other person with presents. His hyperactivity is "talk" rather than implementation. Though he appears glib on the surface, his use of words does not comprise a one-to-one relationship with other events. A psychopath frequently is branded as a liar. Because of his mistrust of his own words, he does not trust the words of others and believes that the only thing to rely upon is action. Feedback from others in terms of advice, admonitions, or recommendations is not heeded, and he has to try everything himself. A psychopath tends to maximize the mandatory aspects of information. When he speaks, it is an order; and in turn, any word addressed to him he considers a command. He cannot imagine that anyone might address him without an ulterior motive in mind. His picture of himself, vain and powerful, thus remains unaffected by verbal intercourse.

Since **action is language,** the communicative aspects of action are so thoroughly maximized that the implementary aspects are minimized. The psychopath is notorious, for example, for getting caught. Inasmuch as he needs an audience which will acknowledge his action statements, he cannot afford to work alone and to remain undetected. Many a hero has performed his deeds because his spectacular action was observed by others. Inasmuch as the psychopath is out to elicit a response and knows little about the concept of appropriateness, his activities, by and large, are not subtle. His feeling of gratification is almost exclusively bound to the acknowledgment of his actions. The real pleasure he gets out of life is related to having achieved a deep impact by means of action.

The action person **neglects propriofunctions** and overexaggerates exterofunctions. Thus, the psychopath can accurately gauge the mood of another person but has no words to express his own feelings. He cannot correctly evaluate his own roles, his own needs, and his own intentions—he does not know what is good for him. Frequently he shows a high I.Q. on intelligence tests. But inasmuch as he possesses little if any information concerning propriofunctions, the utilization of his intelligence is rather inadequate. One might say that his knowledge of machines is rather small, that his information pertaining to other people is considerable, but that, above all, his skill in using other people to his advantage reaches unusual perfection.

So far, no evidence has been brought forward to show that the above-described disturbances of communication should be thought of as constitutional defects of the communication apparatus. Thus, we still have to conceive of the psychopathic personality as a functional disorder. The **childhood** events which contribute toward the overemphasis of action as language in the communicative endeavors of the psychopath are tied up with the parents' responses to the actions of the child. When the infant crawls, walks, climbs, pushes, or makes noises—in brief, proceeds with some action—notice is taken of him; but when he is still and silent he remains unnoticed. Therefore, he has to act as a means of survival; he has to bring, steal, break, and throw things; he has to attack people and play tricks; and, above all, he must be impressive and achieve an effect. Since he senses that a premium is placed on action, he becomes an astute observer of the behavior of others.

THE DEMONSTRATIVE PERSON

There exists a group of people who, instead of handling those persons or situations with which they are in conflict, deal with the symbols that stand for these events. Many persons, variously labeled as hysterical characters, conversion hysterics, and exhibitionistic personalities, among others, belong to this group. Such a person not only deals with conflicts in a symbolic manner but conveys the content of such conflicts to the outside world. In contrast to the infantile person, the demonstrative person displays a remarkable **system of symbolization** which enables him to express inner events in verbal, action, or somatic terms (41). In order to appreciate fully the overfacilitation of symbolization, one has but to think of people with functional blindness and paralysis of the limbs, impotence, frigidity, or functional anesthesia of the extremities; or of the blushers, the emotionally labile individuals, the stutterers, and the people with tics; or the amnesia victims, saints and fanatics, the prophets, and the hypnotic media. All these people are demonstrative persons (72, 90, 137).

The demonstrative person is a social individual, and withdrawal is not one of his difficulties. Psychoanalysis and psychotherapy have been particularly successful with these patients because their intrapsychic conflicts are expressed in interpersonal or group difficulties.

The demonstrative person is relatively **blind to action.** He does not seem to know that actions and events have two aspects: a practical and a symbolic one. Characterized by what is commonly called "naïveté," he listens to words and promises but does not heed the actions of others. This unawareness of action is perhaps directly responsible for the difficulties of the demonstrative person. The hysterical girl, for example, can be rather intimate with a man and then is shocked when she becomes aware of his sexual intentions; or she takes a walk on a dark street and is surprised at being accosted by strangers; or she may get lost in the streets without recognizing familiar localities or remembering her identity; or she can ignore danger and walk along precipices that would make others shudder.

Demonstrative personalities are notorious for using **somatic language** for purposes of expression. But in contrast to the infantile person whose autonomic nervous system mediates primitive statements about wanting to be touched or cared for, the demonstrative person uses somatic language for symbolic purposes. Smooth muscles are treated as if they were striped muscles and are pressed into service for communicative action. There are known cases that could reproduce localized bleeding in a distribution that followed Christ's wounds, a feat over which ordinary people have no influence. Contractions of the skin vessels, which in most people escape voluntary control, are used by hysterics to flash signals to others by means of blushing or blanching, and contraperistaltic movements for purposes of vomiting can be produced almost at will. In their way of expression, the spirit truly triumphs over the flesh, and they willfully suspend or exaggerate the functions of their sensory and motor systems. Thus, the separate contraction of one of the two heads of the gastrocnemius was not a special feat for one of my hysteric patients.

The demonstrative person coordinates **word and action** in a peculiar way. In transmission, he does one thing and says another, the emphasis being on action rather than on the word; conversely, when perceiving he pays more attention to word than to action. Seeking always the hidden rather than the obvious meaning, he possesses good connotative abilities, but as compared to a truly creative character he possesses poor denotative facilities. And perhaps this inability induces him to rely more upon nonverbal codification in order to express himself. It must be presumed that demonstrative personalities possess an **analogic codification** system which in complexity far exceeds their verbal and digital codification systems. From experience we know that hysterical personalities tend to develop insight when a therapist helps them to integrate the nonverbal with the verbal. In their minds, they do not coordinate pictorial-analogic with verbal-digital systems of codification. And much of what is achieved through the lifting of repression has been known to them in other terms all along. What the psychiatrist commonly terms the unconscious is reflected in these persons as a block in logical-verbal thinking; the memories and fantasies which are inaccessible to verbal discourse, however, seem to be expressed in analogic ways.

This particular dichotomy makes the hysterical personality a poor technician, a poor engineer, and a poor theoretician. His predictive capacities are inadequate because he cannot extrapolate or interpolate or engage in extensive logical thinking. Instead, such persons are concerned with the **intuitive assessment** of social events. Particularly in the case of girls, their diffusely erotic qualities charm others to yield to their wishes. Always with an eye on how to remain in the limelight, they treat others as a prospective audience which is supposed to admire their nonverbal exhibitionistic tendencies. Hysterical personalities are easy to hypnotize; they are suggestible because they interpret the words of others as if they were commands. Some are capable of using their own words to produce a magic, command-like effect upon other people. Thus, the enlightening aspects of information tend to be neglected and the mandatory aspects are vastly maximized. For this reason, the mutual exchange of messages with others is restricted. Instead, demonstrative persons tend to establish a one-way flow of communication, either from self to others or from others to self. But they have difficulty in viewing communication as an ongoing bilateral process. One-way communication lends itself, of course, for purposes of control. But unlike the psychopath, who controls others to achieve personal power, the demonstrative person frequently makes his conquests not for himself but in the name of another person, a movement, or an idea.

The **childhood** development of the demonstrative person apparently proceeds favorably up to a certain point. Between three and five years of age, coincident with the discovery of the facts of life, the concern with problems of identity, and the beginnings of group communication, however, something disturbing seems to occur. Encouraged by the parents not to face the problems of sex differentiation, these youngsters continue pretending that they are not interested in bodily anatomy, the birth of babies, and other aspects of sexual reproduction. At the same time, however, they learn all the gestures and words that characterize their gender. The children thus relate to parents and adults by displaying their sexual, social, and psychological identity in symbolic terms; but since they are children, the parents do not expect their erotic behavior and innuendoes to be backed up by facts. In such families, the parents usually enter separate father-child and mother-child relations; they enjoy the exhibitionistic tendencies of the youngsters and prevent them from functioning as a full partner in the family group. The home atmosphere thus is characterized by particular conditions which, on the one hand, prevent the growing child from being aware of the real world and, on the other hand, promote the playful symbolic management of events which cannot be faced in actuality. For example, I remember one hysterical person who when in her teens was not permitted to go out with boys, while her re-enactment of a love scene on the stage was thought to be perfectly proper and was not only tolerated but actually encouraged. When certain things cannot be said out loud, when facts are denied or actions prohibited, nonverbal expression and symbolic elaboration become the only means by which pressing problems can be handled.

THE LOGICAL PERSON

The person who repeats the same statement or action without regard for the impact or the effect achieved traditionally is referred to as an obsessive or **compulsive character.** In daily life we meet this person as the overconscientious, meticulous, orderly individual who endeavors to classify experiences into categories. Such an individual is unaware that his statements convey little meaning to others and that they serve principally to alleviate his own anxiety. In extreme cases, such a person is apt to engage in repetitive actions which assume a ritualistic character (84, 85, 87).

Our **contemporary civilization** rewards this type of personality. With the rapid changes in materials and machines that people have to adapt to, it is increasingly difficult to accumulate a relevant body of knowledge about experiences involving complex patterns. The interaction between people and machines, and therefore between people themselves, is not given enough time to be stabilized in integrated patterns. For example, modern airplanes rapidly become obsolete, sometimes even before they have left the drawing board. The resulting lack of experience and its integration into patterns of living vividly contrasts with man's integrated experience involving horses and boats. The cumulative body of knowledge about these ancient methods of transportation evolved slowly in the course of thousands of years, and man had time to adapt to it. But the rapid changes which confront us today create anxiety in the individual and, as in all forced development, lack of mastery is managed by obsessiveness and compulsiveness.

Interested in rational appraisal, the compulsive person tends to neglect emotional and nonverbal aspects of living. He is inclined to operate at the **intrapersonal level,** regardless of the situation. His evaluation is selectively geared to the interpretation of verbal statements of others. He prefers to deal with syntactic and semantic rather than with pragmatic aspects. He does not care for the impact that a statement produces upon others, nor is he capable of viewing the effect that the statement of another person may have upon him. In evaluating external situations, he concentrates upon the appraisal of interference that might upset his systematic procedure. Therefore, operational assessment of what is actually happening at a given moment tends to be replaced by a variety of predictions about eventualities. These tendencies are especially marked in the paranoid patient.

In order to make **logical statements,** an individual must adhere to precise usage in language. Therefore, the compulsive person's vocabulary, his gestures, his way of phrasing and slicing statements, are remarkable. Inasmuch as he tends to specialize in making statements about the statements of others, he possesses an appropriate critical vocabulary. Personal satisfaction is derived from the ability to make a pertinent statement at the right moment. Thus, he judges success and failure not necessarily in terms of achieved effects but rather in terms of whether a statement was or was not made, for the record, as it were. Among these logical, verbal persons we find many lawyers, mathematicians, and philosophers, as well as the people who make a living out of engaging in petty bureaucratic practices.

The perfection of logical thinking and expression in word or number is matched by an **inadequate appreciation of feeling and emotions.** These facts are borne out in therapy, for example, when compulsive characters have to be helped to experience anxiety. This end is achieved by interfering with the compulsive performance while it is in progress. When the patient cannot complete his statements or finish his ritual, anxiety appears. This experience demonstrates to the patient that a compulsion is not designed to achieve a goal; instead, it is designed to keep the individual free of anxiety. Compulsive performance is frustrating to others inasmuch as it precludes any reply, it is repetitive to the point of being mechanical, and it offends others. A compulsive person overcontrols and underadapts, and his classificatory tendencies do not lend themselves to flexible behavior. Inasmuch as he doesn't observe the effects of his own actions upon others, correction through feedback leaves much to be desired. The compulsive person acknowledges only the face value of a statement. He **does not** care to **acknowledge** the intent of the other person, nor does he care to observe whether the other person received his message in the way it was intended. The reader may be reminded of the endless discussions that compulsives may have about who made what statement, when, and where, rather than analyzing what the perceived effects of such statements might have been. And the interchange between compulsive characters frequently results in mutual monologues: first one person talks and the other listens, waiting for the moment when he can talk so that the other will listen.

The events that force children at an early age to make logical statements are related to **premature demands** on the part of the parents. Activities that cannot be mastered and things which are not meaningful to the child cannot be integrated, are isolated, and escape future modification. Under such circumstances, the child cannot cope with the situation in any other way but by memorizing some external criteria, by forsaking opportunities for experimentation, by avoiding failure at all cost, and by doing things "just so" and in no other way. These children do not acquire experience in the realm of action; they cannot generalize from one action to another, and therefore they never obtain the freedom of action that characterizes a master. The history of compulsives shows that they were reprimanded if they did not busy themselves; idleness of the child provoked anxiety in the parent. But as soon as the child was "at it," rewards came forth, and thus he learned that "doing" provided him with approval. Thus, the compulsive has to do things, regardless of whether or not the outcome is meaningful. The parents did not underline the pleasure of the activity or the pleasure of mastery; they rewarded the effort made rather than the effect achieved, and the inherent frustration that the child sensed in his premature attempts was rewarded with affection. Henceforth, the feeling of gratification became linked with **doing things in the proper way;** action, regardless of the results achieved, became gratifying and guaranteed freedom from anxiety. Because of the premature demands for mastery, the logical person learned early in life to ape the verbal statements of adults; the memorizing of words and sentences rather than the inquiry into what these words stood for on the part of the youngster satisfied the parents of precocious children. The time needed for developing analogic understanding was not granted them, nor were they shown how to react to other people in non-verbal terms. Pleasure thus was taken out of the process of communication, save for the critical, biting, and sarcastic performances which usually took place in the family.

THE WITHDRAWN, NONPARTICIPATING PERSON

People who suffer from the condition traditionally labeled dementia praecox (34) or schizophrenia (135) are characterized by a lack of participation in social relations, inasmuch as observation tends to displace participation. This feature is most pronounced in catatonics, less in hebephrenics, and least in paranoids. As a result of scant participation, the schizophrenic person lacks social skills and tends to compensate for this deficiency by a number of inferences which derive from self-observation. The features attributed to other people are, by and large, projections of intrapersonal phenomena (210).

Persons with observer qualities are greatly appreciated in abstract fields such as mathematics, theoretical physics, and philosophy; there they can put their observer qualities to good use since their professional activities require little, if any, action. Here their innate disposition is particularly useful, since participation is often detrimental to the sort of observation that scientists wish to make. **Modern technical civilization,** then, favors in some measure the withdrawn personality (75). If one compares the way of life of people at the beginning of the eighteenth century with modern urban conditions, one discovers a progressive tendency toward limitation of activities. American citizens in centuries past had to know how to bear arms and how to cope with nature and Indians—techniques which were necessary to survival in a pioneer and frontier setting. With progressive industrialization and with specialization of roles and skills, modern craftsmen, artisans, and skilled workers are not allowed to practice more than one trade. The versatile and rounded craftsman of days past has disappeared. Today, the specialist delegates to others the activities which fall outside of his field. In the social sphere, the modern citizen is an impersonal entity; he is known only by the number on his social security card or by his dog-tag rather than by his name and address. His civil responsibilities have lessened, and his voice in the election of officials is minimal. Instead, his role as spectator is fostered by the availability of radio, movies, television, and football and baseball games. We are moving in a direction which is so often depicted by the cartoonist—of Homo sapiens as a species with a frail body and an oversized head, the personification of the concept of schizophrenia.

If properly trained, an individual with an observer personality may become a basic **scientist,** or if he has a certain tendency toward participation he becomes an engineer. The withdrawn personality feels at ease when alone, and he carries on conversations with himself; but when brought together with others, in either an interpersonal or a group situation, he feels anxious. Being introspective, he views other people with curiosity or disdain and sometimes treats them as if they were things or numbers, always assuming that he is not an integral part of the situation. As a result, he treats people as nonidentifiable particles such as atoms or molecules. His emotional reactions are bound to concepts and ideas rather than to people or things.

But in some ways the individual with an observer personality also is a **realist;** not being encumbered with feelings for people, he can observe social events with a clear head as long as these events are accessible to nonparticipating observation. Thus, he is adept at evaluating exterofunctions, the other person, the outgroup, the machine, the gadget. His understanding diminishes, however, when evaluation has to be based upon participant-gained information and when it comes to evaluating body functions, personal relations, ingroup ties, or other interofunctions. This inability does not detract from his observing the actions of others with the intent of detecting signs of coercion. He is extremely aware of the impact of the actions of others upon him, while he remains blind to his own social effect upon the surroundings.

The individual with an observer personality usually is highly gifted in dealing with **digital and verbal language,** while he tends to neglect analogic, pictorial, and nonverbal languages. His intelligence is high, his vocabulary rich, and his fondness for unusual or even bizarre words is proverbial. However, his expressions are frequently unintelligible because he does not use verbal signs in the sense which society has agreed upon. Every psychiatrist remembers the veteran schizophrenic in the back ward of the hospital who day after day handed him long letters and drawings, or made long speeches. The schizophrenic is capable of symbolizing externally his internal events in an idiosyncratic manner. However, he does not wish to share with others his private system of symbolization.

Equipped with a gift for abstraction, the withdrawn person perceives relationships and **processes** rather than fixed states (209), and one might assume that he thinks in terms of formulae rather than in terms of pictorial images. Such abstraction lends itself to the recording of process and change, and this perhaps explains the mathematical talent of many an ambulatory schizophrenic. His ability to predict is great if propriofunctions are not involved. His capacity to design machines is likewise astounding. But his actions are often clumsy and his coordination is poor. He is not good at sports or crafts. He is capable of making theoretical contributions of a social or psychological nature, and he clearly sees the theoretical underpinnings on which certain values or procedures are based, eliciting the antagonism of other people when he points to existing contradictions. His ability to accept events at their face value is limited, and his management of his daily affairs leaves much to be desired. As a result, the withdrawn person is not intimidated by cultural pressures, and socially he appears to be somewhat of a deviant. He is an underadapter and at times an overcontroller. To control the impositions of others, to forestall harm to himself, and to take revenge on those who have coerced him are some of his goals. Although he possesses some skills, they rarely involve the muscular system.

In the **exchange of messages**, the difficulties of the observer personality are most clearly revealed. Such an individual finds it hard to acknowledge the presence of another person, and he is even less capable of acknowledging the other's communicative intent; therefore, it is difficult for him to interpret the messages of others. When he expresses something, he demands to be acknowledged then and there; but he denies others the gratification that he seeks for himself. In fact, he makes the task of acknowledgment extremely difficult for others because he does not give any hints as to how his statements ought to be interpreted. Because of his idiosyncratic symbolization system, his minimization of emotions, and his failure to acknowledge others, he is a lonely person who rarely achieves the pleasure of mutual understanding. Unloved and incapable of loving others, he is destructive without being aware of his self-destructiveness (9).

From the study of autistic, withdrawn, or outright schizophrenic children we can surmise the conditions that led to the development of this particular disturbance of communication. The parents' unresponsiveness in nonverbal terms prevents the child in the early years of life from learning how to relate through **movement and action.** The absence of early appropriate and gratifying communication through action, gesture, and object leaves traces. The movements of many schizophrenics are angular, jerky, and uncoordinated, and they are carried out with uneven acceleration or deceleration, at either too slow or too fast a tempo. The primitive or uncoordinated movements which appear in individuals suffering from severe functional psychoses may be viewed as attempts to re-establish an infantile system of communication through action. It is as if these patients were trying to relive the patterns of communication that were frustrating in early childhood, with the hope that this time there might be present another person who would reply satisfactorily in nonverbal terms. It is as if these patients knew that the basis for human relations is established in the nonverbal mode and that successful communication cannot be achieved before this step is mastered. This view is supported by the observation of the behavior of psychotic children (219, 220, 221), who tend to play with their fingers, make grimaces, or assume bizarre body positions. Their movements rarely involve other people; instead, they are directed toward themselves, sometimes to the point of producing serious injuries. But as therapy proceeds, interpersonal movements gradually replace the solipsistic ones, and the response of the child becomes matched to stimulus of the adult. Once these children have had satisfactory experiences in the nonverbal mode, they are willing to learn verbal communication and discursive language.

The withdrawn personality frequently is found in families where the meaning of verbal messages does not coincide with the meaning of action. This contradiction the child solves by attentively watching the actions of others and by ignoring their words. Thus, he is cut off from communicative exchange and as a result he devises compensations by which he can entertain himself in order to overcome his desperate loneliness. It isn't that the schizophrenic did not in his childhood receive food or clothing, or shelter; it isn't that he was beaten or punished. No; on the contrary, all these things were usually attended to properly, but what was denied him was the pleasure of acknowledgment. He was not appreciated as a person, and his **intentions** to communicate were **not acknowledged**. Most of the time he didn't even obtain a tangential response; and if he received a response, it probably contained references to the anxiety of the other person. He learned to shut himself off from the anxious communications of others, and he felt that there was greater safety within himself.

There are authors who maintain that schizophrenia is **genetically determined** and that it is the child who does not respond in the first place (36). If such is the case, we must assume that even more adaptiveness, appeal, leniency, and interest are required on the part of the parents. If such additional effort is not forthcoming, the unlovable child does not receive appropriate social exercise. One frequently finds that in the families of schizophrenics manipulative schemes were developed in order to influence the child where communication failed. The disappointment and anger of the parents over their failure to establish contact usually was camouflaged by proper behavior, and only in the subtle means of coercion did the child sense the diabolical truth. Thus, he grew up in a family in whch he was cut off from communication and sharing within the group. Although he did not participate, he was allowed to remain as a passive observer.

THE ANXIOUS AND FEARFUL PERSON

Intense, strange, or dangerous stimuli alarm the individual and set him into a state of physical and psychological alertness which prepares him to cope with the forthcoming situation. The emotional components of the **alarm reaction** are described in terms of anger, fear, or anxiety. If the organism feels that it can lick the danger, fight will ensue; if the danger is thought to be overwhelming, flight is the result; and if neither fight nor flight is feasible, anxiety will develop. While upon initial stimulation the alarm reaction increases the responsiveness of the organism, a state of general disorganization sets in if such an alert persists for an undue length of time. Anxiety, therefore, results when the organism is continually bombarded by stimuli which cannot be avoided and which exceed the tolerance limit of the organism (216). The general disorganization inherent in an anxiety state is highly frustrating, and it is obvious that the individual will aim at avoiding this particular condition. While the initial alarm reaction is man's best friend, the chronic state of anxiety with its resulting disorganization is dreaded by all.

An analysis of the communication network in which **anxious people** (92, 112) participate reveals the existence of excitation which exceeds the capacity for reception, evaluation, or transmission of that particular person. Overexcitation results in a jamming and disorganization of the communication network. A phobic person consciously avoids the situations and conditions which will produce such overexcitation, to the extent of avoiding communications about the fear-inspiring topic altogether. In anybody's life there exist situations which have to be avoided; but the normal person has the ability to repress anxiety-producing perceptions, which distortion enables him to cope with the danger in a modified form. A phobic person has no such ability, and he invariably perceives the anxiety-arousing stimulus. Rather than explore the thing that creates alarm, he avoids the event altogether; direct exploration, thinking about it, or interpersonal elaboration is avoided, and therefore all chances to modify such behavior are forfeited.

The life of the **phobic person** (84, 86) is organized around the management or avoidance of anxiety. While the acutely anxious person has not yet learned to defend himself against the bombardment of those stimuli which disorganize his communication network, the chronically fearful person has learned to avoid anxiety. Phobias are the result of a concerted effort to avoid anxiety-provoking situations such as crowds, darkness, small rooms, social encounters, and so forth.

Avoidant and anxious persons may use **interpersonal relations** to alleviate anxiety and fear in themselves. Regardless of whether their excitation is due to inner or outer conflicts, their organism has to reduce the number or the intensity of the stimuli. Unfortunately, an anxious person frequently reduces the number of incoming messages by curtailing social contact with others; thus, he abandons the only anxiety-reducing mechanism at his disposal. In so doing, he makes the assumption that all outside contacts produce an over-stimulation which will disorganize his precariously established equilibrium, and he often is unaware of the fact that the flood of stimuli frequently originates within his organism rather than on the outside.

It sounds almost like a contradiction to state that the anxious person tends to overemphasize **proprioceptive functions** and to neglect exteroceptive functions. Actually such an individual does not concern himself with real danger but is preoccupied with internal elaboration of purportedly external dangers. Watching for external stimuli which might contain some cues in support of his preoccupation, he will tend to magnify the essentially disrupting influences. Internal pressures thus are conveniently projected onto an outside source and the inside source becomes sufficiently obscured.

Anxious and phobic persons can **infect others** with their anxiety (204). The anxious person transmits alarm directly by the use of muscles and glands for purposes of expression. Instead of words and gestures, somatic and action language are employed to express the state of excitation. The phobic person transmits alarm indirectly and by being avoidant conveys the idea that there is something worth being avoidant about. Overcontrol of alarm or avoidant behavior thus serves as a danger signal for other people.

Avoidance of a great many situations leaves anxious and phobic persons without appropriate knowledge about the world. When they meet a new situation, the flight reaction sets in so quickly that no exploration of the anxiety-producing situation is possible. While their general body of information is frequently rudimentary, their ability to predict anxiety-producing situations is unusually good. Such predictions frequently are made unconsciously and the persons in question may be unaware of their anxiety and avoidant behavior. The need for control often induces such persons to disregard the gratification of some vital needs. This leads not only to an impoverishment of experience but also to some sort of starvation in terms of pleasure. As a result, the exchange of messages with others is disturbed. Frequently they acknowledge in a negative way as if to say "Go away; your statements frighten me." Anxious persons tend to give tangential replies and rarely do they really acknowledge the intent of the other person. Their instructions to others for interpretation of messages are primitive and revolve around the topic of danger or anxiety. In turn, the metacommunicative messages of others are misinterpreted since the focus of observation is likely to be centered on the presence or absence of alarm rather than on encompassing the full meaning of the statement. Progressive avoidance leads to increased immobilization, until every self-assertive action is avoided and the person becomes confined—first to the house, then to one room, and finally to the bed.

Like all other people, anxious and phobic persons were in their **childhood** exposed to situations which they could not master. But in healthy families the child is helped to deal with his anxiety. The benevolent adult shares with the child the alarm-arousing experience and inspires confidence by not getting anxious himself. Above all, he teaches the youngster that communication is a means of elaborating experiences, which process eventually may supply the information necessary to manage the anxiety-provoking situation or may help in adapting to unalterable circumstances. With anxious or avoidant parents, in contrast, children have no way to ventilate their anxiety; the adult, being disturbed himself, is usually unable to respond appropriately (242) and may actually transmit his own anxiety to the child. As a self-protective measure, the child tends to curtail his contact with the adult, and left to himself, he has to learn to control the anxiety with his own resources.

THE DEPRESSED PERSON

Melancholia (88), manic-depressive psychosis (1), cyclothymic constitution (138), and holergasia (164) are terms which denote the recurrent condition in which a person reduces or increases communication with the outside world and avoids or seeks interpersonal contacts. In the depressive phase, group participation is minimized, hope for progress is abandoned, and the person's outlook becomes gloomy. This general withdrawal from social life, the lack of interest in the outside world, and the increase in self-recrimination are usually the result of imaginary or real failures. Loss of a beloved person, collapse of an ideal, or failure to achieve some aspirations may be associated with psychomotor retardation. Many psychosomatic patients and some persons described as oral incorporative personalities suffer from depressions.

The communicative behavior of a depressed person is characterized by an attempt at reducing participation in group and interpersonal networks and confining the personal operations to repetitious performances, the content of which emphasizes the irreversible changes which have taken place in the past and are anticipated in the future. The hypomanic person, in contrast, participates in numerous networks without being able to do justice to many of the engagements that have been entered initially. One of the reasons for the over- or underactive behavior is the organism's **inability to stabilize input and output.** The stimulation is either too much or too little; the depressed person compensates for too little external input by an increased internal input—by stimuli which arise in the memory. The hypomanic person compensates for too little internal input by exposing self to heightened external input. In manic-depressive states, each phase seems to generate the next one, whereby the swing of the pendulum exceeds the commonly observed limits.

The depressed person operates in an **intrapersonal network,** and whenever interpersonal contact is necessary the other person is treated as if he were a part of the self. The other person is assumed to be interested in manifestations of guilt, shame, and wrongdoing of which the depressive person accuses himself. The manic person believes that others are interested in all the activities which he initiates. The manic-depressive person thus assumes that his inner world and the environment are one and the same; awareness of the delineation of boundaries, of different language systems, and of different procedures and interests therefore is rudimentary.

The depressed person has lost the ability to use information for the purpose of action. The topics that he is concerned with are ruminated about with such intensity that he is frequently **unable to perceive** the cues of real danger which may surround him. The slowing down of his evaluative functions is revealed in many tests which are designed to assess speed and accuracy of decision-making. His processes of expression are inefficient. All the depressive cares for is to make statements; he does not care whether he is understood. Propriofunctions, although emphasized, are evaluated as being inferior to exterofunctions. Such emphasis on inferiority constitutes, on the one hand, an attempt to solicit support from the outside and, on the other hand, an attempt to discourage it.

Changes affecting the **language and codification systems** of the manic-depressive person during a psychotic episode warrant special scrutiny. When not psychotic, the cycloid person makes ample use of analogic codifications; he is warm, interpersonal, and frequently artistic. The works of many poets, painters, and musicians who suffered from depressions can attest to the excellence of both verbal and nonverbal skills of their creators. When sane, the cycloid person has well-rounded and coordinated movements that express the close relationship between analogic thinking, imagery, feeling, and the muscular system. But during manic or depressive phases, this connection seems to get lost. Frequently one hears the comment that such-and-such a person seemed so well adjusted, that his movements and poise were so convincing that nobody expected him to suffer a breakdown. The difficulties that therapists experience in establishing rapport with depressed patients—difficulties which at times are much greater than those experienced with schizophrenics—are in part related to this loss of genuine expression. Therapists repeatedly have commented upon the somewhat phony and fraudulent impression these patients create. The explanation of these facts is not difficult if we assume that during a depression the synchronization between the nonverbal and the verbal systems of denotation is impaired or lost altogether. If we remember further that following shock therapy, psychotherapy, or drug therapy, depressed patients have been observed to improve in a matter of hours or days, the theory of lack of synchronization between verbal-digital and nonverbal-analogic forms of denotation becomes more plausible (207).

Initially, the lack of synchronization seems to result from a speeding up or slowing down of verbal functions, including speculative or logical thinking. The **analogic functions,** including imagery and body movements, tend to lag behind both in the depressive and in the manic phase. The resulting disorganization produces the impression of insincerity and is responsible for the fact that depressive persons do not acknowledge the messages of others, that they do not detect another person's intentions or interpretative instructions, and that they do not understand the context of the situation or their own predicament.

The observation that depressives are hostile and that they turn their hostility against themselves becomes understandable when one considers another condition in which **lack of synchronization** between analogic-nonverbal and digital-verbal codifications occurs—namely, in certain forms of aphasia. The anger of the depressive resembles that of an aphasic patient who knows a word but cannot speak it, or speaks it but is confused as to what it means. In desynchronization, action becomes impossible because the extrapolated goal of an activity is conceived in verbal or digital terms and cannot be matched with the body image, which is represented in analogic terms and controls movement. In such states, only automatic, repetitive movements can be initiated, a condition which is frequently observed in agitated depressions. If meaningful action cannot be instigated and inadequate expression prevents others from properly acknowledging the patient's messages, the resulting tension diminishes self-respect. Intuitively, such a person senses his inability to cope with things, especially with the implementations of daily living. The inability to act is responsible for the gloomy predictions that the depressed personality tends to make, and suicidal ideas may appear.

The conditions that promote the development of a depressive character can be traced to some of the educational measures of the parents. If **parents emphasize end results** rather than the pleasure of the moment, ideals and conscience grow to the detriment of skill. Such parents attach more importance to having succeeded in climbing a mountain, in making good grades, in achieving social dominance, than to the acquisition of skills. Therefore, the youngster learns to anticipate and to extrapolate—functions which seem to be mediated by the forebrain of man and his ability to use verbal-digital codifications. In the process of making such extrapolations, the goal of action is projected more and more into the future and becomes progressively more difficult to attain. Thinking races ahead of doing and being, and all actions leading up to the goal are viewed as necessary chores. Once such a person perceives that the delineated goal has no actual value, total collapse may occur.

Parents who emphasize ideals distort reality; and by distorting the character of life they prevent the youngster from learning co-ordination of action in time. When the child recognizes the arbitrariness of the **goal** and admits to himself that life is an ongoing process and that no resting or final state really exists, his whole training for achieving or holding some fixed point on a continuum becomes meaningless. Depressive personalities are somewhat static individuals who long for fixation of ongoing processes; a depression is an attempt at fixating the eternal flux in the hope that finally an attitude can be acquired which will enable them to cope with this continuous change. The schizophrenic, in contrast, is a dynamic personality who knows about the processal nature of life; his trouble is related to his inability to accept social organization as a necessity and to show perseverance in the pursuit of somewhat fixed or stabilized goals.

Chapter Six

Social Pathology:
Disturbances of Communication
in Groups

SOME DETERMINANTS OF GROUP PATHOLOGY

COMMUNICATION in groups differs from that in two-person situations, inasmuch as there is less opportunity to correct errors. For effective functioning of a group, the flow of messages must be organized, the language shared, and the assumptions understood. One person's failure to function as part of the network may disorganize the network, and therefore members are expected to endure tension or even to sacrifice their lives for the benefit of the group as a whole (117). Consideration of individual or interpersonal pathology is not sufficient for full appreciation of group pathology. When living with others, the individual becomes part of a larger organization which influences his behavior. If the individual is suffering from some kind of pathology, the group will react either by forcing him to adapt or by excluding him. There also exist **disturbances of** communication which affect **the group as a whole,** the symptoms of which become apparent in one or a few individuals only. Just as medicine has long since abandoned the notion that because a patient has a pain in his abdomen he must have an intestinal disease—for he might have a cardiac condition or suffer from a general infectious disease—so have group experts abandoned the concept that the carrier of symptoms necessarily is the diseased entity. He may or he may not be. Thus, in some instances treatment of the "patient" alone is indicated; in other cases—particularly in those involving children

—treatment of the whole family is necessary. If the therapist deals with a group disturbance, he himself will have to see all members in succession or together, in order to understand the disturbance that besets the group. If, however, the breakdown in communication is due to the presence of one or two disturbing individuals, these may be seen by separate therapists once the group has decided to function without them.

Group process and its deviations

Just as a biological organism, a group is an entity and its organization is determined by rules. The members of a group are connected with each other by some means of communication. Therefore, the data bearing upon group functioning can be gathered only when the group is in action. The events that are germane to collective functioning are generally summarized under the heading of group process, which term refers to hypothetical constructs used by experts to explain the complex communication system of people in groups (105). Among the more significant constructs are:

The task of the group or the collective goal. Unless a group subordinates its symbolic and physical activities to a well-defined task, it generally falls apart. Group functioning apparently imposes such frustration upon the individual that he can endure it only if he is able to achieve goals that he cannot reach alone. In order successfully to organize cooperative activity, high morale and cohesiveness of the group are necessary, which features are in turn dependent upon the task awareness of the group members.

Disturbances arise in the group if tasks are conflicting or unrealistic, if verbally stated goals differ from implied purposes, or when the goals are destructive to the group and to its individual members.

Cohesiveness and identification with group. Feelings of belonging, of being accepted, of playing a vital role, of security—all are factors in what might be called identification with the group. This process is facilitated when members are dedicated to the task or when external threats weld the group into a unit. When group cohesiveness does not exist, the members fail to understand one another, they cannot agree on compromises, and they feel frustrated and work against one another. Benign mutual correction of information is reduced to a minimum—as is help to the laggard members.

Rules and group norms. Group functioning is governed by rules which indicate who can talk to whom, about what, when, and for how long, as well as who has to do what. These rules may be made up as the group goes along, they may be imposed by some individual, or they may be established by tradition. Any rule established in a group implicitly carries provisions for how to circumvent, alter, or break it. Of special importance, therefore, are those provisions which instruct members in how and how not to observe laws, rules, and regulations. Similar to rules of a game, social traditions, police regulations, and laws of the land limit the field and the nature of action. Specifically, such rules define:

1. Duration of the situation
2. Place of situation
3. Status assignment
4. Rewards and punishments
5. Provisions for eventualities
    a) Provisions for initiation of situation
    b) Provisions for interruption of situation
    c) Provisions for extension and restriction of the situation in time and space
    d) Provisions for outside interference with situation
    e) Provisions for violation of rules by participants
    f) Provisions for change of rules
    g) Provisions for total abolition of situation

Pathology may develop if separate rules are applied to different members of a group. The creation of social differences prevents the establishment of uniform assumptions about communication, which in turn precludes effective communication. Disturbances also arise if rules are made that violate common sense or when man-made rules are in conflict with the realities of nature.

Status and roles. In order to define one another's functions in the group, members assume roles—that is, functional attitudes—which help in the interpretation of messages. Awareness of role enables a person to communicate succinctly and efficiently with any other person, in spite of specialization of functions.

In groups, disturbances arise when people assume overlapping roles with duplication of functions, when they assume roles which are unessential while necessary functions are not attended to, when the horizontal (intimacy) and vertical (status) definition of relationship is inappropriate, or when the distribution of roles within the organization is top-heavy or lopsided.

Leadership and control. Any large group has to have a control center. Similar to a command post, the control center has the function of disseminating information, coordinating constituent elements, and issuing orders. Pathology develops either when the position of leader is not filled or when a person does not function properly in this role. Among the most frequent errors is the favoring of partisan interests which frequently disrupt the growth and proper functioning of the group (19).

Conflict between intra- and extra-family communication

Some families keep to themselves and the members mingle only with other members of their clan; other families welcome outsiders into their midst. Children raised in the latter kind of family have infinitely more advantages than those raised in the former type. In order to learn versatile communication, a child must be raised in a system in which he can assume roles which exercise his functions of reception, evaluation, and transmission; he must be exposed to different ways of codification and correction and must practice communication with a variety of people. Unless the child assumes **varying roles** and positions, he will be unable at a later age to participate in different systems of communication. When children have an opportunity to check their views and beliefs with outsiders, they are faced with the necessity of integrating contradictory opinions and of finding some way of reaching agreements with others. Children who are raised in families that stay strictly within their clan are taught uniformity, and they lack the opportunity to cope with diversified opinions. When such children are confronted with facts which contradict the accepted views of the family, they become anxious, a situation which is conducive to the development of prejudice (3).

The foundations of group communication are learned in the **family unit**, which consists of father, mother, and child. The basic three-person system ensures a greater degree of variability and flexibility than the two-person system, but retains the intensity of emotional experience which is lost in a five- or ten-person system. Multiple three-person systems may exist within the same family; the constituent members may be mother, brother, and sister; father, brother, and sister; mother, grandmother, and son; or perhaps other combinations. In most families composed of more than two people, the child will learn group communication; and if the exchange breaks down in one combination, he has recourse to another. In every multiperson group, one finds not only role diversification but also a distribution of functions with regard to authority, affection, and skills which may vary with the age of the child. Around the age of four, the child's usually healthy adjustment to mother and to the family group becomes somewhat disturbed until at the age of about six or seven a new pattern of adjustment has been achieved. This consists of participation in nonfamily groups at school, the establishment of a relationship to father, and perhaps the treatment of the parents as a unit. The mastery of the fundamentals of group functioning outside of the family circle coincides with the resolution of the oedipal conflict and the beginning of the latency period. Disturbances which prevent the child from making a successful transition from interpersonal to group functioning and from intrafamily to extrafamily participation are reflected in the transference phenomena of later life (206).

Thus, there exist certain **family constellations** which prepare the child for later group activities, while there are others which prepare him inappropriately or not at all. The mastery of communication in groups, which is basically different from that in two-person situations, is the mark of the healthy person. Patients, in contrast, are characterized on the whole by their inability to function in groups. This may be due to the fact that in the family the child may learn ways of communication which are difficult to apply later on. For example, the mother may be the authority and the father may be weak and peripheral; or the father may be authoritarian and the mother may be submissive; or the father may have no status compared to the mother, or the mother may be much older than the father. All these differences set the expectations of the child; he learns specialized ways of communication and unless he is exposed rather early to other systems he may not be able to adapt to other types of group communication. Family patterns with peculiar distribution of functions have been shown to be characteristic of patients suffering from psychosomatic diseases (211, 212, 213).

Among the deviant family structures, the two-person family is the most rigid. Mother and son, mother and daughter, father and son, father and daughter, two sisters, and other combinations are examples of **two-person family** systems which, when they continue to exist during the formative years of the child, have a profound influence upon his communicative behavior. Since in two-person systems there is no diversification of roles and relationships or of such functions as authority and affection, all functions are concentrated in one and the same person. This concentration of functions makes this one person all-important to the child. Certain things may not be asked or said; different views about this all-important person cannot be gathered from other members of the family. When there is conflict with this dominant figure, there is no recourse to another person and therefore conflict has to be avoided at all cost. Commonly such a situation leads to the development of dependent personalities who are unable to express their emotions freely (213). Furthermore, this intimate living together with one older person leads to specialization which unites the two persons into a symbiotic team, of which neither member can function without the other. In later life, the disturbances of communication observed in persons raised in two-person families are frequently expressed in their decision-making. Either such a person makes decisions for others or others make decisions for him. Since he believes that differences of opinion are abnormal, he does not know how to assert himself tactfully. Also, such a person loses the ability to check information, because through intimate living with another individual both are exposed to the same events and both can assume that the other has the same body of information. **Communization** thus substitutes for communication. Mutually interdependent people are attentive listeners and perceivers, but they have lost their ability to gauge the effect they produce upon others. Their self-assertion is not a continuous smooth process but occurs in outbursts. For a while they submit to the decisions of the other person, then they rebel against them; as a result, they feel guilty and begin to redeem themselves by submitting anew until frustration builds up again and the cycle starts all over.

Pathology is not confined to small families. The turn of events may be such that out of a sizable group only females or males survive, and in such a setting particular ways of communication will prevail. Distortions may be produced through the **ordinate position of the child** among his siblings. The first-born frequently becomes a test object for the educational methods of the parents and tends to be overburdened with responsibility. The youngest child has to

absorb the impact of the older siblings in addition to being separated from them by a gap of several years; he usually receives all
the tender affection of the parents and sometimes is deluged with
indulgences (213). The sex distribution likewise matters, particularly if all the children are girls or if all are boys, or if after several
boys or several girls a child of the opposite sex is born. Within the
family, coalitions may be formed; the youngest may gang up with
the oldest and the mother, the second youngest with the father and
the second oldest. Each position in the birth order of the family—
the oldest, the youngest, the second youngest—entails its particular
problems. Contradictions in a large family are more easily resolved
because the pressure of circumstances forces the parents to be practical and not to waste time with individual issues. Furthermore, the
leadership required for the functioning of the large family necessitates maximization of one opinion and minimization of another. Although most children who grow up in large families theoretically
have a better chance to be exposed to a variety of situations and
changing systems of communication, there still may be one child
whose experience is limited due to specialization of roles; in effect,
he then is confronted with the same difficulties as the child who was
raised in a two-person family.

Conflict between ingroup and outgroup communication

The problem of group pathology is complicated further by the
fact that an individual does not belong to only one group; almost
every person participates in at least a family, an occupational group,
and several informal social groups, and many have additional memberships in military, church, or recreational organizations. When
the ways of communication in the nonfamily groups contrast and
conflict with those of the family group, pathology may arise (46).
Many families lead a happy family life as long as the children are
young. However, one day the children discover that the values and
the ways of communication of the family do not match the practices
encountered on the outside. Obviously the parents are not liars, but
their world and their ways of relating may correspond to a set of
values which exists in Europe or Asia or which was prevalent in the
past. The teen-agers then are faced with a conflict: either they have

to accept the ideas and ways of communication of the parents or they have to adopt the ways of the outgroup. If their relation to the family is a friendly one and they wish to preserve the family ties, they will have to endure a certain isolation from the outgroup. If, however, their relation to the parents is not rewarding and communication with them is not very satisfactory, they will leave the family at the price of feeling disloyal and guilty. If neither solution is adoptable, the children are likely to exhibit the typical second-generation problem characterized by rebellion, lack of identification, and delinquency.

Culture change

Value systems, practical implementations, language, and methods of communication differ from group to group and give to each that particular flavor which we identify as culture. When a person migrates from Europe to America, from the Atlantic seaboard to the Pacific coast, when he changes from civilian to military life, or when he moves from one social class to another, he is exposed to culture change (214). Leaving a group of which he has been a member for over twenty or thirty years has serious repercussions for the individual. In attempting to gain a foothold and in adapting to the ways of communication of the new group, an individual cannot avoid carrying with him some of the old ways of communication. In the end, he is at best a tolerated stranger; never will he share completely the secrets of his adopted culture.

Although the majority of people involved in the process of culture change manage to adapt satisfactorily to the new surroundings, a number of conditions may exist which retard adaptation and interfere with successful communication. When **whole groups migrate** to a new country, the old communication system is transplanted into the new surroundings; as a result, the group may experience difficulties with the natives, and the history of the first settlers abounds with pertinent examples. The ensuing struggle revolves around the question of whose ways of communication and which values are to prevail. Continued friction, persecution, and even war follow if one or the other system does not gain dominance. Another situation arises when a newly arrived individual does not join the native core group but settles in an established **colony** of his own people in a foreign land. A Japanese who migrates to the United States and settles among other Japanese may not learn the ways of communication of his adopted country. As a result, he may remain dependent upon interpreters and other members of his group to transact business with the native population. The individual who joins neither a colony nor the native core group and settles in a **marginal group** by himself encounters a similar predicament. Such a person may be found among bohemians, hobos, and all those who live in mixed settlements of large harbor cities such as Shanghai, New York, and London. Such a marginal individual may be restricted to a pidgin-English type of communication which limits exchange to the practical implementations of daily life. Finally, when an individual attempts to move directly into a society which is new to him without passing through transitional groups first, the core group may put serious restrictions upon him. While the individual who moves against such resistances usually suffers greatly, the exclusion effort leaves the core group not unscathed; although it usually unites, it may occasionally split or break up the group.

Functionally unsuitable networks

A network of communication has to be functionally organized and the flow of messages has to be adapted to its capacity. If one station is overloaded and another is not used, breakdown of the communication system is likely to occur. Overload is prevented in various ways. An executive, for example, who is liable to be exposed to overload, protects himself by reading only condensed reports, delegating technical details to subordinates, and discussing decisions in committees. With this rerouting, some of the load of the executive is shunted into auxiliary networks and the quantitative regulation of the network is assured. More often than not, a network breaks down because **qualitative aspects** of communication have been neglected. If the content of a statement is not relevant to the function of a certain station, the recipients usually fail to react and the flow of messages may peter out. If in a hospital the nurses are instructed about the latest intricacies of biochemical tests and not about the management of the patient, and the physicians are informed about the latest kitchen equipment and not about the interpretation of recently introduced laboratory tests, communication becomes inefficient. Since statements pass through many hands, and particularly through hands that may not recognize the significance of a message, the organizers of a network are faced with the crucial problem of relaying relevant information to the right person at the right time. Most experts have discovered that the best method of implementing this problem is to create **trouble-shooting** teams who check the already established networks; they can crisscross established pathways, are able to establish new connections, can compensate for overload and underload in parts of the network, and can see to it that the information reaches the right person. Unless such safeguards exist, an individual working at a station of the network where an emergency arises may get blamed for what happens. He may become the scapegoat for deficiencies of the system, although he himself is a perfectly capable, healthy, and competent person who functions well in an appropriate network.

Unresolved conflicts

In almost any group there exist unresolved conflicts. In medical circles one finds various conflicting theories about the etiology of diseases; in families, individual members may not agree with each other about the expenditure of money or about political and moral issues. Among the military there may exist disagreement about the type of armament to be used in a future war. While in due time these personal disagreements usually are resolved, conflicts between groups or coalitions of people are more difficult to settle. Particularly resistant to change are conflicts which involve different factions of the family. If one set of rules applies to males and another to females, if one set of actions is rewarded by father and disapproved by mother, the children are exposed to unresolved conflicts. Though it is quite feasible for parents to defend their individual views, it confuses the child if they do not demonstrate through example how to resolve interpersonal conflicts and disagreements. For example, if a father believes that the son should play baseball to the exclusion of music and the mother believes he should practice piano to the exclusion of sports, the child is faced with a serious conflict which he may not resolve without outside help. Matters are even worse when the conflict pertains to differences in **emotional attitude.** If father is hard and punitive and mother tries to compensate for father's harsh discipline, the child becomes an involuntary participant in the struggle between the parents. Father becomes more punitive when mother tends to be lenient; and the child, in order to cope with the situation, has to expose himself to the attack of the father in order to avoid the overcompensation of the mother, which in turn brings about more punishment from the father. The vicious circle could be avoided if each parent would acknowledge the other's temperamental disposition. Then the child would learn that father copes with problems in one way and mother handles them in another way, and the parents' mutual respect would indicate that no conflict need arise because of differences in personality.

Station-to-station communication

The "station-to-station" call is an impersonal type of communication used in daily life when sender and receiver are not personally known to each other. Letters are addressed to the Commanding General of the Sixth Army, to the Superintendent of a State Hospital, to the Chief of Police of San Francisco. These messages usually deal with matters related to the occupational role of the addressee and do not refer to his personality. Though this procedure is useful in public life, it cannot be applied to more intimate relations. Family members know each other too well to address each other exclusively in terms of impersonal roles.

A station-to-station call can deal only with **generalities;** it can never acknowledge the uniqueness of circumstances. The impersonal station-to-station call is used in emergencies, in casual contact, and on occasions when people wish to express their dislike for each other. Pathology arises when station-to-station calls are used improperly—for example, when a husband talks to his wife in impersonal terms as if one or the other of them were a public figure. Here the station-to-station call substitutes for the appropriate "person-to-person" call. There are many individuals who do not understand how to behave in personal situations and hence falsely assume the attitude of officials. Communication also is ineffective when station-to-station communication is based upon false identification of roles —for example, if a child asks the schoolteacher what kind of clothes to wear, when this decision is the function of the mother. Serious disturbances may arise when specialists in station-to-station communication have to face intimate personal problems; when the salesman has to be a father to his son, or the advertising woman a wife to her husband.

Person-to-person communication

In "person-to-person" calls, the role—the mask that somebody wears—is disregarded while emotional features become prominent. Person-to-person calls are used between lovers, between a mother and her baby, and between personal friends. In this form of communication, the child learns to evaluate such matters as the intent of the other person, his motivation, his particular ways of expression, and all those things which make a person or a relationship **unique.** A child who is exposed only to person-to-person calls usually has some difficulty in coping with the more impersonal aspects of public life where it matters that he assume a role or position and disregard his personal feelings and reactions. Children raised in families where person-to-person calls predominate lean toward artistic, religious, and philosophical pursuits or learn the skills taught by the various crafts, arts, and professions. Those raised in families with prevalence of station-to-station calls where appeals are made to the role of the bearer rather than to his feelings tend to become organizers, administrators, salesmen, and civil servants.

Disturbances of communication may arise when person-to-person specialists have to deal with social institutions, large private organizations, or the law. They dislike the communication practices inherent in bureaucratic organizations where violence is done to the individual, and they tend to rebel or to withdraw from participation in organizations. On the whole, the extravert (130) fits better into the bureaucratic machinery than the introvert, even though he may occasionally be punished for infractions of rules and too-spontaneous behavior. The introvert, who develops ideas, makes scientific discoveries, and rises above the platitudes of conformity, fits much better into informal organizations. He prefers person-to-person communication, although if he should choose to become a civil servant he rarely if ever is involved in disciplinary problems.

Ambiguous roles

A mother may create confusion if she advertises the father's ability and success in the eyes of the children and gives him the label of strong father, devoted husband, upright citizen, and successful man, although these statements are not supported by fact. If the children observe that father comes home and complains about his inability to get along with his boss, if they feel that he pinches pennies because of lack of income, if they sense that he is not attractive to mother, they learn that the verbal statements of mother and the facts of life do not correspond to each other. In such a family there exists a conflict between what is said and what is done.

The same discrepancy between **stated and actual roles** can be observed in politics. A candidate is built up before an election and is praised in superlative terms; but once he has assumed office, his incompetence may show. People may be in doubt whether to treat such a person according to his performance or according to his role and reputation. If not enough deference is shown to such a titular leader, he will invoke sanctions to reinforce his role; if too much deference is shown, he is seduced to cast aside the last doubts he may have had about his competence. This kind of ambiguous position is frequently responsible for the perpetuation of a very damaging kind of communication. If the people become aware that the statements of a politician are not representative of what he actually thinks or feels, they become contemptuous, give up the attempt to be honest, corrupt communication for the achievement of material ends, and find no gratification in straightforward and enlightening exchange of messages. Under such circumstances, breakdown of group communication is unavoidable.

Stated rules and actually observed rules

In many households parents have a tendency to lay down the law and to establish rules which regulate the life of the family. One doesn't sing at dinner; one washes before supper; one scrapes one's feet on the mat before entering the house; one does not drink alcoholic beverages; one eats what is on one's dinner plate; and so on. Such rules may be arbitrary but not damaging if the family really lives up to them. Frequently, however, the children will observe that the parents shout at dinner, do not wash their hands before supper, walk in with mud on their shoes, get intoxicated at home, and violate all the rules they have themselves laid down. Confusion results because there are two kinds of rules—the rules that are stated and the rules that are observed. Thus, the children will learn to **proclaim one thing and do another.** Under these circumstances, the generalization emerges that one can do anything as long as one claims to observe the standards. Stating the rule thus becomes the sanction for doing the opposite. But when the individual juxtaposes verbal statement and action in an ill-fitting or contradictory manner he lays the foundations for moral turpitude and corruption. Rules regulate the communicative interchange between people, and if only lip service is given, the flow of messages becomes confused, content cannot be trusted, and the very means by which a group is held together is undermined.

A similar situation arises when there exist simultaneously **two sets of rules:** those applicable to insiders and those that pertain to outsiders; or rules that apply to adults and those that apply to children. Different rules for different people is an axiom that is valid only in a culture where differences in class and caste are acknowledged and where communication and transportation are undeveloped. But modern trends toward equality have an operational foundation; equality provides the matrix in which globe-encircling communication can thrive. The more uniform the rules of communication are, the better the dissemination of information becomes. Different rules for different people lead to misunderstandings, loss of information, and distorted feedback.

Many parents confuse universally valid limitations of human nature with arbitrary rules. If a mother declares, "We go to bed when we are tired and you already are half asleep," it is unlikely that a dispute with the child will develop. If, however, a mother says, "Children go to bed at seven," she is making a rule which does not apply to adults, and the child tends to resent this double standard. As a result, children are induced to make their own equally arbitrary rules, feeling excluded and excluding the parents in return. Later on, such an attitude of discrimination prevents understanding and communication with outgroups.

THE RELATION OF INDIVIDUAL TO GROUP

For practical purposes, it is safe to assume that nobody lives completely alone and that every individual is an occasional or regular participant in one or more groups. If an individual develops symptoms of a psychiatric breakdown, the disturbance may lie within himself or he may reflect the disturbance of another person or he may be the victim of certain processes which involve the whole group. Any physically sick individual becomes a potential threat to the group—a fact which is well recognized in infectious diseases. But a mentally sick person is equally threatening to others, and therefore the whole machinery of mental health institutions and private psychiatrists is called into action to treat the patient and to **safeguard the group.** The effect that individual pathology has upon the group can be observed when an epileptic has a fit on the sidewalk. His misfortune attracts so many onlookers that traffic is congested. A man who is readying himself for a suicidal jump from a skyscraper can disturb hundreds of people, and the fire and police departments, the clergy, and relatives may be kept busy for several hours to attend to both the potential victim and the public. Unfortunately, the methods used to protect the group from the sick frequently result in the exclusion of the sick individual, with all its deleterious effects upon both the excluded and the excluder.

Although it is understandable that people want their mentally sick relatives hospitalized and isolated so that children and other members of the family do not become disturbed, this **expulsion** leads in many instances to undue prolongation and fixation of individual psychopathology. Comparison of the treatment of combat casualties through evacuation to mental hospitals with the treatment of casualties on or near the front line reveals this fact particularly well. When military patients are treated on or near the front lines and are given food, clothing, shelter, rest, and encouragement, and if they are not separated from their units, they tend to recuperate in a matter of days (10). If they are evacuated, their disturbance may last many months. Likewise, when certain psychiatric emergencies are treated at home and the sickroom is established within the fold of the family, the feeling of group belonging and common responsibility may lift the patient over the hump (187).

When a group wants to **retain an individual** in spite of his desire to leave, another kind of disturbance develops inasmuch as the group cannot tolerate attack upon magic beliefs regarding its own attractiveness and supremacy. When someone leaves, these magic beliefs are shattered, and therefore every effort is made to hold the individual back. A mother who induces her grown daughter to live with her may achieve her end through bribery or blackmail; unfortunately, both methods interfere with communication. Refugees who desire to escape from a totalitarian country usually are put into concentration camps, and racketeers, political radicals, and religious groups may invoke severe sanctions against the one who wishes to leave.

A complete interruption of the flow of messages is usually not so destructive as **distorted communication.** When a system works halfway, distortions can exert their destructive influences for years because people do not dare give up what little they have; they do not realize that such distortions prevent adaptation and growth (159). Persons who suffer complete breakdowns are willing to relinquish a system that did not work satisfactorily in the first place and begin to learn anew, provided that the group supports them in their new venture (198). Individual and group are interdependent—a fact which justifies the procedure of examining the groups in which psychiatric casualties occur as carefully as the patient himself. Individual psychopathology and group pathology are so closely interwoven that we can hope to interrupt the vicious circle that keeps disturbances of communication alive only by approaching the problem through a combination of group and individual measures.

The healthy individual in a sick group

When a person changes place of residence, nationality, occupation, or position, he may discover to his own dismay that he has become associated with a sick group. The members of such a group cannot develop their potentialities and frequently they head toward their own destruction. A healthy individual who joins a sick group thus is faced with the following alternatives: he may conform and share in the disturbed communication of the sick group; he may attempt to stay outside of the sick group; or he may alter the existing system of communication. Particularly the military have experience with such reorganization. When an infantry division or a ship's crew has low morale, the following steps are used to improve it: change of location, duty, food, and shelter; change of command; infusion of the unit with new men. If these measures are unsuccessful, breaking up of the unit and reassignment of the men has to be resorted to.

That the psychiatrist may be faced with similar problems is illustrated by the following **example:** A middle-aged woman who lived for twenty years on the West Coast returned east to visit her brother. This is the situation she met: The father of the family, her brother, had banished his daughter because she had married below her status. He had rejected his son, who preferred to play in a jazz band rather than to join the family business. The mother, who was dependent upon the father's large income, did nothing to improve the relation between the father and his children, and she had become a chronic alcoholic. Our visitor, upon her arrival, was asked not to see the son and daughter. Faced with such disrupted group relations, her first impulse was to leave and to "let them rot"; her second was to conform to the request; while her final decision was to do something about the situation, and she consulted a psychiatrist. Since neither her brother nor his wife wanted to cooperate with the psychiatrist, arrangements were made for the daughter to undergo psychiatric treatment. The son moved to the West Coast and became a professional jazz player. After his wife had been institutionalized, the father consented to see the same psychiatrist that his sister and daughter had consulted, and gradually the family re-established normal relations with each other. When the mother returned from the institution, she did not find any of the previous tendencies of exclusion; father was friendly with his children and their mates, and the mother became a teetotaler.

The changes that occurred in this family group were brought

about because the aunt remained outside the family squabble and was thereby able to extricate her brother's son and daughter from the sick group. The successful establishment of new group relations between the aunt, her brother, and the two children eventually made her sister-in-law desirous of joining such a successful group and to abandon her drinking.

Most **sick groups exert** such **a hold** on their members that few dare to escape. This hold consists of particular ways of behavior whereby group approval is given for self-denial and submission to ways of communication prevalent in the group. Although the individual may be aware of the prevalence of erroneous assumptions, false statements, and the destructiveness of the relationship, he is helpless to change the general system. In the groups around Hitler, Napoleon, and other dictators, feedback from the population, from the army, and from intellectuals was disregarded; facts were distorted; decisions were based on unrealistic considerations; and tolerance for contradiction was minimal. The progressive distortion of the body of information held by such groups made it impossible for them to cope with events, and complete breakdown was the result. The healthy individual in such a sick group senses the distorted values held by the majority; but being himself in the minority he is branded as the unstable or "sick" individual; measured by objective standards, he is of course the one who possesses the more successful means of communication.

The sick individual in a healthy group

In some groups one may find that the sick unit is the individual and not the group. This is the case in families that have a child with a birth injury or one who suffers from some congenital anomaly like mongoloid idiocy. The standards and practices of large families are geared to healthy functioning. But a disabled or sick child needs more attention, greater tolerance, and perhaps an entirely different upbringing. A mother with four healthy children and one that is disabled has difficulty in maintaining two sets of rules or standards— one for the healthy and one for the sick. With a compromise solution, all children seem to suffer. Since the healthy ones are in the majority and in order to prevent unfairness, the sick child is usually given separate instruction, sent to a boarding school, or placed in an institution. Special schools for the mentally deficient, epileptics, spastics, the blind, and the deaf have been created to meet these needs. Often such a child is taken back into the family after he has been trained and when the other children are grown. At such a late date, special attention does not interfere with the welfare of other family members.

The **isolation of the sick** is even more pronounced in adult groups. In combat, the wounded are taken over by the medical corps and separated as soon as possible from the healthy. Burial details remove the dead from sight as soon as feasible to prevent undesirable effects upon the morale of the unit. In wartime, trains with wounded soldiers are moved at night and disfigured soldiers are kept in hospitals so that the civilian population is not upset. In hospitals, people are placed in separate rooms when they are about to die in order not to shock the other patients. Deep down, every individual and every group likes to believe in its own immortality (158), and sickness and death are irrefutable proofs of the frailty of human beings.

In modern times, great efforts have been made to reduce the disastrous impact of isolation upon the chronically sick, and the population is being educated to accept the disabled, to give them jobs, and not to treat them as outcasts. In order to achieve more tolerance for abnormality, mental health campaigns are designed to alleviate the normal person's fear of disease. Employers are shown that disabled people—and this includes certain mental patients—can work and support themselves, provided the right occupation can be found. With the advancing average age of the population, such attitudes of tolerance have to be extended to include the infirmities of the aged. Since people do not like to be reminded of the fact that one day they are going to be old, left without strength and beauty, and dependent upon others, the triumphs of modern medicine necessitate a revision of the attitudes of people toward infirmity and age. Inclusion rather than exclusion thus becomes the goal of social therapy.

The sick individual in a sick group

There are groups whose functioning is based upon the dysfunction of one or more of their members. If in such a group one of the sick members gets better, becomes independent, and leaves the group, one or more of the heretofore "healthy" members tend to get sick. The psychiatrist is familiar with the **black sheep** problem of prominent families. Occasionally there appears a member who violates all the rules; he gambles, contracts debts, drinks, provokes scandals, and his existence seems to be an unending source of embarrassment to others. But if he should have the misfortune to die or be reformed, frequently another member will assume his role. Some experts explain these events on the basis of vicarious gratification; the healthy members who have to behave in a respectable way can do so only when, through identification with another nonconformist member, they are allowed to misbehave, as it were, by proxy. Others maintain that the black sheep draws the hostility of the healthy members who, instead of attacking each other, attack him. Therefore, he indirectly contributes toward the unity and respectability of the family. The same principle applies to certain organizations which intentionally retain the services of a person who carries out devious transactions, engages in illegal practices, and maintains contact with people of dubious character. Thus, military and government officials frequently use henchmen, informers, or agents who mix with the underworld to achieve their purposes. But should such persons be caught, connection with their principals is usually denied.

In some groups, the disturbance of communication is based upon a mutual adaptation of the psychopathology of individuals. Homosexuals live with other homosexuals, sadists associate with masochists, dependent people get together with those who wish others to be dependent upon them. As long as the psychopathology of one individual is balanced or compensated for by the psychopathology of another person, the group seems to function. But, nonetheless, the group as a whole is sick, and so are the individual members. Careful analysis of these networks reveals the precariousness of the exchange; certain topics are taboo; certain responses must be avoided; certain sentiments must be expressed repeatedly. The feedback circuits are selective and certain kinds of information are magnified while other kinds are disregarded. When situational stress appears, the group tends to fall apart. On the whole, such pathological groups provide well-being for their members on a temporary basis only. The term "marginal group" describes such situations best.

Such pathology can be treated in different ways: the psychiatrist treats each member of the group separately; or he attempts to influence the sick group as a whole; or he introduces the sick individual into a new group. A combination of these approaches was adopted by Jones (129), who established therapeutic communities in which the sick individual had a chance to learn new ways of communication. Once the patient has experienced the pleasure of healthy exchange, his desire to continue frustrating communication is minimal, provided he can return to healthy surroundings. But as long as slum areas breed addiction, crime, and other forms of pathology, rehabilitation is limited. What is needed, of course, is a kind of social therapy that would break up areas that foster delinquency, schizophrenic withdrawal reactions, and marginal groups in general. On the other hand, there is no denying the fact that some patients can exist only within such marginal groups; therefore, the complete abolition of such groups would probably give rise to other forms of individual psychopathology. But management of the ecological factors of disease alone is not enough. Facilities are needed for the treatment of families so that when the hospitalized patient returns home the group will no longer feed into his particular kind of pathology.

TEAM PATHOLOGY

Division of functions occurs as a prerequisite of all group activities. In healthy groups, each person can, if necessary, assume to a certain extent the function of another person. In **pathological teams,** however, this is not the case. In such group formations, where one person's pathology feeds into another's, the functions are so distributed that one individual without the other remains a psychological cripple. Thus, there are teams in which pathology is based upon the division of functions: one person specializes in theory, the other in group management; or one person is technically gifted and socially clumsy while the other possesses social know-how and lacks technical skill. In some teams the members specialize in hurting each other, one being the aggressor, the other the victim; or one acts as audience to an exhibitionistic person, and another as parental figure to an infantile character. One person can function only in conjunction with an invalid, and another may seek the company of a famous individual.

The symbiotic team

The symbiotic team is usually made up of two persons who are **mutually interdependent** (201). In our civilization, it is customary to allow the children to remain symbiotic up to the time of puberty. Thereafter they are thrown out into the world and are expected to live with contemporaries rather than with elders. If the symbiotic relation with the parents lasts for more than two decades, it is usually considered abnormal; however, an invalid or a sick person is permitted to live in symbiosis even as an older person. American public opinion condemns dependency in the male but expects it of the female, who is supposed to be helpless. However, if the female chooses to be independent she can do so, and although she will be accepted, she will not always be popular.

Symbiotic relations are established not only with close relatives or friends but also in occupational situations between employer and employee or between fellow workers. In public life, symbiotic persons are found, by and large, in dependent positions. If they are not dependent upon individuals, they are **dependent upon** the state or upon **large organizations.** The symbiotic needs involve not only the giving or receiving of approval but also the availability of a convenient target for hostility. When two persons are used to hostile exchange with each other, neither seems to be capable of living without such drainage of hostility. In these teams, the removal of the partner represents a stress situation (59).

The symbiotic team operates almost exclusively at the interpersonal level. Each participant needs the affinity and proximity of the other person, and because of this need tends to overadapt. The other person is not treated as a separate entity but is considered part of the self, or the self is considered as part of the other person. To achieve unity is the unverbalized wish of any participant in a symbiotic team. For this purpose, the participants distort reality and make certain distorted assumptions regarding the demarcation of ego **boundaries**. They assume that no boundaries exist between people so that anything that comes within reach is assumed to be an extension of their own organism or sphere of influence. They assume that a message given to another person is understood and acted upon immediately just as an impulse that reaches their own leg results in contraction of the muscles. This state of affairs is described best by saying that the symbiotic persons are primarily concerned with propriofunctions. They perceive primarily the stimuli that arise within themselves and within the realm of the team and neglect or ignore messages that arise in organizations which do not fall within their immediate sphere of interest.

Since symbiotic persons suffer from loneliness when alone and are somewhat irresponsible when in a group, they **cannot tolerate** awareness of an **outside boundary**; such awareness produces frustration, and immediately every resource is mobilized to blur the demarcation line. This is most easily achieved by the consumption of alcohol. An alcoholic is chummy with everyone around him; he assumes that all the others feel the same as he does, that they understand his messages, and that they have the same perceptions. He acts as if all the people formed one happy brotherhood. As a result, the alcoholic's system of evaluation suffers. Not being able to put himself into the position of an outsider, he is unable to compare his attitudes, actions, and roles with those of others. His body of information, therefore, is based almost entirely on data derived from propriofunctioning, and correction of information through communication with others leaves much to be desired. Therefore, the alcoholic seeks the company of others who operate like him. The informal organization of the bums on "skid row" enables the alcoholic to live in a brotherhood in which all participants are exposed to similar experiences and where no boundary between him and his fellow drifters has to be recognized. The methods employed by Alcoholics Anonymous are built upon this same principle. This very successful organization provides the alcoholic with an "inside membership" while it helps him gradually to recognize and acknowledge the outside boundary. He is enabled to maintain his own individuality and sense of responsibility in spite of the fact that the group exerts a certain control.

As far as family life is concerned, the male **alcoholic** tends to marry a domineering, frigid, and rejecting wife, whose personality problems make it difficult for her to associate with normal men. Such a woman, by and large, has to associate with cripples or men who have to be nursed, supported, or educated; with healthy males she becomes too competitive. Similarity threatens her, and difference puts her at ease. As long as the man is sick, she feeds him, keeps house, and works for him. But as soon as he gets better her competitive striving makes him aware of the boundary problem. If he should be successful, her hostility becomes so intolerable that he may return to drinking. The cycle starts all over, and she begins to rescue him anew.

When such a symbiosis has lasted for a number of years, the breaking up of the relation frequently means disaster. One participant does not possess the means of carrying out the functions that the other person had assumed, and after separation he literally feels lost. Overspecialization of input functions and underspecialization of evaluation is the lot of **the underdog** in the symbiotic relation. Such a person is extremely sensitive in perceiving signs of approval or disapproval, of like or dislike. He tends to evaluate matters in terms of the flow of things that come his way. When incoming messages refer to his well-being, he feels gratified. But the symbiotic underdog is unrealistic. He does not know what is good for him; he only knows what is good for the symbiosis. In perceiving, such a person is extremely sensitive to words; however, he is rather blind to statements of others that are codified in terms of action. He believes the word but neglects the evidence presented in terms of action. He himself is inarticulate in terms of vocabulary, gesture, and other means of expression. He does not dare to express his thoughts and feelings lest someone might be offended. This inefficiency of expression is in part related to the assumption that within a symbiotic relationship the other person knows what goes on and consequently communication, which appears as a necessary daily chore, remains undifferentiated. If necessity dictates that he communicate with strangers, this difficulty becomes particularly noticeable. Usually the stranger experiences the symbiotic person's inability to cope with discursive language as coercive, inasmuch as demands are made in terms of decision-making and action which far exceed the stranger's readiness to comply.

One example of symbiotic functioning occurs in certain **mother-child relationships.** Some mothers are unduly concerned with certain body areas and functions. The preoccupation with constipation, diarrhea, menstruation, pregnancy, development of breasts in girls, dental hygiene, cleansing of skin, diet, clothing, or hairdo transmits to the child the idea that these functions are of importance for maintaining the relationship. In order to accommodate mother, the child shares her preoccupation, and such body function then becomes the mediator of interpersonal contact. Thus, when an overprotective mother is incapable of expressing her affection verbally or of acting without ambivalence, she resorts to subterfuges. Combing of her boy's hair offers an opportunity for caress; his constipation offers an opportunity to perpetuate, by means of enema, the much-beloved scene of diaper change; cleaning of mouth, nose, and ears presents an excuse for touch. These mothers feel rather uneasy about touching the body of the child without stringent indications, and they feel compelled to hide their pleasure in bodily contact. Under such circumstances, the child experiences ambiguity. The mother verbally states, "This is done for your interest and health," but the child senses the gratification that mother experiences during these activities. By complying or denying, by being sick or healthy, the child can exert leverage on mother's gratifications.

One of the reasons for entering into a symbiosis in adult life is the lack of mastery of **verbal-digital language.** The analogic, nonverbal means of expression which such persons possess are suitable for mutual understanding only; they are not suitable for purposes of discourse. Thus, various aspects of events cannot be taken up in succession and different shadings discussed. Symbiotic persons rarely are capable of dealing with abstract fields such as mathematics, physics, or philosophy; instead, they are concerned with the more trivial matters of daily living. Since abstract analysis is precluded, prediction of events becomes impossible. In view of these limitations of communication, loneliness becomes terrifying and only immediate physical contact may alter this feeling to a certain extent. In symbiotic homosexual, invalid-nurse, or parent-child teams, physical contact frequently becomes the central function around which the relationship revolves. This down-to-earth attitude gives these people the appearance of cheerfulness, practicality, and warmth, which features are responsible for their popularity.

In their formative years, symbiotic persons usually were prevented from learning by trial and error. They were not permitted to act, to initiate, or to undertake things; instead, they were forced to over-adapt. **Overadaptation** is always associated with control of communication which facilitates such overadaptation. Healthy adaptation, in contrast, develops only if discursive language and relative independence are maintained. In symbiotic teams, inarticulateness of verbal expression requires the use of action as a means of communication. Since they use action for communication rather than for implementation of practical tasks, symbiotic persons rarely become very skilled. For them, mastery is not pleasurable but is a disagreeable "must." Since they tend to overadapt or **overcontrol,** they cannot afford to make errors, and therefore their inappropriate implementations rarely serve their needs.

Among the genetic childhood events that promote symbiotic living one finds with frightening regularity an uneven distribution of functions of communication within the family. Either mother or father was reported to have an overbearing personality and one of the parents then assumed over-all importance (211, 212, 213). Situational disequilibrium through death or disease, the nature of the occupation, or the personality of the parent may have been responsible for such developments. Thus, the remaining parent, by reason of either personality or circumstance, became the important person, and the growing child was deprived of the experience of **group communication.** In the process of maturation, support or criticism of the group, supply of valuable information, and opportunities for correcting distorted views take the place of bodily reliance upon the protective actions of the parent. The symbiotic persons thus cannot function in large groups; multiple roles cannot be assumed; and inclusion of another person can only occur in two- or three-person situations. Because of this disability, they possessively cling to one other person and in so doing prevent their own further growth.

Mutually destructive partners

The game of "I hurt you and you hurt me" can be carried out in purely communicative terms. The sadistic-masochistic exchange of messages is founded, on the one hand, on the principle of hurting by skillful use of **offensive content** and, on the other hand, on the principle of withholding or distorting acknowledgment. Calling a person names may be brutal, coarse, or unfair, but as long as the other has a chance to retaliate the performance is not considered sadistic. Open attack, sneak attack, and fencing with words are acceptable ways of communication. Here the impinging and traumatizing force hits directly from the outside, and the individual can defend himself. But the situation is much worse when the words used impinge upon an intrapsychic mechanism of the other person. Verbal sadistic attack usually is aimed at lowering the other person's self-respect. Words that set in motion anxiety, guilt, or shame, or words that expose a carefully hidden weakness or disability are designed to defeat the individual by sabotage from within. But the individual so attacked usually is asking for cruel treatment. By disemboweling himself in front of the other, by exposing dispositions toward self-reproach, ambivalence, exasperation, self-abasement, or doubt, he extends an invitation and offers himself as target.

The second and more veiled form of sadistic-masochistic performance is found in those people who do not give their partners the satisfaction of acknowledgment. By disregarding a hesitant and shy approach, by omitting a clarifying explanation, or by elaborating the self-evident, the other person may be hurt. Failure to perceive an intent may be awkward or inconvenient and the other person may be disappointed; to **ignore** an **intent** that has been perceived, and letting the other person know that acknowledgment is purposefully omitted is cruel. When a child wants to go and visit his divorced father, an open "no" may be temporarily painful; but when the mother regularly schedules visits to homes of friends when she perceives this intent, the child may be deeply hurt.

The perniciousness of the sadistic-masochistic game lies in the fact that the build-up to and the preoccupation with the painful exchange becomes an **all-absorbing performance** which makes all other emotional reactions appear anticlimactic and pale. All other considerations, such as rationality, dignity, satisfaction, and health, are renounced in favor of an opportunity to play the game. The range of such deviant emotional experiences is varied. With his impotence in heterosexual relations, the homosexual may embarrass himself and at the same time withhold pleasure from his partner. The employer may enjoy keeping his employees insecure with regard to the permanence of their work, sometimes raising hopes and then extinguishing these a little later. In return, he is served poorly and the employee will get back at him by making embarrassing mistakes. People who become addicted to this game deliberately seek only partners who provide for this all-absorbing experience.

The **language of the sadistic-masochistic game** is usually such that when the verbal exchange is superficially polite and reserved the nonverbal elements are violent and insulting. Conversely, when verbal language is traumatic, the nonverbal element is frequently gratifying. The principle thus is clear: gratification occurs in response to one type of codification and frustration occurs in response to the other. Those persons who hurt others frequently can prove that they obeyed the law and observed all conventions to the letter, and those who use abusive language can often convince their partners of their honest intentions. The leverage exerted upon the other person is achieved by promising some forthcoming action which then is withheld, or by making a statement in action which is later verbally denied. In both instances, the other person is induced to act on assumptions which at first are made to appear very probable and then are treated as if they always had been improbable. This game operates effectively only when a person's wishful thinking can be stimulated by innuendoes, whereupon the partner goes about to destroy these fantasies in equally subtle ways. Realistic people rarely get trapped in such a game, but if they do they quickly correct their erroneous assumptions. The sadistic-masochistic person, in contrast, overcorrects and lets the partner know of his disappointment and asks of him that he repent. By reversing roles, he then becomes the avenger, a role which stimulates the other person's wishful thinking, and on goes the game.

The circumstances that lead to the development of such personalities are related to **double talk.** When father reads his little daughter a story and at the same time directs her attention to his physical prowess, when a mother openly encourages her son to feats of adventure and then secretly manipulates the scene in such a way that he cannot leave home, the situation becomes loaded and the child learns to respond in an equally roundabout manner. The same double talk occurs when parents indicate that they would appreciate confidences and then betray the child by telling everybody the secret. However, when action, talk, thinking, and feeling of the parent are coordinated and, in terms of signifying, refer to the same events, then the chances for the development of sadistic-masochistic games are eliminated. With progressive age, the intensity of these games diminishes. As people's fantasy becomes duller, as wishful thinking gives place to disappointment, as people feel unloved, they become resigned and cease to rise to the bait. Such persons then have grown less self-destructive at the same time as they have lost some of their zest for living.

Part Two

The Clinical Observation
of Communicative Behavior

Chapter Seven

The Systematic Assessment
of Communication

COMMUNICATION is that human function which enables people to relate to each other. By means of signals and signs, human beings exchange views, express inner thoughts and feelings, make agreements, and state disagreements. In communication theory, the assumption is made that **information controls behavior** and that by studying information and its exchange one can obtain a better understanding of human behavior. Among the behavioral disciplines, psychiatry is that field of human endeavor which is devoted to the study and treatment of conditions which prevent the successful interrelation of people. Specifically, it is concerned with those structural and functional disturbances which arise within the individual or in small groups and interfere with the successful exchange of messages.

In the systematic assessment of communication, the **message** has become the focus of observation. A message can be defined as a series of statements which originate in one place and terminate in another; when the receiver acknowledges the receipt of the statement and when the sender perceives this acknowledgment and acknowledges it in turn, a message has in fact been exchanged. The advantages of dealing with messages rather than with behavior are great. Regardless of whether a system of communication consists of a single individual or of a social structure, and regardless of whether the scientist's emphasis is on linguistics or on the nature of feedback, the message can remain the entity of study. A message can be followed and traced through a variety of networks, both large and small, and therefore the systematic assessment of communication begins with the human participants, then proceeds to the assessment of two-person and small-group networks, and finally encompasses larger societal structures.

In proceeding from the observation of messages circulating within the organism to those circulating in large societal structures, the scientist follows the fate of the message as it passes through different fields. Unfortunately, the methodology has not as yet been worked out completely and some difficulties remain. These are related, on the one hand, to the use of language and of technical vocabularies and, on the other, to the position of the observer vis-à-vis the events he observes. In person-to-person contact, the doctor is within a few feet of the patient; each remains within reach of the other, and each reacts to the other in certain ways. If, however, the doctor is in a convention hall, he may see the patient at a distance only; the latter may not see him, and what the doctor observes on such an occasion is the group behavior of the patient who is surrounded by his family, which in turn is surrounded by strangers. In this situation, the doctor is concerned not only with individual but also with mass behavior. Although these observations may be as accurate as those reported in a two-person situation, they are nonetheless of a different order. The problem thus consists of making the observations about individuals comparable to observations about groups. But there exists an additional difficulty. Observations about one individual may not be comparable to observations about another individual if these two persons do not engage in similar activities. Empirical propositions or statements of fact, therefore, have to be translated into more abstract terms which lend themselves to comparison of individuals with individuals, groups with groups, and individuals with groups.

In scientific procedure, concrete observations can be condensed into more abstract terms through the use of hypothetical constructs, or **intervening variables.** These, in turn, are interconnected by means of theoretical propositions which make possible the testing of the predictions made (157). Thus, when an observer gets through with his observations he can summarize his report in terms which are understandable to his follow workers and which lend themselves for purposes of comparison. The reader has to be warned, however, that in psychiatry intervening variables are not so strictly definable as in physics, chemistry, or even experimental psychology. More often than not, the doctor has to be content to have available one or several indices rather than a complete assessment of all aspects which make up an intervening variable. Since most of the hypothetical constructs, or intervening variables, have been extensively described in earlier publications (203, 205, 207, 210, 211), a brief recapitulation may here suffice.

SIX HYPOTHETICAL CONSTRUCTS

Systems of communication

A communication system is delineated in space by the network in which a given statement travels from its origin to its destination. Thus, human communication networks can be limited to one single person, to two persons, or to small groups, or they can embrace societies of people. Every individual operates voluntarily or involuntarily in a network of communication, the size of which depends upon the person's occupation and his importance in society. Since participation in a network is such a ubiquitous feature, it lends itself for observation and prediction particularly well. For psychiatric purposes, the one-person, the two-person, and the small-group network are of particular relevance. Not every person is capable of operating with the same skill and ease in networks of different sizes, although most people have some notion of how to behave under differing conditions. Differences in the skill of communication and specialization in certain functions begin at birth, inasmuch as the infant is born into a two-person communication system without being able to express any choice in the matter. This situation continues for a number of years until the network begins to include other family members. The involuntary participation in these "natural" and not self-chosen **two-person systems** is responsible for many of the distortions of communication; were the child to be exposed for the first time to frustrating two-person communication at an age when he could choose, he probably would quickly sever such relations or avoid them altogether. Later in life, any person enters selectively a variety of two-person situations which satisfy needs dictated by circumstances as well as those dictated by earlier conditioning. The choice of partners is based on the expectations that the relationship raises, and the prevailing form of communication is by necessity the result of compromise.

As the child matures, he has the choice of associating with a variety of groups. These may differ as to their status, organization, formality, activity, and, above all, with regard to the satisfaction they provide for the individual. On the whole, one can observe that individuals tend to adhere to the same type of group. If they prefer casual groups, they will seek organizations in which each member can easily be replaced; and if they prefer organized groups, they will seek organizations that enable them to exercise their particular specialty. The organizational differences between groups are reflected in the characteristics that govern the exchange of messages. Some groups have far-flung systems of communication which are spread over the whole nation and require extensive written correspondence and superficial contact with many people. Other groups are made up of local members, providing for the intimacy of shared experience.

Information bearing upon an individual's past experience with certain communication networks makes prediction of future choice of systems possible. Information about the structure of the network enables the examiner to forecast certain aspects of the communicative behavior of an individual, provided he knows at which spot in the system the individual operates.

Functions of communication

Any biological or social entity is characterized by the ability to receive, to evaluate, and to transmit messages. At the one-person level, all three functions are located inside the same organism; at the two-person level, functions are divided between two people; and as the groups increase in size, functions are shared by many individuals leading to the development of subspecialties in the areas of reception, evaluation, and transmission (203). With age, almost all people experience a progressive change away from perception and action and toward evaluation. In his first few months of life, the baby can perceive but is limited in action. By the time the child is ten or eleven, coordination of movements and physical action have been mastered, but evaluation is lagging behind. In young adulthood, perception and action are reoriented more toward social action, and finally, after forty or more years of experience, evaluation is mastered. Thus, determined in part by biological and in part by social factors, people tend to exhibit selectivity for either perception, evaluation, or transmission.

At the **two-person level,** this selectivity may reveal itself in the choice of a partner who compensates for or reinforces an existing tendency; a passive-receptive individual may choose an active partner who specializes in transmission. At the group level there is an even wider variety of choices. An individual may join the body of people who are concerned with perception, observation, intake, and reception; he may become part of the section concerned with evaluation—the planning or executive body, or the general staff; or he may in turn be part of the transmitter and effector system of an organization, being the errand boy, the leg-man, or, in brief, the doer. The three basic functions—perception, evaluation, and transmission—always have to be treated as a unit. Information about an individual's specialization in perception, evaluation, and transmission, his skills in attending to these functions, and the distortions he produces enables the examiner to predict future communicative behavior with regard to these functions in specific situations.

Language and codification

The process by which one set of events represents another set of events is referred to as **codification.** The term "language," then, is reserved for a series of codifications which, in order to qualify as language, have to be known to at least two if not more people (167). Idiosyncratic expressions of a schizophrenic, for example, which are unintelligible to anyone else, cannot, therefore, qualify as language. Inside the organism, signals are coded in terms of nervous impulses traveling along certain pathways. Outside the organism, people use spoken language, gesture, and action to signal to each other; a more durable form of codification is found in written language, sound recordings, photographs, moving pictures, and three-dimensional models.

Formal education trains people in the use of words and numbers

—that is, in verbal communication. Family life and interaction train people in nonverbal communication. In individual development, the nonverbal precedes the verbal for many years, and the integration of the two forms of language gives rise to highly individualistic patterns. Information about codification systems and language used by individuals and groups enables the examiner to predict the way information will be recorded, the limitations and distortions which may occur, the durability of such codifications, the universality or specificity of the statements, and the distribution that these might attain.

Content and information

A message may be said to have content when sender and receiver can reach an agreement regarding the events to which the signs refer. But, unlike the signifying function of a single sign such as a word, the term "content" implies **signification** of complex action sequences. Content, therefore, always implies the identification of a subject and object, respective qualification, and some statement of process or action which connects the various elements with each other and perhaps even with more remote events (167). A meaningless and unintelligible message would be one in which part of the message is so garbled that no agreement can be reached with regard to a clear-cut identification and qualification of its significance.

The term "content" carries no implication regarding truth or falsehood. This occurs only in a subsequent step in which statements made, either to self or to others, are tested against what is called reality. If the statements hold up, a person may be said to have knowledge which enables him to reconstruct past events, to predict future events, and hence to engage in successful action. That part of knowledge that can be transferred to others is generally referred to as **information**, while the other part, which cannot be transferred through a simple process of communication, is generally referred to as skill.

Correct evaluation of the past and appropriate decisions for the future are largely based upon the relevance, accuracy, and completeness of information. This can be achieved only when information derived from outer sources is combined with information derived from inner sources, inasmuch as an insider's view rarely coincides with an outsider's perspective. In order for information to be intelligible, its human source and intended destination must be reported. Discrepant views can be reconciled when the position of the observer and the time of observation are known to the interpreter of a message. In two-person situations, agreement and **disagreement** are usually easier to ascertain than in a group situation, and misunderstandings can be prevented. In group situations, information has to be so condensed and compressed that for the sake of brevity many interpretative and instructive statements are omitted. In group situations, a speaker cannot tailor his presentation entirely to the needs of one person, lest he be not understood. When talking to many people at the same time, the necessary condensation, the short span of time allotted to a speaker, and the use of a popular vocabulary bring about a loss of information. The choice thus rests between saying a lot to a few or saying a little to many. The referential property of signals and signs, the amount of knowledge, and the problem-solving property of information are features which lend themselves particularly well to prediction.

Metacommunication and instruction

The individual's instructions and interpretative devices, his communications about communication, have to be viewed from the standpoint of both perception and transmission (210). The ability of a speaker to instruct others about the way his statements ought to be interpreted and the listener's proficiency in understanding these instructions contribute equally to successful communication. Instructions about interpretation of messages can be given explicitly; but more often than not, when reliance is placed upon role recognition, knowledge of rules, or appreciation of context, they are implicit. In contrast to the two-person situation, where subtle, nonverbal instructions can be used, the group situation necessitates a certain **explicitness** of instruction and interpretation. Together with this explicitness in metacommunication goes an implicitness of personal management. In group situations it is more difficult to direct people, unless, as in the military situation, the channels of communication have been set up and are rigidly maintained; and the task of management is usually achieved with **implicit devices.** In two-person situations, where metacommunicative statements usually remain implicit, the management of the other person presents hardly any problem and can be achieved explicitly and directly.

Although it must be granted that individual variations exist, a certain code pertaining to the giving and interpreting of instructions prevails in each social group. Interpretation of metacommunicative statements thus requires knowledge of the social matrix or the culture in which the exchange of messages takes place.

Correction, feedback, and reply

Correction of information occurs when within a communication system the results of action are fed back to the control centers; this feature is characteristic of social organizations, individuals, animals, and some machines (257). Correction of performance can occur only when the effect of action is observed and necessary revisions in the body of information are made. Correction is basic to all forms of learning and hence to adaptive, healthy behavior and successful communication.

The best approach to the study of feedback in human communication consists of observing action and message sequences. Correction of information is dependent upon which statement of Person A is followed by which statement of Person B, upon the clarity, distinctness, and relevance of the statements, and upon their timing. All these factors are more important than the actual subject matter and its formulation. In healthy interpersonal and group situations, people learn to influence one another with tact and tolerance. If, however, individuals or groups cease to react to the influence of others, if they stop learning and do not bring their information up to date, or when they in return do not feed back information to others, then the communication system eventually breaks down. The stability of a communication system thus depends largely upon the feedback circuits and the use to which they are put.

EMPIRICAL NOTIONS ABOUT COMMUNICATION

Many observers do not report their findings in terms of abstract hypothetical constructs of the type mentioned above. This is particularly the case if they do not wish to compare notes with others or to make scientific predictions. In this case, they are content to phrase their findings in popular terms. These, handed down through the centuries, are of course far superior to the scientific terms when it comes to conveying to another person the full flavor of a communicative situation. Mythology, folklore, and slang are full of concepts and terms that pinpoint and illustrate man's views on the subject of communication.

For the psychiatrist, familiarity with the empirical and popular notions about communication is essential if he wishes to utilize the reports of lay people. Such comments are of great value because they cover the behavior of individuals in situations which are not accessible to him directly. Although this information may offer clues and hints which guide the psychiatrist in his future explorations, it is in part of course unreliable, inconsistent, or fictive. A systematic assessment of communication, therefore, has to combine these pieces of information that are advanced voluntarily with firsthand information obtained by means of direct observation of action and of speech. Since most people spend part of their time alone, part of their time in two-person situations, and part of their time in groups, the systematic explorer of communication does best to follow an individual in his daily activities through various situations. Where he cannot be present, he has to rely upon self-reports and reports of others, which undoubtedly will be phrased in popular terms. The total information derived from various sources and situations then has to be combined into a whole, which by necessity will be phrased in scientific terms—that is, in terms of intervening variables. A brief review of the popular notions about communication may familiarize the reader with the scope of people's knowledge about communication.

The label of the situation

Whenever people are alone, in two-person situations, or in multiperson groups, they tend to give the prevailing state of affairs a label. This practice corresponds to what the scientist would call the delineation of the field in which an event takes place. The label of the situation is determined sometimes by the goal of action which is deemed the most characteristic feature, sometimes by the emergency nature of the situation, and in other instances by the prevailing atmosphere. In daily life, alert and intelligent people are well aware of what a situation is about and consequently adopt roles, apply rules, instigate actions, and think and feel in a manner which has proved successful in the past. Behavior appropriate to the circumstances of course makes the accomplishment of a task more likely. Almost anyone who gives an account of past events unwittingly furnishes information about the label of the situation and gauges his own and other persons' actions with regard to their appropriacy. Since disturbed people frequently tend to misidentify the situation and hence adopt inappropriate behavior which is not likely to accomplish the task, the kind of information given by the relatives is invaluable to the psychiatrist, as it helps him to understand the difficulties of the patient.

The identity of the participants

"Who spoke to whom?" and "For what audience was a statement tailored?" are questions which frequently are raised in daily life. More abstractly speaking, one might say that every person or group attempts to find out where statements originate, for whom they are intended, and whom they actually reach. Both origin and destination of statements and the resulting exchange of messages are best understood in terms of the identity of the participants. Identity can be defined in terms of name, age, sex, past experiences, roles, status, and a host of other features (74). Recognition of individual and group identity sets the expectations, and therefore most people spontaneously inform others who they are. Disturbed patients frequently misidentify themselves or others and disturbances of communication may develop. The psychiatrist usually has no difficulty in spotting the true identity of patients, either at the time of the transaction or later through secondhand reports; however, it is much more difficult for him to reconstruct the identity that the patient falsely assumed during a given interaction.

Designation of relationships

The interrelatedness of people may be expressed in terms of the **roles** they occupy in various social systems. Among the military, rank and unit designation afford means of recognition and therefore of relationship. Family relations such as father and son or husband and wife are usually determined by a multitude of behavioral clues which participants rely upon if they wish to communicate with others. Roles, so to speak, are the keys for the interpretation of messages, and almost all patients talk about the persons they live with in terms of such roles. Disturbances of communication arise, of course, when roles of self and of others are misinterpreted or not clearly expressed. In psychotherapy, a good deal of time is spent on the elucidation of the patient's roles vis-à-vis the therapist and his family members. Roles, of course, cover only the somewhat repetitive and institutionalized aspects of a relationship and do not include information about the spontaneous and unique interactions between people.

The intent of the speaker

The intentions and motives of people are subject to continuous scrutiny. "He did not mean to offend you" and "He is sincere in wishing you good luck" are sentences which express such empirical judgments. In daily communication, **conscious or unconscious** intentions of people are subject to interpretation by others. Whether statements about intentions can be taken at face value is another question; nonetheless, conscious intentions are verbalized by most people. The role of unconscious intentions and motivation is rarely treated in daily life save in courts of law and in the therapist's office.

The goal of action

When boys on the playground radially converge to pick up a football, the indicated goal of action is the ball. When a candidate makes speeches in order to be elected to the office of governor, his long-term goal is likewise clear. When the goal of an action is not apparent, people may inquire, "What is he after?" and **"What** does he want?" and, if factual information is not forthcoming, they volunteer to interpret the intentions and goals of others as readily as they view with suspicion the absence of any apparent goal. Once the goals have been identified, the question is raised as to whether they are realistic or fantastic, appropriate or inappropriate, conventional or unconventional—aspects which the man on the street is vitally concerned with.

The appropriacy of implementations

"This was a foolish thing to say" and "His aim was perfect" are statements which refer to efficiency, appropriacy, and relevance of implementation. Apparently such **judgments** are the result of matching with one another the goal of action, the nature of the implementation, the efficiency or economy achieved, and the gratification obtained. Inappropriate implementations in terms of both action and speech are the subject of extensive comment. They give the psychiatrist a clue in the reconstruction of what happened in the past. In the absence of any criteria concerning appropriacy of implementation, a man's record as measured in terms of his monetary success is frequently taken as an index of appropriate behavior.

Emotional reactions

"He was terrified" and "He has the blues" are expressions which denote emotional reactions. Likes, dislikes, disappointments, hopes, resentments, fears, and many other emotional nuances are reported by newspapers, radio commentators, novelists, or are commented upon by ordinary people. Much of what relatives report about patients' emotional reactions refers to deviations from the expected. In any culture, a set of emotional expressions is deemed appropriate for certain occasions. When people do not show the expected appropriate reaction, bystanders tend to comment on what they consider an abnormality (142).

Explanation of causal connections

"High city taxes have induced people to move to the suburbs" is a statement that implies motive, cause, and effect. In ordinary life, people volunteer causal explanations which point to the way in which different events are connected with each other. Whether such explanations really correspond to scientific facts or are merely misconceptions, prejudices, or superstitions matters less than the fact that the listener gains insight into the assumptions that the speaker makes.

Observation of rules

"He drove through a red light" is a statement that points to a violation of rules. "Beyond and above the call of duty" is a comment that expresses a person's extension of rules to a situation where such behavior is not expected. People, and particularly the press, take note of the violation as well as the scrupulous adherence to and extension of rules, while average observance of laws and regulations does not rate special comment.

The location of the disturbance

Almost all people, and particularly the physician, want to know where a disturbance is located, inasmuch as knowledge of the **where** facilitates the work of those who have to initiate remedial measures. Conditions which interfere with successful communication may be divided into two groups: those located within the individual and determined by his physical and psychological structure, and those beyond an individual's control and related to interference with the free flow of messages. The latter disturbance is located between people, and the participants per se may be healthy people who are capable of rational behavior. But if they cannot exchange messages with each other—for example, because of language difficulties— then an interpersonal or group disturbance of communication develops. This distinction is diagnostically important. There where the physician feels that he deals with communication pathology due to sensory, motor, or central nervous system abnormalities, he will treat the individual. There where he feels that communication pathology is due to functional disturbances located inside the person, he will also treat the individual. If, however, he recognizes that communication pathology is the result of inappropriate intercommunication between people, he will treat the group, either as a whole or by working with the various members individually. More often than not, these three forms of pathology may be intertwined. And the comments of relatives, physicians, and police officers may help the psychiatrist to locate the place of the breakdown in communication.

THE CONCRETE OBSERVATION OF COMMUNICATIVE BEHAVIOR

In climbing down the ladder of abstraction from the lofty heights of theory via the intervening variables—and their popular counterparts—we come now to the discussion of how to make concrete observations. Immediately the question arises, what out of the wealth of possible observations is worth retaining and what out of the experience of the observer is worth reporting? Not only does communicative behavior change from situation to situation and from time to time, but verbal reports about behavior are even more variable. A scientist listening to a report is usually in doubt as to whether contradictions are related to inconsistencies in the actual events or in the interpretation of the observer. Difficulties encountered both in making and in reporting pertinent clinical observations, however, may be overcome in part if foci of observation are made explicit. This procedure compensates to a certain extent for the inconsistencies of the human observer and it brings to the attention of the psychiatrist the various aspects of communicative behavior which people observe in each other. Therefore I have drawn heavily upon the data collected in therapeutic communication with patients to formulate more systematically some of the elusive and unconscious aspects around which human interaction revolves. The selection of these foci of observation was dictated by both theoretical considerations and the existing empirical data. When engaged in the exchange of messages with others, people use many of the principles set forth here. Often these are not expressed in words but are merely acted upon, and in some instances they are phrased in terms different from those found in this book. But regardless of the form of codification used, every person continuously perceives, evaluates, and reacts to the communicative behavior of other people. In subsequent pages, the reader will find an outline which has been designed to suggest possible ways of studying communicative behavior rather than to establish a mandatory procedure. The guide has been divided into three profiles, each with a different emphasis. Analogous to map projections of the globe, each emphasis introduces a different type of distortion.

In the **Personality Profile** (Profile A), repetitive, intense, and unusual behavior features are emphasized; successive events which occur over the course of years are telescoped into such constructs as preferences, attitudes, potentialities, and dispositions. In this instance, the temporal characteristics of behavior are neglected and it is assumed that the individual, regardless of time and place, may exhibit these features. The specificity of behavior with regard to social situations obviously has to be neglected.

In the **Interaction Profile** (Profile B), repetitive, intense, and unusual action sequences which occur in two-person situations are emphasized; attitudes, dispositions, and other more time-enduring features of the personality as well as behavior in group situations have to be neglected.

In the **Group Profile** (Profile C), intense, repetitive, and unusual behavior which a person may display in group situations is emphasized. Group processes which may influence a person's behavior are considered, and individual and interpersonal behaviors are neglected.

The difference between the three profiles can be paraphrased in the following terms:

A. Personality Profile: "He does," "He is," regardless of the situation

B. Interaction Profile: "He reacts to what the other does or is," "He does to her," "She does to him"

C. Group Profile: "He reacts to others and to the nature of the situation," "He does to them, they do to him"

Instructions for the use of the guide

Profile A, entitled "Personality Profile, or The Individual's Communicative Behavior Regardless of the Situation," is assembled by using all possible sources of information and observation. Since the most frequent and the most intense events are considered the most characteristic features, successive events occurring at different dates have to be condensed in such a manner that they appear as if they occurred simultaneously. Abstractions of the more time-enduring, repetitive, or unusual features of a person's communicative behavior are in effect statements of probability which indicate that, since such behavior occurred in the past, it also can be expected in the future. Terms like "attitude," "disposition," "inclination," "habit," and "tendency" subsume this probability. Accuracy of prediction increases if one knows particulars about the situation in question. Since in most instances this information is incomplete, predictions frequently have to be confined to general personality features rather than to be concerned with action behavior in a concrete situation. For want of a better expression, the term "personality profile" has been adopted to refer to these very general aspects of the communicative behavior of a person. However, the profile is based upon a distortion—the assumption that an individual can exist in relative isolation from others. The paradox of the matter is that the communicative behavior of one person can be observed only in two-person or group situations and that self-reports which are addressed to other people likewise have to be considered as interpersonal communications. But in spite of all the variations introduced by the presence of other people, this type of profile is the only means by which one essential element in a complex communication network—the individual communicator—can be characterized.

Profile B, entitled "Interaction Profile, or The Individual's Communicative Behavior in Two-Person Situations," will vary with the complexity of the subject, the nature of the situation, and the character of the other person. In the case of complex personalities, the variations will be greater than in the case of immature, abnormal, or undifferentiated personalities where the profile may be similar for all interactions studied. The profile is primarily based on actual observations, and inferences derived from historical material and characteristics of group membership are minimized. Although the data bear upon the interaction of two people, the profile has been constructed in such a manner that the behavior of one person—the test subject or patient—is emphasized. This facilitates the comparison of behavior in two-person situations with behavior in groups.

A two-person interaction has been conceived of as consisting of a set of stimuli—the statement of the first person—and a set of responses—the reply of the second person. By considering the way in which the reply is tied to the initial statement, it is possible to emphasize the selectivities which operate in two-person situations and which contribute to or interfere with successful communication. The communication engineers define successful communication as the establishment of identical information in sender and receiver. In the study of human communication, this criterion cannot be applied because neither participant nor observer can ascertain whether the statement of the first person has been completely understood by the second person. Instead, one has to rely on indices of tension or tension reduction. When an individual makes a statement, it produces in him a state of tension which is subsequently altered by the reply of another person. If the reply hits the nail on the head, the individual experiences tension reduction. The pleasure of having been understood, of having received a reply that fits, of having been acknowledged—all that produces a sense of well-being in the individual. Conversely, when a reply does not hit the nail on the head, when a statement is acknowledged inappropriately or not at all, then the tension increases and may even have some halo effects upon the person who gave the inappropriate reply. The criterion of successful communication thus is bound to at least one person's feeling of having been understood. When this is verified by the second person, then we are on safer ground with the assumption that communication has been successful.

The present profile thus has been constructed around the reactions of one person to the behavior of another person. The terms "action" and "reaction" have been used interchangeably because in practice it is impossible to decide which action is primary and which is secondary. While the Personality Profile specifies preference in communication and assumes that there exists a variety of choices in the selection of situations and persons with whom to associate, the Interaction Profile details the specific communicative reactions which occur in two-person situations.

Profile C, entitled "Group Profile, or The Individual's Communicative Behavior in Group Situations," intentionally contains little information bearing on personality structure and on situations other than group situations. The Group Profile is not concerned with an analysis of the group as a whole and of events which are commonly subsumed under the term "group process"; instead, it emphasizes the constituent parts of the group—that is, one individual at a time. The communicative behavior of one individual is separated from that of the rest of the group. The individual under consideration then becomes an identified person, whereas for simplicity's sake the other members are lumped together and are known by the generic term "group" only. The procedure of considering one person at a time is particularly relevant in psychiatry because an ordinary group may be disrupted when people with disturbances of communication and psychopathology join it. The disruption of a group is frequently more a function of the pathology of an individual than of the group as a whole. Although on occasion the introduction of a disturbing member can be handled through the adaptive processes of the group, more often than not the disturbing individual has to be taken aside, instructed, treated separately, or removed from the group entirely. In a well-functioning group, people cooperate with each other. Sick individuals may be incapable of such cooperation, and therefore the study of a sick individual in a group is therapeutically more relevant than the study of disrupted group processes as a whole.

Each of the three profiles bears upon different situations, gives different views, and introduces different distortions. In combination, the profiles constitute a device which enables the examiner to scan the communicative behavior of an individual in different situations and to spot possible areas of disturbance. **Disturbed and undisturbed communication** has been outlined **as one continuous function:** the disturbances are considered either as quantitative exaggerations of normal behavior or as behavior that does not fit a given situation. Occasionally, the cutoff point which separates normal from abnormal is difficult to locate. In case of doubt, the following criteria should be applied: if a subject shows rigid adherence to a given pattern over a period of time, indicating inability to choose other responses when the need arises; if his responses show quantitative exaggeration or diminution; and if he exhibits symptoms of stress whenever he cannot use his favorite response, then we are allowed to talk about pathology. Furthermore, if the individual is a participant in one or more systems of communication that do not function satisfactorily and in which the other participants experience tension, there exists further supportive evidence for the existence of pathology.

As to the **technical details,** each focus of observation has been given a number and a letter. All items labeled *A* refer to the Personality Profile, items labeled *B* to the Interaction Profile, and items labeled *C* to the Group Profile. Single letters (A, B, C) refer to undisturbed behavior; double letters (AA, BB, CC) refer to disturbed behavior. Items with the same number refer to analogous observations in the three profiles. For example, A-1, B-1, and C-1 all refer to observations regarding the nature of the communication system in which the individual participates. Each focus of observation has been defined in somewhat abstract language and illustrated by examples derived from everyday life or condensed from case records. The examples are not exhaustive but are intended to delineate the area of observation and to remind the clinician of the background associations which he must possess in order to engage in effective scanning of the events in question.

In practice, the examiner will observe the patient on different occasions: he will interview him alone, with one significant relative, and perhaps in the presence of several family members, or he will observe the patient on the ward and in group gatherings. After observing the individual in interpersonal and group situations, the examiner needs information about those aspects of communication which seem to be a function not of a single person but of the actual multiperson network which defines the system. Therefore, communicative events may be restricted in space, as in the case of quarrels which take place in the fold of the family, or they may be widespread, as in rivalry between competing members of a national organization. The combination of individual-determined with system-determined aspects will help the examiner to understand how individual pathology is kindled and fed by the existing interpersonal and group relations and how, in turn, individual pathology can contribute to the breakdown of groups.

Chapter Eight

A Guide to the Clinical Observation of Communicative Behavior

FOCI OF OBSERVATION

I. Systems of Communication

A-1	Preference for systems of different magnitude	AA-1	Disturbances
B-1	Structure of two-person systems	BB-1	Disturbances
C-1	The structure of group situations	CC-1	Disturbances

A-2	Concurrent participation in systems of different magnitude	AA-2	Disturbances
B-2	Concurrent participation in several two-person systems	BB-2	Disturbances
C-2	Concurrent participation in several group systems	CC-2	Disturbances

A-3	Successive participation in systems of different magnitude	AA-3	Disturbances
B-3	Successive participation in various two-person systems	BB-3	Disturbances
C-3	Successive participation in various group systems	CC-3	Disturbances

II. Functions of Communication

A-4	Preferred functions of communication	AA-4	Disturbances
	Some details of functioning at the individual level:		
A-4.1	Perception	AA-4.1	Disturbances
A-4.2	Memory patterns	AA-4.2	Disturbances
A-4.3	Principles of evaluation	AA-4.3	Disturbances
A-4.4	Decision-making	AA-4.4	Disturbances
A-4.5	Reasoning	AA-4.5	Disturbances

III. *Language and Codification*

IV. *Content and Information*

A-10	Interests and approaches	AA-10	Disturbances
B-10	Preferences for certain universes of discourse	BB-10	Disturbances
C-10	Task orientation in group situations	CC-10	Disturbances
	Some details about task orientation:		
	C-10.1 The change of tasks in group situations	CC-10.1	Disturbances

A-11	Reactions to conflicting information	AA-11	Disturbances
B-11	Congruity and ambiguity in expression	BB-11	Disturbances
	Some details about contradictory information:		
	B-11.1 Subject matter, role, and personal consideration	BB-11.1	Disturbances
	B-11.2 Personal reference in the exchange of information	BB-11.2	Disturbances
C-11	The management of discourse in group situations	CC-11	Disturbances

V. *Metacommunication*

A-12	Instructions	AA-12	Disturbances
B-12	Social techniques	BB-12	Disturbances
C-12	Interpretative devices in group situations	CC-12	Disturbances

A-13	Contexts and situations	AA-13	Disturbances
B-13	The frame of reference in two-person situations	BB-13	Disturbances
C-13	Preferred atmospheres in group situations	CC-13	Disturbances

A-14	Rules	AA-14	Disturbances
B-14	Observation of rules in two-person situations	BB-14	Disturbances
C-14	Observation of rules in group situations	CC-14	Disturbances

A-15	Roles	AA-15	Disturbances
B-15	The choice of roles in two-person situations	BB-15	Disturbances
C-15	The choice of roles in group situations	CC-15	Disturbances
	Some special characteristics of roles:		
	C-15.1 Preferences for family roles	CC-15.1	Disturbances
	C-15.2 Roles of decision-makers	CC-15.2	Disturbances
	C-15.3 The choice of persons addressed in group situations	CC-15.3	Disturbances
	C-15.4 Switch from passive to active participation	CC-15.4	Disturbances
	C-15.5 The mode of speaking in group situations	CC-15.5	Disturbances

VI. *Correction, Feedback, and Reply*

A-16	Tolerance limits	AA-16	Disturbances
B-16	Responses to quantitative variations in two-person situations	BB-16	Disturbances
C-16	Responses to quantitative variations in intensity in group situations	CC-16	Disturbances

A-17	Attitudes toward people	AA-17	Disturbances
B-17	The selection of communication partners in two-person situations	BB-17	Disturbances
C-17	Position of self in relation to others	CC-17	Disturbances

A-18	Ways of replying	AA-18	Disturbances
B-18	Preferences in appealing in two-person situations	BB-18	Disturbances
	Some special forms of appeal in two-person situations:		
B-18.1	Personal leverage	BB-18.1	Disturbances
B-18.2	Leverage through manipulation of needs of other person	BB-18.2	Disturbances
C-18	Appealing in group situations	CC-18	Disturbances

A-19	Ways of replying	AA-19	Disturbances
B-19	Ways of responding in two-person situations	BB-19	Disturbances
	Some special forms of reaction in two-person situations:		
B-19.1	The selective response	BB-19.1	Disturbances
B-19.2	Reaction to the other person's way of perceiving-evaluating	BB-19.2	Disturbances
B-19.3	Reactions to the other person's decision-making and exertion of control	BB-19.3	Disturbances
B-19.4	Reactions to the other person's modality of action	BB-19.4	Disturbances
B-19.5	Emotional gratification given by replying in different ways	BB-19.5	Disturbances
B-19.6	Agreement and disagreement in two-person situations	BB-19.6	Disturbances
C-19	Ways of responding when addressed	CC-19	Disturbances
	Some special forms of reaction in group situations:		
C-19.1	Ways of responding when action is called for	CC-19.1	Disturbances

A-20	Learning and correction	AA-20	Disturbances
B-20	Learning, teaching, and correction in two-person situations	BB-20	Disturbances
C-20	Learning and cooperation in the group	CC-20	Disturbances
	Some details about efficiency of communication:		
C-20.1	Criteria of effective communication in group situations	CC-20.1	Disturbances

A-21	Social conflict	AA-21	Disturbances
B-21	Management of conflicts in two-person situa-tions	BB-21	Disturbances
C-21	Management of conflicts in group situations	CC-21	Disturbances

A-22	Adaptation and control	AA-22	Disturbances
B-22	Adaptation and control in two-person situa-tions	BB-22	Disturbances
C-22	Adaptation and control in group situations	CC-22	Disturbances

PERSONALITY PROFILE
or
The Individual's Communicative Behavior
Regardless of the Situation

A-1. *Preferences for systems of different magnitude.* A person's preference for participation in small or large communication systems is expressed in terms of the time spent within networks of a certain magnitude, the avoidance of certain magnitudes, and the importance of the person's presence for the functioning of a given system (210).

AA-1. *Disturbances.* Since each network is governed by certain characteristics which may not apply to another network, any individual's communicative behavior has to fit into the network in which he operates if he wishes to receive satisfactory replies. But sometimes people tend to behave as if all systems were alike, and in this case disturbances of communication arise. The circumstances that lead to distortions may be related to inaccurate perception of the situation, to lack of experience with a particular system, or to inability to adapt to the existing system; distortions may also be introduced intentionally for political purposes.

a) Functions most comfortably alone:
—Spends a great deal of time thinking, meditating, reading, or working by himself
—Does not seek the company of others in his spare time
—Transacts necessary business with others as quickly as possible

a) Tends to distort interpersonal, group, or societal situations by behaving as if he were alone:
—In a social situation, ignores others; he attends to his own comfort or pursues his own interests without consideration for others
—Manipulates people as if they were extensions of himself
—When lecturing, his communications are not geared to the audience; he is thinking out loud without attempt to explain his thoughts
—Does not inform others of his intentions; he goes without taking leave

b) Functions most comfortably in a two-person system of communication:
—Prefers to work with one other person rather than alone
—Lives with one other person
—In his spare time, seeks the company of one other person
—Tends to discuss matters in intimate, tête-à-tête situations

b) Tends to distort personal, group, or societal situations and to treat them as two-person situations:
—When alone, engages in lively interactions with an imaginary partner
—When with others, reduces ideas or problems to a simple dichotomy even though most issues are more complex
—When in a group, tends to split it into two factions—himself and his adherents, on the one hand, and his opponents, on the other—thus reducing the group to a two-member structure
—When in a group, may address one individual only, neglecting the others, and artificially producing a two-person situation

c) Functions most comfortably in small groups composed of several persons:
—Travels in a crowd
—Avoids two-person situations
—Lives with several others
—Works for a small enterprise

c) Tends to distort personal, interpersonal, and societal situations and to treat them as group situations:
—When quick individual response is required, proceeds to deliberate and debate
—When an individual decision is required, as, for instance, in ordering a meal, makes his decision dependent upon the decisions of others
—Instead of facing issues by face-to-face talk, resorts to devious schemes and intrigues. Involves other people and uses them as tools to achieve personal ends; e.g., mobilizes a gang of friends to settle a personal difference with another individual

d) Functions most comfortably in a large system:
—Influences masses of people through speeches, writing, or acting
—Seeks administrative or other controlling positions
—Is active member of large organizations
—Works for large enterprises or the state

d) Tends to distort personal, interpersonal, and group situations and to treat them as societal situations:
—Treats personal problems as if they had universal social importance
—Talks at people, as if he were broadcasting, instead of addressing them in a personal way
—Feels entitled to special considerations although the situation does not warrant such treatment; e.g., the political figure on vacation who demands special attention

A-2. *Concurrent participation in systems of different magnitude.* An individual can relate to other people within a variety of systems. The way in which his membership is distributed between small and large systems constitutes a rather significant personality feature.

a) Interacts with the same individuals in two-person and group situations over a period of years:
—Father sees each of his children alone and also together at dinner and on weekend outings
—Chief of staff in hospital discusses work with each member separately and then meets with all in a group

b) Interacts with the same individuals in two-person and group situations but frequently varies the individual partners:
—Innkeeper meets each guest individually and during evening entertainment

c) Interacts with different individuals in two-person and group situations and maintains the same membership over an extended period of time:
—Boy has a steady girl-friend and plays music in a band

d) Interacts with different individuals in two-person and group situations and exchanges partners at all levels frequently:
—Man plays cards with a constantly changing company and switches girl-friends frequently

AA-2. *Disturbances.* Disorders of communication develop when people are incapable of simultaneously participating in both small and large systems or when they are incapable of replacing their partners. This disability may be reflected in people's rigid affinity for one person, group, or idea; others may restrict themselves to certain activities or procedures; and still others can function in one kind of system only. Each of these behavior patterns constitutes a disturbance because its bearer cannot operate well under other circumstances.

a) Person addict; flexibly goes through changes of systems provided that the significant person remains the same:
—The "man Friday"

b) System addict; operates within one kind of system, disregarding persons, purposes, or goals:
—The socialite who is able to function only at large parties
—The person who functions well only in the pursuit of his official duties

c) Special-situation addict; functions successfully only with certain people in certain situations:
—Actress who functions well only when working, and this with a certain director
—Alcoholic who functions well only in bars

d) Change addict; unable to tolerate the same system for very long:
—Repeated change of marriage partners, friends, circles, cities, occupations, and associations

A-3. *Successive participation in systems of different magnitude.* The sequence of being alone, in two-person situations, and in groups usually is determined by such features as fatigue, satiation, or communicative skills, although it may in part be dictated by the demands of others. These sequential patterns reveal significant subtleties of communicative behavior.

a) Alternates between being alone, in two-person situations, and in groups without particular selectivity of sequence

b) Alternates between being alone and in two-person situations:
—Terminates two-person communication after several hours

c) Alternates between two-person and group situations:
—After a group meeting, seeks a two-person situation

d) Alternates between being alone and in groups:
—Interrupts his group activities primarily to stay by himself

AA-3. *Disturbances.* In an adult person, failure to participate at all three levels—alone, in two-person systems, and in group situations—usually is indicative of serious limitations in communicative skills.

a) Can tolerate neither being alone nor being with people:
—Acute disorganization in anxiety state

b) Cannot function in groups:
—Unable to assume multiple roles, to subordinate himself to others or to group tasks, or to tolerate criticism and rejection

c) Cannot tolerate being alone:
—Needs external stimulation to control disturbing fantasies, thoughts, and feelings arising in self. Unable to think things over

d) Cannot tolerate two-person situations:
—Experiences intense stimulation of proximity receivers with temptation to fight or make love. Unable to discuss intimate problems and hence does not avail himself of interpersonal feedback

A-4. *Preferred functions of communication.* Although perception, evaluation, and transmission are inseparably linked, each individual tends to emphasize one function more than the other (205). Knowledge about an individual's preference for perception, evaluation, or transmission is derived from observing the time spent in pursuing each function and the gratification that it provides for the individual.

a) Functions most comfortably as perceiver:
—Tends to observe himself
—Attentive to the needs of others
—Acts as the eyes and ears of organizations
—Is military, technical, and economic observer
—Has hobbies such as birdwatching or listening to music

b) Functions most comfortably as evaluator:
—Tends to judge himself and others
—Tends to predict events to come
—Tends to make up his mind easily
—Tends to be in responsible, decision-making positions
—Tends to be a technical adviser or expert

c) Functions most comfortably as transmitter or doer:
—Seeks every opportunity to express himself in word and deed
—Tends to engage in physical activity
—Tends to engage in "field work"
—Tends to choose situations where he can transmit his own and other people's opinions

AA-4. *Disturbances.* Exaggerated emphasis on one of the functions of communication must result in neglect of another function. Undue emphasis usually is associated with rigidity—that is, inability to shift flexibly from one function to the other in accordance with the requirements of the occasion.

a) Disturbances associated with exaggerated or restricted input:
—The hypnotic medium
—The passive-receptive person
—The eternal student
—The person with illusions and hallucinations
—The blind or deaf person
—The autistic person

b) Disturbances associated with over- or underemphasis on evaluation:
—The judgmental person
—The person who has delusions
—The person with a memory defect
—The disoriented person

c) Disturbances associated with excessive or restricted output:
—The compulsive talker
—The person with a tic
—The person with mannerisms
—The catatonic person
—The mute
—The person with motor aphasia
—The nonagitated depressed person

A-4.1. *Perception.* At birth, the child perceives the external world primarily through the mediation of his mechanical and chemical endorgans; in the next few years, he learns to rely more upon vision and hearing which enable him to scan and explore the more distant environment. In our culture, maturation is linked to the preponderant use of distance perception, while closeness perception is primarily reserved for children. A person in whom dominance of closeness perception continues to exist well into adult life is considered immature (218).

a) Preference for closeness perception:

Perceives predominantly through the senses of smell, taste, touch, temperature, pain, and equilibrium; emphasis upon small details and relative ineptitude in scanning.

—Explores texture, surface, and temperature of objects by touching, stroking, moving them
—Emphasizes smell, taste, weight, and movability of things and persons
—Engages in handicraft as a hobby

b) Preference for distance perception:

Perceives predominantly through vision and hearing and is skilled in scanning.

—Studies others by means of visual inspection
—Goes on "Cook's tours" and enjoys the "bird's-eye view"
—Emphasizes appearance of people and objects and is sensitive to the way things sound
—Engages in photography, painting, or music appreciation as a hobby

AA-4.1. *Disturbances.* Inability to use the most effective sensory modality for exploration of the environment is one of the foundations of disturbed communication. The world of the senses is specific: that which has to be tasted cannot be assessed by vision, and that which has to be heard cannot be appraised by touch. Use of one mode of perception when another one is called for may occur in organic disease affecting the sensory pathways, in functional disease affecting sensory experience, and in all those conditions which favor one sensory modality more than another (17).

a) Distorted closeness perception:
—Undereats or overeats
—Is teetotaler or chronic alcoholic
—Does not smoke, or is chain smoker
—Explores other persons by touch—the blind
—Rarely touches objects and people, or has to handle everything
—Does not engage in physical exercise or is physical-culture adherent
—Practices sexual abstinence or excess

b) Distorted distance perception:
—Has defective vision or is inept at visual scanning
—Has defective hearing or is inept at auditory scanning
—Specializes in visual observation; is voyeur
—Specializes in auditory observation; over- or underreacts to noise

A-4.2. *Memory patterns.* Every individual is selective with regard to retention and recall of past events. In turn, this selectivity influences subsequent observation and retention and therefore helps to shape the individual's view of himself and of the world. The past prejudices the future.

a) Selectivity with regard to past experience:
—The man who quotes cases of precedent
—The man who does not pay attention to what went on before

b) Selectivity with regard to certain periods of the past:
—The memory for "highlights"
—The memory for college days
—The forgotten childhood

c) Selectivity with regard to certain types of events:
—The man with the social memory
—The man who cannot remember names

d) Selectivity with regard to configurations, patterns, and Gestalten:
—The man without perspective
—The theoretician
—The historian

e) Selectivity with regard to details:
—The expert with a rote memory
—The man who remembers figures
—The man who cannot recall technical details

AA-4.2. *Disturbances.* Central nervous system disease usually is characterized by memory disturbances which affect the recent past more than the remote past. In the functional disorders, the memory for certain kinds of events may be blotted out altogether. In defects of the sensory endorgans, an apparent memory disturbance exists which in actuality constitutes a missing sensory perception.

a) Poor memory for or exaggerated concern with past experience:
—Defective retention of events in the recent past
—Acute memory for remote past

b) Poor memory for or exaggerated concern with certain periods of life:
—Hysterical amnesia; retrograde and anterograde amnesia
—Embellished and repeatedly told anecdotes of past glory

c) Poor memory for or exaggerated concern with certain types of events:
—Traumatic, repetitive memories
—Repression of experiences
—Brooding over affront to honor

d) Poor memory for or exaggerated concern with patterns, Gestalten, and configurations:
—Diffuse and vague theoretician

e) Poor memory for or exaggerated concern with details:
—Disturbances in rote memory
—Selective recall of unrelated details

A-4.3. *Principles of evaluation.* The process of experience consists of combining input from external sources (exteroception) with input deriving from the organism itself (proprioception) and with input originating in past experience (memory). The result is something that is labeled, in terms of immediate output, a decision, and in terms of delayed output, a value. These selectivities, or value systems, which embody the principles which in the past have proved helpful, put a steady and predictable bias into the evaluation process of adult people.

AA-4.3. *Disturbances.* In the face of stringent circumstances the healthy person can relinquish pet principles and adopt better-suited ones; the disturbed person, however, seems to cling to the once-chosen principles, even though these prove inappropriate. Under such conditions, decisions either cannot be made or cannot be implemented. As a result, breakdown of the communication system in which such a person participates is likely to occur.

a) Temporal emphasis: the historical person
—Emphasizes development, evolution, growth, process, and change

a) Overemphasis on past or future at the expense of the present:
—Inability to see opportunities of the moment
—Daydreamer who reminisces about the past and dreams about the future

b) Spatial emphasis: the orderly person
—Emphasizes classification, order, and neatness

b) Overemphasis on order at the expense of practicality or usefulness:
—The logical, compulsive person who has difficulty in adapting

c) Normative emphasis: the conformist
—Conforms to standards set by public opinion; is concerned with averages

c) Overemphasis on conformance at the expense of personal development:
—The dependent "yes sayer"
—The immature social climber

d) Emphasis upon rules, laws, tradition, and precedent: the legalistic person
—Emphasizes regulations, bureaucratic practices; is a stickler for details
—Emphasizes protocol and etiquette

d) Overemphasis on rules at the expense of getting things done:
—The legalistic obstructionist

e) Emphasis upon means: the methodological person
—Emphasizes technical methods and the orthodoxy of procedure

e) Overemphasis on means at the expense of ends:
—Ritualistic performance or ritualistic thinking

f) Emphasis upon ends: the dedicated person
—Emphasizes purpose, goals, and ideals

f) Overemphasis on ends at the expense of means:
—The monomanic pursuit of one goal: the fanatic

g) Emphasis upon ethics: the moralist
—Relies upon the cumulative body of knowledge of the group as it is expressed in good-bad labels

g) Overemphasis on ethics with neglect of experience:
—Saints or sinners

h) Emphasis upon success: the socially mobile person
—Emphasizes popularity, social effort,
status, prestige, or rebels against
these

h) Overemphasis on success or failure:
—The social decliner: the hobo

i) Emphasis upon esthetic principles:
the artist
—Emphasizes syntax and the relationship of various symbols to each
other; concerned with style

i) Overemphasis on esthetic considerations:
—The empty concern with ornamentation and decoration

j) Emphasis upon social progress: the
person with social consciousness
—Emphasizes social security, mental
health, insurance programs, charity,
and the impact of political events
upon people

j) Overemphasis on social progress:
—The militant reformer who, in the
name of progress, hurts other people

A-4.4. *Decision-making.* The elements of timing, novelty, risk, and social impact seem to characterize the process of decision-making. A decision can be conceived of as an input of information which, when combined with memory material, leads to an output which will alter the parameters of a given social situation (66).

a) Timing:
—Emphasizes optimal timing; does not make decisions ahead of the critical moment or wait for circumstances which force his hand

b) Novelty:
—Emphasizes novelty and new combinations rather than precedent and tradition

c) Risk:
—Is inclined to take reasonable and calculated risks instead of being concerned with security

d) Social impact:
—Emphasizes the human consequences of decisions rather than being concerned with the technical aspects of action

AA-4.4. *Disturbances.* A wise man has patience, moderation, and balance and is able to reverse or alter a decision in view of changing circumstances. But quantitative deviations in the elements of timing, novelty, risk, and social impact, as well as rigid adherence to any one of these factors, may lead to decisions which contribute toward a breakdown in communication.

a) Timing:
Makes decisions prematurely and as a consequence is forced to make a new decision at the critical moment
—Premature ejaculation
Excessively late so that decision is ineffective and becomes a gesture
—Handing in his resignation after having been fired

b) Novelty:
Reconfirms past decisions and sticks to clichés because he is unable to cope with the new
—The paranoid bureaucrat
Excessive preference for novelty with rebellion against the traditional
—A psychopath's choice of a new but bizarre way of dressing

c) Risk:
Excessive concern with security and self-preservation to the extent of being phobic
—The phobic who, before he registers, makes sure that no black cat is living in the motel
Excessive risk-taking and self-exposure to the extent of being self-destructive
—The daredevil who descends Niagara Falls in a barrel

d) Social impact:
Excessive concern with human consequences
—"I cannot fire him; he has a family to support."
Neglect of human consequences
—The military commander whose unit has a low morale because he neglects the needs of his men

A-4.5. *Reasoning.* An individual's way of reasoning seems to remain fairly constant, although it must be granted that with a change of circumstances he might be capable of adopting a different pattern (186).

a) Nominalistic reasoning is based on the assumption that the human mind merely establishes hypotheses which must be verified by concrete experience: it proceeds from the particular to the general

b) Universalistic reasoning is based on the assumption that the human mind can grasp directly the order of the universe: it proceeds from the general to the particular

c) Intuitional reasoning is based on the assumption that intuition is an independent means of understanding which is distinct from systematic cogitation and logic

d) Dialectic reasoning is based on the assumption that nature can be understood rationally through consideration of the flux of events and the contradiction of forces

AA-4.5. *Disturbances.* When, irrespective of the situation, a certain kind of reasoning is rigidly adhered to or completely neglected, disturbances of communication and social conflict can arise.

a) Exaggerated nominalistic or concretistic reasoning: The only thing that matters is the concrete experience. Any hypothetical reasoning is to be doubted
—The aggressive action personality

b) Exaggerated universalistic reasoning: The only thing that matters is abstract consideration. Concrete experience and reality testing are neglected
—The autistic personality

c) Exaggerated intuitional reasoning: The only thing that matters is intuition; belief in visions, premonitions, and extrasensory perception
—The metaphysicist
—The spiritualist

d) Exaggerated dialectic reasoning: The only thing that matters is verbal argument and controversy
—The compulsive-obsessive intellectualizer

A-4.6. *Assessment of self.* Opinions about self are based on many detailed evaluations of which the individual may remain unaware. These evaluations are concerned with the appraisal of affective and intellectual aspects of the self.

a) The happy self: views self as a balanced unit that takes care of events as they arise

b) The anxious self: views self in a state of alarm and disequilibrium

c) The concerned self: views self as concerned with some immanent difficulties

d) The irritated self: views self as intolerant of interference

e) The ridiculous self: views self as object of ridicule

f) The obligated self: views self as obligated by self-imposed duties

g) The disappointed self: views self as victim of false hopes

AA-4.6. *Disturbances.* When feelings of pleasure, anxiety, fear, anger, shame, guilt, and depression become so dominant that they displace other considerations, neither the state of the organism nor the social situation can be appropriately assessed.

a) Disturbed evaluation of pleasure:
—The austere puritan
—The playboy

b) Disturbed evaluation of anxiety:
—The panicky person
—The overcalm schizophrenic

c) Disturbed evaluation of fear:
—The phobic patient
—The fearless psychopath

d) Disturbed evaluation of anger:
—The self-destructive person
—The homicidal person

e) Disturbed evaluation of shame:
—Cannot live in shame; suicide because of injured pride
—Brazen person

f) Disturbed evaluation of guilt:
—Overburdened by guilt; the depressive
—Denial of guilt; the remorseless criminal

g) Disturbed evaluation of depression:
—Denial of grief; the celebrating mourner
—The manic

A-4.7. *Transmission.* An individual's verbal expressions, gestures, movements, and social actions can be characterized in terms of amount, speed, efficacy, and distinctiveness. Because these features distinguish one person from another they have been used by detectives, scouts, and handwriting experts for purposes of identification.

AA-4.7. *Disturbances.* Unintelligibility of the speaker or distorted interpretation on the part of the perceiver can lead to breakdown in communication. A distortion of expression can be said to exist when the majority of qualified listeners are incapable of understanding the statements made by the speaker. This lack of understanding frequently is due to maximization or minimization of such aspects as amount, speed, efficacy, or distinctiveness of action or speech.

a) Emphasis upon amount:
—Talks or moves a lot or hardly at all

a) Disturbances in amount
Greatly increased output:
—Incessant, compulsive talking
—Involuntary movements: athetosis, chorea, tremor
—Tics
Greatly reduced output:
—Catatonic behavior
—Mute child
—Paralyzed or somnolent adult

b) Emphasis upon speed:
—Talks or moves fast or slow

b) Disturbances in speed:
—Psychomotor retardation or acceleration
—Uneven speed as in Parkinsonism

c) Emphasis upon efficacy:
—Capable of or negligent in producing desired result

c) Disturbances in efficacy:
—Active, overdramatized expression: the hysterical patient
—Underactive, undramatic, and boring expression; incapable of achieving and controlling effects as in infantile, ineffectual patients

d) Emphasis upon distinctiveness:
—Pays considerable or little attention to distinctiveness of signals

d) Disturbances in distinctiveness:
—Overconcern with the distinctiveness of signals; overcareful articulation of speech, as in some manneristic compulsives
—Underconcern with distinctiveness of signals: slurred speech

A-4.8. *Organ systems used in expression.* Almost every individual tends to use one channel of expression more than another. The preferred mode of expression is clearly revealed when the individual is under stress and particular organs or systems are relied upon to discharge tension.

a) Preference for verbal action:
—When tense, elaborates in words, or thinks, but does not show somatic manifestations of tension

b) Preference for expression in terms of physical action:
—When tense, engages in projects such as cleaning house, painting, pruning trees, chopping wood

c) Preference for expression in terms of social action:
—When tense, seeks the company of people; attends parties or club meetings or flirts with members of the opposite sex

d) Preference for locomotive expression:
—When tense, clenches fists, becomes restless, paces floor, goes for a walk

e) Preference for urinary-intestinal expression:
—When tense, must eat, drink, smoke, urinate, or eliminate

f) Preference for respiratory expression:
—When tense, sighs, breathes rapidly, coughs, clears throat

g) Preference for vascular expression:
—When tense, gets flustered, blanches or blotches, gets cold hands and feet, shows changes in pulse rate and blood pressure

h) Preference for cutaneous and glandular expression:
—When tense, perspires, cries, has dry mouth

AA-4.8. *Disturbances.* Inappropriate use of organs and functions can result in either underdevelopment of one system or compensatory overtaxation of another. Displaced, exaggerated, or restricted expression of a person can seriously interfere with his own functioning as well as with his interpersonal communications.

a) Verbose reaction:
—Chronic complaining; logorrhea; verbalization of delusions, illusions, or hallucinations

b) Reaction in terms of deviations in activity:
—Compulsive action, rituals, hyper- or hypoactivity

c) Antisocial reaction:
—Violence, conduct disorder, withdrawal

d) Motor reaction:
—Convulsions, cramps, tics, paralysis

e) Urinary-intestinal reaction:
—Dyspepsia, ulcers, colitis, spasms, anorexia, aerophagia, incontinence

f) Respiratory reaction:
—Bronchial asthma, hay fever, nervous coughing

g) Vascular reaction:
—Hypertension, Raynaud's disease, vagotonia, sympathicotonia, extrasystoles

h) Cutaneous or glandular expression:
—Eczema, exanthema, white flow, continual crying

A-4.9. *Tension-release mechanisms.*
After excessive concentration, tense waiting, or the skirting of dangers, people show a variety of tension-release mechanisms. These are also observed in the course of conversation, and usually they have a significant impact on all the other participants (223).

AA-4.9. *Disturbances.* It must be assumed that in certain psychopathological conditions the patient's attempts to discharge tension through the repeated use of the same release mechanism may exert an effect which in turn produces more tension. This paradoxical effect is in part based upon positive feedback from other people who are affected by the bearer's tension and in part upon the fact that the patient is aware of the inefficiency of the mechanism but is unable to correct it.

a) Spontaneous indication of release:
—Stretching, grunts

a) Spontaneous release mechanisms either absent or constantly in operation

b) Joking:
—Telling jokes
—Clowning and mimicking
—Kidding and teasing

b) Continued and inappropriate joking and clowning, or inability to joke

c) Griping:
—Cussing and complaining, usually audible to others but without expectation of a reply

c) Continued griping and cussing, or inability to complain

d) Laughing:
—Smiling, roaring, or unwinding laughter

d) Frequent or continued laughing, or inability even to smile

e) Crying:
—Tears of pleasure or sorrow
—Sobbing and sighing

e) Frequent or continued crying, or inability to cry

f) Startling movements:
—Slamming down fist
—Throwing objects
—Pointing at a person

f) Sudden startling movements, or hardly any spontaneous movements at all

g) Pacing and walking:
—Pacing the floor
—Walking around the block
—Going out for coffee
—Intense exercise

g) Continued pacing or walking, or complete immobilization

h) Eating, drinking, smoking
—Lighting a cigarette
—Chewing gum
—Eating a snack, having a drink

h) Exaggerated food or drink ingestion, or refusal to eat or drink

A-4.10. *Voice patterns.* Respiration, range, register, resonance, and rhythm determine the principal acoustic dimensions of the human voice, which is further characterized by such features as melody, intensity of sound, speed, accents, emphasis, pathos, and exactness in phonation. In certain voice patterns, the above-mentioned characteristics have been combined in various ways (168).

a) The healthy, self-assured voice: Sonorous, deep voice; relaxed, operating diaphragm; coordination of various components; expiratory phonation

b) The voice of pleasure: Speed-up or slowdown of rate of speech; changes in intensity; wide range in pitch; mucous membranes are moist

c) The voice of aggression: Words are started with a hard attack; last syllable strongly accented; too many words crammed into one breath

d) The voice of defeat: Slow speed; unclear articulation; little variation in the dynamics of volume, intensity, and rhythm; lack of inflection; chest registers not prominent

e) The voice of complaint: Deep voice with upward tendency in melody over the longer range; constantly up-and-down gliding pitch over the shorter range

f) The voice of alarm: Loud voice fading into soft, and high pitch sinking to low; components of fear or anger may be mixed in

g) The voice of indifference: Middle loud, without emphasis; does not trail off; no variation in dynamics

AA-4.10. *Disturbances.* The most common disturbances in voice patterns are characterized by pressure problems affecting respiration, the vocal mechanism, and the resonators. Uncertain intonation and unsure pitch lead to early fatigue. The content of particular disturbances may reflect itself in tonal qualities of the voice.

a) The voice of indecision: Voice too soft or too loud; upward inflection of voice on last syllable may twist statements into questions. Voice may be lowered to a murmur. Mucous membranes are dry. Enunciation sometimes overcautious

b) The voice of excitement: Wide pitch intervals; absence of lower tones; contraction of pharyngeal and neck muscles; increased changes in pitch and rhythm

c) The voice of resentment: Dry, tense vocal cords; excessive pathos; sudden increase in intensity and overemphasis at a given moment

d) The voice of depression: Uniform phonation; narrow vocal range; falling rhythm; monotonous voice, may trail off

e) The voice of quarrelsome complaint: Beginning loud, the voice glides into a lower pitch with decreased intensity. Prominence of chest registers

f) The voice of anxiety or fear: Rough or wavering tone (respiratory pressure weaker than pressure of the glottis); frog in throat; breathy hoarseness; inspiratory phonation; whispering, aphonia, or mutism

g) Schizophrenic voice: Rhythmic verbal and vocal patterns; alternating head and chest registers; repetition of words or sounds, often well separated and spoken with intensity

A-5. *The sequential order of perception, evaluation and transmission.* The functions of perception, evaluation, and transmission can follow each other in various ways. For example, when circumstances do not permit extensive preliminary observation, people are forced to make quick decisions; under such circumstances, perception follows evaluation. Although a healthy individual should be capable of dealing with any particular sequence, experience usually prepares people more for one kind of sequence than for another.

a) Perception-evaluation-transmission: the usual approach to the new
—Procedure of the naturalist

b) Perception-transmission-evaluation: transmission of information gathered by observation with postponement of evaluation until feedback of other person has been obtained
—The dependent person
—The action person

c) Evaluation-transmission-perception: preconceived notions are transmitted and perception of the real situation follows last, if at all
—The opinionated person
—The authoritarian parent

d) Evaluation-perception-transmission: preconceived notions are checked with the real situation and the result is transmitted
—The imaginative person

e) Transmission-perception-evaluation: talking and acting occur before the situation has been observed and evaluated
—The frightened person

f) Transmission-evaluation-perception: talking and action are undertaken for the sake of thinking things over; check with real situation follows last
—The statement as trial balloon

AA-5. *Disturbances.* Persons who cannot adapt to certain prescribed ways of communication are severely handicapped in interpersonal and group relations. Disturbances are particularly prone to be noticed when the individual, arbitrarily and regardless of appropriacy, applies his favorite function: perception, evaluation, or transmission. The intensity and rigidity of his pursuit and the inability to correct an obviously erroneous performance indicate the severity of the disturbance.

When the situation calls for observation:
a) Proceeds to evaluate:
—Makes snap judgments in terms of good and evil
—Generalizes from insufficient information

b) Proceeds to transmit:
—Acts prematurely
—Prevents himself from observing by talking all the time

When the situation calls for evaluation:
c) Proceeds to transmit:
—Talks or acts before he has made a decision
—Engages in traditional action instead of evaluating the situation anew

d) Proceeds to perceive:
—Waits for more information
—Observes actions of others instead of making decision for himself

When the situation calls for transmission:
e) Proceeds to perceive:
—Instead of lending help to someone in distress, merely watches the situation
—When on the sports field, watches others play instead of participating

f) Proceeds to evaluate:
—Explains future intentions instead of engaging in action
—Instead of making report, passes judgment

A-6. *Codification.* In daily life, the nature of the social situation dictates which type of language is most appropriate (52). The choice falls between somatic, action, and verbal language or a combination of these. Any individual can be characterized by the spectrum of language he uses most of the time (215).

AA-6. *Disturbances.* There are abstract concepts which can be best symbolized in digital ways—for example, in terms of a mathematical formula. There are other abstract concepts—for example, the notion of instinct—which can be denoted in verbal terms only. Finally, there are aspects of experience —for example, feelings—which can be expressed adequately only in nonverbal terms. When a person lacks the ability to apply the appropriate language to a given situation or has not mastered certain types of language, disturbances of communication are likely to occur (201).

a) Prefers somatic language: uses shape, color, or location of organs and organ systems for communication, although these are not commonly intended for this purpose

Uses the smooth muscles of the vascular, respiratory, and intestinal systems to convey signals to others:
—Makes bodily noises: flatus, coughing, sneezing, hiccups
—Blushes, blanches, blotches
—Relies upon personal odors or uses perfume
—Ostensively exposes certain body parts
—Talks about and interprets body functions, usually with some demonstration

a) Uses somatic language for codification of most significant messages in spite of the fact that other language would be more appropriate:
—Undereats or has anorexia; these self-initiated deprivations are communicated to others
—Overeats, drinks or smokes heavily; these self-indulgences are communicated to others
—Discusses abnormal body functions such as constipation, pains, colds, eczema; demonstrates disturbed functions
—Through symptoms, controls the behavior of others; demands silence, support, diets, transportation

b) Prefers action language: uses for communicative purposes movements which are commonly intended for practical implementation

Uses the striped muscles of the skeletal system to convey signals to others:
—Goes out of his way to do things for or to people
—Bakes or cooks to please others; breaks or loses other people's things
—Dances to express himself

b) Uses action language for codification of most significant messages in spite of the fact that other languages would be more appropriate:
—Does bodily harm to others or self
—steals or is kleptomaniac
—Arsonist
—Engages in vandalism to property
—Habitually loses objects
—Is accident-prone
—Carries chip on shoulder and shows lack of success

c) Prefers gestural sign language: uses codifications in which words, numbers, and punctuation signs have been supplanted by gestures. In contrast to action language, gestural language serves the purpose of signaling and has in itself no other value
—Gesticulates
—Responds in kind to changes in facial expression of others
—Uses shorthand manual language; makes the "bull's-eye" or other signs

d) Prefers object language: intentionally or unintentionally uses display of material things such as implements, machines, art objects, and architectural structures for communicative purposes
—Likes to convey his ideas in drawings, arrangements of objects, or photographs
—Is a painter, sculptor, or interior decorator

e) Prefers verbal-digital language: uses codifications which are based on phonetic denotation and Arabic numerals for communicative purposes
—Writes poems, short stories, novels, essays, or scientific reports
—Is accomplished in vocabulary, diction, and oratory
—Occupies himself with mathematics or statistics

c) Uses gestural sign language for codification of most significant messages, although other language would be more appropriate:
—Sign language of the deaf and dumb, who cannot use sound
—Gestural mannerisms
—Compulsive clowning

d) Uses object language for codification of most significant messages although other languages would be more appropriate:
—Expresses care for others through gifts of food, money, or other objects
—Engages in drawings when words would be more appropriate

e) Uses verbal-digital language for codification of most significant messages although other languages would be more appropriate:
—Attempts to verbalize nonverbal phenomena
—Intellectually analyzes art and reduces it to some kind of formula
—Reduces love to a verbal game

A-6.1. *Verbal denotation.* Each person tends to develop a verbal style of his own, in part dictated by education and occupation, in part determined by other life experiences (127). Some people even possess the ability to adapt their verbal style to the situation and the purpose of their communication, although such skill is not encountered too frequently (145).

AA-6.1. *Disturbances.* From simple preference to pathological exaggeration range the idiosyncrasies of style. However, extremes, although valuable as personal expression, usually are unsuitable for discursive purposes (102).

a) Abstract, condensed denotation: the language of theory
—Uses abstract or comprehensive words
—Has conceptual orientation
—Relies upon connotation

a) Vague denotation with generalities and abstractions
—As in the case of some schizophrenic patients

b) Concrete detailed denotation: the language of scientific description
—Uses concrete words
—Qualifies, specifies, and describes
—Has extensive orientation and avoids connotations

b) Minute and detailed denotation to the point of losing sight of the principal idea
—As in the case of certain compulsion neurotics

c) Formal denotation: the highbrow language
—Uses rare or technical words; avoids slang
—Lofty, elevated, rhetorical language

c) Stilted, artificial, and manneristic denotation
—As in the case of some schizophrenics

d) Popular denotation: the language of the people
—Uses slang
—Uses adages

d) Vulgar style, consisting mainly of cusswords and obscenity
—As in the organically deteriorated person

e) Legalistic denotation: the language of bureaucracy
—Redundancy in usage of words
—Interwoven sentence structure

e) Circumstantial denotation with never-ending sentences
—As in the case of some epileptics

f) Brief denotation: the language of instruction
—Economical use of words
—Brief sentence structure

f) Telegraphic style with omission of words
—As seen occasionally in psychopathic personalities

g) Esthetic denotation: the language of prose and poetry
—Esthetic principles govern the use of words
—Words appeal to imagery and emotions of the individual

g) Flowery, somewhat obnoxious denotation, with repetition of words with similar sound; often intermingled with neologisms
—As in the case of some manic patients

h) Clumsy denotation: the language of the illiterate
—Tendency toward inaccurate, irrelevant, and unesthetic denotation
—Grammar ignored

h) Inappropriate and erroneous denotation, often with syntactic misuse of words
—As in the case of the mentally deficient

A-6.2. Syntactical orientation. Any sentence can be divided into the subject, on the one hand, and the predicate, on the other. While the subject is expressed by a noun or a pronoun, the predicate, expressed by a verb with or without further elaboration (54), contains qualitative and quantitative descriptions of the subject. The subject-oriented person, with preference for the "what," leans more toward structural-static appraisal and the predicate-oriented person, with a preference for the "how," tends toward dynamic-processal (209) approaches to life.

a) Subject-oriented denotation:
Formulations are grouped around a central idea or theme which can be expressed by a noun
—Horse, engine, arm
Statements of goals refer to the "what" or the identity of people or things; "We must ask Dr. X to join us."

b) Qualification-oriented denotation:
Formulations are grouped around a central idea or theme which can be expressed by qualifying statements contained in the predicate
—Green, long, fast
Statements of goals refer to the "how," subordinating ends to qualifications; "Red is becoming to you."

c) Action-oriented denotation:
Formulations are grouped around a central idea or theme which can be expressed by a verb
—Run, work, dive
Statements of goals refer to doing, subordinating ends to action; "They are ready to go anywhere."

AA-6.2. Disturbances. Persons who are in the process of learning a new language or children who have just learned to speak use nouns primarily, tend to be concerned with the identity of things and people, and are subject-oriented. Extremes of predicate orientation with emphasis upon qualifications are found among schizophrenic persons, and with emphasis upon action in psychopathic and paranoid personalities (9).

a) Classification:
Prevalent use of nouns with relative absence of verbs, adverbs, and adjectives
—Compulsive personalities who are concerned with identity and classification of things

b) Qualification:
Prevalent use of adjectives and adverbs with relative absence of nouns
—Hypercritical, aggressive persons who are concerned with qualifications, using terms such as "too short," "too long," "too little," "too late"

c) Movement:
Prevalent use of verbs with relative neglect of nouns and qualifications
—People with hypochondriacal and paranoid delusions and ideas of reference who show extreme concern with action and movement

A-6.3. *Nonverbal denotation.* Variety is achieved in the process of nonverbal signaling by the combination of kinetic, directional, topographic, and sequential indices of movements. Because of the innumerable possible combinations, each person develops his own idiosyncratic ways of expression which are superimposed on the culturally determined patterns of nonverbal language (132, 215).

a) Signaling through changes in intensity of movement:
—Increased or decreased activity
—Sudden stillness or abrupt initiation of a movement

b) Signaling direction:
—Walking toward or away from
—Looking in a certain direction

c) Signaling through posture:
—Shifting position, slumping, sitting erect, leaning forward or backward

d) Signaling through topographic combination of body regions:
—Flag semaphore utilizes different positions of arms to indicate alphabet
—The snakelike motions of certain native dancers, where motion begins at one end of the body and gradually spreads to other parts

e) Signaling through modulation of the voice and other noises:
—The voice of admiration, disgust, condemnation, resentment
—The sound of a person's gait

AA-6.3. *Disturbances.* When an individual's movements can be meaningfully and consistently interpreted by others, they fulfill language function. But when a person makes movements which appear to be strange, he is not understood and arouses suspicion. The greater the deviation, the more unanimous the opinion of the observers becomes that he is a foreigner, a sick man, or a lunatic.

a) Quantitative disturbances of movement:
—No movement, or sporadic movement as in the catatonic
—The jerky, fast movements of the irritable catatonic
—Excessive, uncoordinated movements as in the agitated, manic, or delirious person

b) Directional disturbances of movement:
—The person who walks backward
—The psychotic with his aimless movements

c) Postural disturbances of movement
—The abnormal position of the limbs in cases of bone, joint, or nervous disease
—Camptocormia

d) Exaggerated or diminished regional movements
—Grimacing
—Involuntary movements as in chorea, athetosis, multiple sclerosis
—Paralysis

e) Disturbances in the production of tone and noise
—Screaming with anguish or pain
—The labored breathing of the unconscious patient

A-6.4. *Gestures.* People are not equally familiar with all gestural signs. The verbally oriented, on the whole, understand more the emphasis-giving gesture, the nonverbally oriented, the illustrating gesture (215).

a) Uses and understands gestural symbols employed as substitutes for words:
—The hitchhiker's sign
—The bull's-eye sign

b) Uses and understands gestures made for purposes of illustration:
—Gestures indicating speed, acceleration, or direction of motion
—Gestures outlining the contours of objects or bodies

c) Uses and understands gestures made for the purpose of emphasizing speech:
—Oratorical gestures which are analogous to the written signs of interpunctuation, such as beating the rhythm or indicating the end of a sentence

AA-6.4. *Disturbances.* Breakdown of communication occurs when people who are handicapped in gestural expression try to communicate with people who use different gestural symbols or talk another language altogether.

a) Does not use or understand gestural signals used as substitutes for words, or uses or interprets them inappropriately:
—The untrained deaf person who cannot lip-read

b) Does not use or understand illustrating gestural movements, or uses and interprets them inappropriately:
—The compulsive person who understands only words and ignores illustrative, gestural language

c) Does not use or understand emphasis-giving gestures, or interprets or uses them inappropriately:
—The person who winks, smiles, or shakes his head, regardless of the statement made
—The person with mannerisms and tics

A-6.5. *Body areas.* In nonverbal communication, the topographical location of muscles can be used as a means of codification. Almost all people reveal habitual preferences for body areas, and this in turn dictates the characteristics of the movements involved. Body zone and modality of movement become inseparably linked (74).

AA-6.5. *Disturbances.* Movements characteristic of one system, organ, or area can, with limitations, be carried out by other systems, organs, or body areas. Such displacement—well known in sexual perversions—when visible to others may give rise to serious disturbances of communication. Displacement also occurs when disease or trauma interferes with the functioning of an organ, and other organs compensate for the deficiency. In the process of communication, the observer notices when a movement is not made that should be made or when a movement occurs which ordinarily does not occur.

a) Mouth:
—Sucking, biting
—Yawning
—Tongue clacking
—Spitting
—Salivating
—Hissing

a) Mouth:
—Copulation by mouth
—Vomiting
—Facial paralysis

b) Eye:
—Winking
—Blinking
—Staring
—Rubbing

b) Eye:
—Squinting
—Ophthalmoplegia

c) Head:
—Throwing head back to get hair out of face
—Shaking head to say yes or no
—Tilting head to the side to be cute

c) Head:
—Headache

d) Neck and throat:
—Swallowing without food intake
—Clearing throat
—Exposing neckline

d) Neck and throat:
—Torticollis
—Stuttering

e) Chest and breast:
—Intercostal respiratory movements
—Modeling of breasts; décolleté

e) Chest and breast:
—Coughing

f) Abdomen:
—Abdominal respiratory movements

f) Abdomen:
—Pain

g) Arm and hand:
—Draping arm over chair
—Folding arms
—Finger tapping
—Making fists
—Punching
—Grasping
—Pointing

g) Arm and hand:
—Paralysis and contracture of muscles
—Scratching

h) Leg and foot:
—Crossing knees
—Swinging leg
—Kicking
—Dragging feet

i) Hip and shoulder:
—Wiggling hips
—Turning away (cold shoulder)

j) Genito-urinary and perineal region
—Passing flatus
—Itching
—Urination and elimination
—Erection

h) Leg and foot:
—Paralysis and contracture of muscles
—Abnormal gait
—Amputee

i) Hip and shoulder:
—Waddling gait in hip lesions

j) Genito-urinary and perineal region
—Diarrhea or indication of diarrhea resulting from repeated use of toilet
—Urinary frequency
—Frigidity
—Impotence

A-7. *Switch of codification.* Successful communication is achieved when in a conversation the same events are treated from different viewpoints. But, in order to be effective, discourse of this kind necessitates the use of several types of codifications. Depending upon the skill of the individual, the switch of codification systems either may entail the use of all systems or is linked to two or three preferred systems.

a) Nonverbal (analogic)-verbal (digital) language switch

b) Organ-action-symbolic language switch

c) Denotative-connotative switch

d) Abstract-concrete switch

e) Highbrow-lowbrow switch

f) Affective-intellectual switch

g) Structure-process switch

h) "Subject orientation" to "predicate orientation" switch

AA-7. *Disturbances.* Inability to switch from one kind of codification to another makes for rigid style and diminished clarity in the transmission of messages. If a person who has difficulties in switching codification systems finally does so, distortions may arise because a less appropriate codification may have been substituted for a more appropriate one.

a) Inability to switch from nonverbal to verbal denotation, or vice versa, may lead to a substitution in which nonverbal codification is identified with lowbrow and verbal codification with highbrow language.

b) Inability to switch from organ or action to symbolic denotation, or vice versa, may lead to a substitution in which organ and action codifications are identified with affective and symbolic with intellectual matters

c) Inability to switch from denotative to connotative codification, or vice versa, may lead to a substitution in which denotation is identified with structure and connotation with process

d) Inability to switch from the concrete to the abstract, or vice versa, may lead to a substitution in which the abstract is identified with "subject orientation" and the concrete with "predicate orientation."

e) See under *a*

f) See under *b*

g) See under *c*

h) See under *d*

A-8. *Philosophy of life.* The attitude toward the world, the management of work and play, the involvement in sexual and social relations, the adherence to certain moral values, and the seeking of certain gratifications are woven into patterns of living which reveal themselves not only in a person's thinking and feeling but also in the way his psychological and social conflicts are managed. Morris has telescoped various ways of reasoning, striving, judging, and acting into thirteen patterns which he calls "ways to live" (166).

a) The Apollonian Path: Preserve the best that man has attained; active social participation; moderation, clarity, and refinement

b) The Buddhist Path: Independence of persons and things; go it alone; self-sufficiency in reflection and meditation; minimum social participation and minimal manipulation of things

c) The Christian Path: Sympathetic concern for others; affection rather than aggression, and avoidance of greed, passion, and power

d) The Dionysian Path: Festivities and solitude in alternation. Life is to be sensuously enjoyed with relish and abandonment, alternating with meditation and awareness of self

e) The Mohammedan Path: Group participation and enjoyment of social life combined with outward living and appreciation of the good things in life

f) The Promethean Path: Constant making and remaking; to compensate for stagnation of daily life, the person seeks physical action, adventure, and realistic technical solutions

AA-8. *Disturbances.* Almost all philosophies of life find their counterparts in psychopathology. In contrast to a well-behaved person, the sick individual arbitrarily maximizes or minimizes one set of values, leading to rigidities of behavior. Interpersonal relations become difficult because breakdown of communication occurs at the moment that disagreement is apparent.

a) Distortions of the values of form, style, and esprit are found in some schizophrenics who concern themselves with decoration or patterning

b) Distortions of the values of withdrawal and solitude are found in the catatonic, the hermit, the recluse, and the symbiotic person

c) Distortions of the values of nonaggression, humility, and piety are found in hysterical characters and in social masochists

d) Distortions of the values of sensuousness, sexuality, and abandon are found in perversion and in puritanical self-denial

e) Distortions of the values of sociability, group participation, and forcefulness may be found in hypomanic persons and in some psychosomatic persons

f) Distortions of the values of action, progress, and technology are seen in the schizophrenic "Rube Goldberg" inventor and in the fighter for lost causes

g) The Maitreyan Path: Dynamic integration of diversity; eclectic attitude and mixture of various philosophies are to be sought. The goal of life is found in the integration of enjoyment, action, and contemplation

g) Distortions of the values of eclecticism, balance, and change are found in the unstable person who cannot concentrate or stay with any topic for any length of time, and also in the compulsive person

h) The Epicurean Path: Wholesome, carefree enjoyment and not a hectic search for intense and exciting pleasure. Relaxed body, gracefulness, good food, and chosen friends are the keys to living

h) Distortions of the values of enjoyment, moderation, and simplicity can be seen in the phobic person, the ascetic, the addict

i) The Taoistic Path: Wait in quiet receptivity until the good things of life come of their own accord

i) Distortions of the values of receptivity and patience are found in the passive, receptive person who feels that the world owes him a living

j) The Stoical Path: Self-control, but not retreat from the world, should be the keynote of life. Too much cannot be expected

j) Distortions in the values of self-control, rationality, and dignity are found in the compulsive and in the impulsive psychopath

k) The Contemplative Path: Knowledge of the inner life of man, of ideals, feelings, and reverie are the keynotes of maturity. In giving up the world, one finds the inner self

k) Distortions of the values of contemplation, introspection, and sensitivity are found in the schizophrenic and the manic-depressive

l) The Path of the Man of Action: Active and adventuresome deeds, the use of the muscles for building, fighting, running; the overcoming of obstacles; and the excitement of power in the tangible present

l) Distortions of the values of action, mastery, and power are found in the social climber, the tyrant, the demagogue

m) The Path of Surrender: In being an instrument of the great powers, one should be grateful, patient, and confident that the great forces silently and irresistibly achieve their goal

m) Distortions of the values of surrender, humility, and devotion are found in the social masochist and the arrogant weakling

A-9. *Internal and external emphasis.*
Any social or physical boundary can be observed from one of two positions: from the inside or from the outside. Accordingly, there are specialists who concern themselves with the internal affairs of a social organization—the Department of the Interior, as it were —and those who concern themselves with what goes on outside of the organization—the Foreign Office or the State Department. On an individual scale, these differences are reflected in daily-life behavior (222).

a) Concerns himself primarily with internal events:
—Self-evaluation, self-awareness, self-concern
—Concern with personal problems, with own family and own group
—Interest in domestic policy and community affairs

b) Concerns himself primarily with external events:
—Concern with gadgets and technical problems
—Concern with other people's problems, other families, and other groups
—Tendency to gossip and talk about others
—Interest in national and foreign policy

AA-9. *Disturbances.* At certain times, every person is concerned with his own affairs, or with "home" politics, as it were, and at other times with his relation to others, or with "foreign" politics. Proper appraisal of situations and wise decisions can only be made if information derived from outside sources is complemented by information from inside sources. Continuous concern with either external or internal events or a temporarily misplaced emphasis may lead to disturbed evaluation which in turn interferes with other processes of communication.

a) When "extero-concern" is required, concerns himself with inside events:
Tends to focus attention exclusively on his own affairs in neglect of other people and events
—Anxious or depressed pedestrian inattentive to traffic
Tends to attribute to others personality features which are prominent in himself, instead of acknowledging the characteristics of others
—Alcoholic in a jovial mood, who does not recognize that others may not want to drink

b) When "intero-concern" is required, concerns himself with outside events:
Tends to focus attention on other people and things in neglect of his own affairs
—The paranoid
Tends to emphasize personality features in others which are not prominent in himself instead of acknowledging the existence of common bonds
—The father who rejects his promiscuous daughter

A-9.1. *Internal sources of information.* Intellect and emotion can be conceived of as two different ways of viewing events. The rational processes constitute an outside observer's view of events, including the individual's view of himself. Emotions and feelings pertain to an inside observer's view of the state of the organism at a given moment. Depending upon the relative weight attributed to intellectual and emotional aspects, the final evaluation of events will bear more or less the imprint of an internal or an external observer. In action, an integration of both views is achieved.

a) Weighting of information derived from thinking, speculation, and meditation:
Tendency to emphasize those aspects of living that can be formulated verbally or digitally
Tendency to emphasize the external aspects—that is, the events that are exposed on the surface
Tendency to emphasize the general and universal aspects of the external world
—Appearance

b) Weighting of information derived from sensation and feeling:
Tendency to emphasize those aspects of living that can be formulated analogically
Tendency to emphasize the internal aspects—that is, the events that occur away from the surface
—Smoldering resentment
—Anxiety
Tendency to emphasize the unique aspects of the internal world
—Self-esteem, pride

c) Weighting of information derived from doing and acting:
Tendency to emphasize those aspects of living that cannot be formulated
—"I can't tell you; you should have been there"
Tendency to emphasize the effects of action in terms of its emotional and intellectual implications
Tendency to emphasize the unique aspects of skill

AA-9.1. *Disturbances.* When the balance between intellect, emotion, and action is upset, disturbances of communication may arise. Any unilateral emphasis greatly reduces the chances of correct evaluation and the possibility of finding people who will agree to such opinions. Unstable human relations are usually the result.

a) Thought and imagination maximized or minimized:
—The schizophrenic person who "thinks"
—The psychosomatic patient who has no fantasy
—The pseudological patient who invents stories
—The speculative thinker and talker who "predicts"

b) Emotions maximized or minimized:
—The hypersensitive person who overreacts inwardly
—The hysterical person who overreacts outwardly
→The emotionally flat person who underreacts
—The cold and calculating person who reacts only in intellectual ways

c) Action and manipulation maximized or minimized:
—The psychopathic person who is constantly "in action"
—The compulsive person who engages in rituals
—The rebellious person who defies authority
—The adventurer who seeks unforeseen action
—The passive person who avoids action

A-9.2. *External sources of information.* The individual's ability to absorb information derived from outside sources varies with the content, its form of codification, and the personality of the transmitter.

AA-9.2. *Disturbances.* Whenever an individual cannot use certain sources of information or whenever he systematically and unduly weights the information derived from any particular source, he obtains a one-sided view of the events in question. Comparison of information derived from various sources compensates for possible distortions, whereas rigid adherence to one source tends to result in disturbances of communication.

a) Preference for information derived from other persons, personally known and qualified to speak on the subject—the professional approach
—From a lawyer
—From a gardener
—From a fishing guide

a) Relies exclusively on or ignores information and decisions made by experts and professionals:
—The ignorant
—The helpless
—The skeptic

b) Preference for information derived from strangers and persons whose qualifications cannot be checked—the amateurish approach:
—From the next drugstore

b) Relies exclusively upon hearsay or ignores secondhand information:
—The suggestible dupe
—The panicky person
—The gossipmonger

c) Preference for information derived from depersonalized sources—the institutional approach:
—From governmental agencies, hospitals

c) Relies exclusively upon or ignores authoritative, institutional sources:
—The seeker of security
—The dependent person
—The nonconformist

d) Preference for information derived from mass media of communication—the popular approach:
—From books, movies, radio, and television

d) Relies entirely upon or ignores mass media of communication:
—The passive person
—The conformist

A-10. *Interests and approaches.* There exist a variety of approaches to any subject matter. The knowledge and skill involved in these approaches are taught by the various professions, arts, crafts, and trades. But aside from occupation, any individual seems to be characterized by his favorite approach to the solution of problems of daily life.

AA-10. *Disturbances.* Exclusive application of any of the special approaches leads to a distortion in the nature of a caricature. Such distortions cannot give a correct view of the problems at hand, and communication with people who use such approaches is likely to be difficult if not impossible.

Exclusive application of:

a) The business approach: dollars and cents

a) The business approach: the human being as a profit or loss organization

b) The technical approach: does it work?

b) The technical approach: the human being as a machine

c) The agricultural approach: eugenics, breeding, conservation

c) The agricultural approach: the human being as an animal

d) The scientific-logical approach: facts and knowledge

d) The scientific-logical approach: the human being as a logical creature

e) The psychological approach: understanding

e) The psychological approach: the human being as a type

f) The political approach: social manipulation

f) The political approach: the human being as subject and object of manipulation

g) The historical approach: the longitudinal study

g) The historical approach: the human being as a creature of fate

h) The creative approach: expression in novel form

h) The creative approach: the human being as an esthetic object

i) The athletic approach: skill and strength

i) The athletic approach: the human being as muscle man

j) The warring approach: fight and victory

j) The warring approach: the human being as cannon fodder

k) The health approach: physical and mental well-being

k) The health approach: the human being as service installation

l) The social approach: manners and popularity

l) The social approach: the human being as a slave to etiquette

m) The motivational approach: intention, effort, and motive

m) The motivational approach: the human being at the mercy of his instincts

n) The efficiency approach: outcome, success, and effect

n) The efficiency approach: the human being as a product of will power

o) The emotional approach: feelings and sentiments

o) The emotional approach: the human being as a bundle of nerves

A-11. *Reactions to conflicting information.* The sorting, ordering, and combining of information with previously accumulated information often results in contradictions. Each individual tends to develop characteristic patterns with which to avoid the stress created by conflicting information (73).

AA-11. *Disturbances.* In the presence of irreconcilable conflicts within the individual or of conflicts with other people, information may be managed in such a manner that through apparent loss of consciously available information the stress situation is temporarily improved; however, this intrapsychic procedure results in distortions of reality and, therefore, is conducive to serious disturbances of communication.

a) In presence of conflict, utilizes contradictions productively:
—When by himself, tends to ask new questions and to further his knowledge
—When with one other person, tends to explore the reason for the disagreement and to find some common ground
—When with a group, attempts to make compromises

a) In presence of conflict, utilizes contradictions unproductively:
—Misuses new information
—Comes to doubt the validity of his past experiences
—Does not learn from disagreements
—Cannot make compromises

b) In presence of conflict, magnifies one aspect:
—When by himself, arbitrarily settles for one side of the issue
—When with one other person, asserts himself and tries to win the other person over
—When with a group, campaigns vigorously and if necessary organizes the minority

b) In presence of conflict, makes arbitrary decisions:
—Goes all out for one aspect and neglects the other completely
—Asserts himself at all costs
—In groups, is difficult to dissuade from premature decisions and impulsive actions

c) In presence of conflict, relies on other people's solutions:
—When by himself, conforms to popular standards
—When in two-person situations, accepts the solution offered by the other person
—When with a group, joins the majority

c) In presence of conflict, surrenders and becomes dependent:
—Accepts solutions of deviant people
—Depends upon one other person or a group to solve his problems

d) In presence of conflict, tends to become indecisive:
—When by himself, is self-absorbed and plagued by doubts
—In two-person situations, shows variable attitude
—When with a group, either does not participate or is hostile

d) In presence of conflict, tends to founder and is self-defeating:
—Tends to disintegrate when exposed to stress; develops nervous or physical symptoms; may become depressed or agitated
—Cannot participate in two-person or group situations without being a burden to the others

A-12. *Instructions.* Each individual seems to develop characteristic patterns of instructing others: some use verbal, others nonverbal methods; some explain the minutest detail, others let the listener struggle along and are content with some inobtrusive hint. People also seem to vary in their ability to perceive different cues: some can observe the minutest changes in facial expression; others are barely able to recognize a temper tantrum; some watch for gestures, others are more alert to words.

a) Gives and perceives explicit instructions:
—A man introduces himself, "I am the plumber"
—"I understand the hint"

b) Gives and perceives instructions contained in gestures:
—Pointing ("Over there")
—Shaking head ("No")

c) Gives and perceives instructions contained in action:
—Leaves the house when he sees an unwelcome guest approach
—When waiting at intersection, turns front wheels of car to indicate a change of direction

d) Gives and perceives instructions displayed by emotions:
—Cries in anger
—Shivers with fear

e) Gives and perceives instructions indicated by role:
—The policeman in uniform
—The salesman

AA-12. *Disturbances.* Inability to transmit instructions to the listener and inability to perceive instructions given by the speaker are responsible for some of the most severe disturbances of communication. In some cases, this difficulty is limited to specific kinds of instructions; in others, it seems to consist of a generalized disability.

a) Difficulties in perceiving or transmitting instructions explicitly in words:
—The feeble-minded
—The patient with aphasia
—The autistic person

b) Difficulties in perceiving or transmitting instructions in gestural terms:
—The inattentive person
—The blind
—The person with involuntary movements

c) Difficulties in perceiving or transmitting instructions in terms of practical actions:
—Cannot learn by being shown: the impulsive psychopath
—Cannot teach others: the autocrat

d) Difficulties in perceiving or transmitting instructions in terms of emotional display
—Does not observe tone of voice, smile, or tears: the compulsive person
—Cannot indicate emotions by means of tone of voice, smile, or tears: the catatonic schizophrenic

e) Difficulties in perceiving or transmitting instructions by indication of role:
—Cannot differentiate between people: the naïve hysterical person
—Cannot state role: the person with brain disease

f) Gives and perceives instructions referring to rules:
—Girl on date makes clear what sex rules apply
—"You will proceed in formation"
—"Play ball"

g) Gives and perceives instructions referring to context of the situation:
—"At the funeral . . ."
—"At a lecture . . ."

f) Difficulties in perceiving or transmitting instructions referring to rules:
—The intoxicated person who does not know when to leave
—The senile person

g) Difficulties in perceiving or transmitting instructions referring to context of the situation
—The gaily dressed schizophrenic at the funeral

A-13. Contexts and situations. Certain individuals seem to gravitate toward particular kinds of physical and social situations which are characterized not so much by the personalities of the participants or the purpose of the gathering but rather by the atmosphere. Apparently the experience of the overall Gestalt of the situation seems to determine the individual's reaction.

a) Tends to participate in ill-defined situations where roles, rules, and physical context seem to be in a state of flux
—Adventurers, pioneers, explorers

b) Tends to participate in structured situations where roles, rules, and physical context are strictly defined
—Politicians, executives, military men, judges

c) Tends to participate in structured situations in an attempt to change the rigidly defined roles, rules, and physical context
—Reformers, revolutionaries

d) Tends to participate as guest or observer in situations organized by others
—Diplomats, military observers, anthropologists

AA-13. Disturbances. When people are exposed to certain situations and are incapable of adapting, they develop anxiety and tend to become disorganized. Such people usually will attempt to avert a debacle by rigidly adhering to one kind of situation. Strict selection or avoidance of situations thus defines the disability.

a) Operates exclusively in ill-defined situations:
—The ambulatory schizophrenic
—Marginal persons and hoboes

b) Is completely dependent upon structured situations:
—The obsessive-compulsive
—The phobic

c) Is completely wrapped up in taking an oppositional or rebellious position:
—The martyr
—The juvenile delinquent

d) Functions exclusively in the position of a nonparticipating guest:
—The schizophrenic

A-14. *Rules.* Any game is governed by explicit rules. Communication can be compared to a game with rules indicating who can talk to whom, for how long, when, on what subject matter, and in what language. Knowledge of these rules is subsumed in daily communication, thus serving as a metacommunicative—that is, explanatory and interpretative—device (217).

a) Perceives and follows existing, explicit, detailed rules:
—The bureaucrat

b) Perceives and relies upon existing, implicit rules:
—The gentleman

c) Perceives loopholes in the existing rules:
—The lawyer

d) Perceives rules but makes exceptions or adopts double standards
—The person with mental reservations

e) Does not perceive rules and does not follow them, but follows rules of his own:
—The newcomer or stranger

AA-14. *Disturbances.* Rules may be perceived and obeyed, perceived and violated, or not perceived at all. Distorted attitudes toward rules can be seen in people who fail to recognize that social order and human relations cannot exist without rules and laws. Failure of communication occurs in these instances because the participants do not apply the same rules to the exchange of messages and do not abide by agreements.

a) Violates explicit rules:
—The rebel
—The criminal
—The undisciplined person

b) Violates implicit rules of tradition:
—The ruthless, aggressive person
—The nonconformist
—The ignorant or feeble-minded person

c) Observes the letter of the law exclusively:
—Captain Queeg in *The Caine Mutiny*
—The child who literally obeys the rule but flouts its meaning

d) Adheres to double standards:
—The gangster who despises and ignores the law but at the same time maintains a code of his own
—The corrupt police official

e) Has no regard for existing rules and substitutes for these rules of his own:
—The conqueror
—The tyrant
—The autocrat
—The fanatic

A-15. Roles. The description of roles has traditionally been in the realm of the writer and the playwright; the impersonation of roles, the pleasure of the actor. But the character of a Willie Loman, a Casanova, a Don Quixote, a Siegfried, or a Hamlet is not limited to fiction (217). Since writers get their inspiration from the observation of ordinary people, the original models are found anywhere.

a) The he-man

b) The hero

c) The adventurer

d) The irresistible charmer

e) The promoter

f) The bohemian

g) The serious moralist

h) The dutiful child

i) The fun lover

AA-15. Disturbances. Inappropriate assumption or unskillful execution of a role easily results in a caricature. People are exceedingly sensitive to inadequate role assumption and tend to respond with hesitancy or ambiguity. Because of the mixed response of others, the individual may become even more confused and communication will break down.

a) The he-man caricature:
—The physical and mental weakling who pads his shoulders, tans his skin, smokes a pipe, and talks tough

b) The perennial hero:
—The former all-American who rests on his laurels

c) The psychopath:
—Looks for adventures and creates adventurous situations at the expense of others

d) The seducer:
—The person who thinks he is irresistible in spite of the fact that others do not respond

e) The perpetual promoter:
—Carries his promotional behavior into his home and plagues his family with empty words

f) The intellectual fringe dweller:
—Identifies himself with artists and intellectuals without being one

g) The value peddler:
—Unable to understand others, he judges and tries to impose his own values upon them

h) The duty addict:
—With high ideals and powerful conscience, this overexacting person puts duty above common sense

i) The pleasure addict:
—Unable to tolerate any kind of frustration, this person resorts to immediate gratification—alcoholism, drugs, gambling

j) The thinker

k) The unfortunate victim

j) The dreamer:
—Instead of thinking, engages in day-dreaming without carrying out his plans

k) The "miserable":
—Constantly dwelling on lack of success, presses into service his failures, misfortunes, and ailments to coerce others

A-16. *Tolerance limits.* In the neonate, the spread between threshold and tolerance limit is narrow. The infant is either disturbed or asleep. With progressive maturation, this spread increases. Eventually people learn to utilize quantitative variation of stimulation as a source of information, provided they can perceive and tolerate that particular stimulus. If it cannot be tolerated, a loss of information occurs.

a) Wide spread between threshold and limit of tolerance:
—Can utilize quantitative variations of stimulus productively; keeps his head

b) Narrow spread between threshold and limit of tolerance:
—Cannot utilize quantitative variations of stimuli; has more of an all-or-none response; panics easily

c) Narrow spread between threshold and limit of tolerance for selected types of stimulation:
—Oversensitive to certain sounds but tolerates visual stimuli well

AA-16. *Disturbances.* The tolerance limits of the individual may be altered in certain diseases of the central and autonomic nervous systems or through endocrine changes and age.

a) Extreme frustration tolerance:
—Sluggishness as in the case of mixe-dematous and demented persons and some hysterical and schizophrenic patients

b) Absence of frustration tolerance:
—Lability of emotions as in the case of sympathicotonic individuals, hyperthyroid persons, and some depressive individuals

c) Disequilibrium between tolerance and intolerance of frustration in selected sensory modalities:
—Absence of pain or temperature sensations in cases of syringomyelia
—Hypersensitivity in tetany

A-17. *Attitudes toward people.* Attitudes toward people not only shape the nature of the interaction but also determine the choice of partners. These attitudes reflect a person's basic beliefs about such diversified matters as responsibility, aggression, education, and human relations.

a) The "dog-eat-dog" attitude:
—Belief that human beings are aggressive by nature and that the expansive qualities of an individual or group are checked and kept in balance by the expansive strivings of another individual or group. To be constantly on the lookout for attack from all sorts of sources and to press one's own advantages in a merciless way become the guiding attitudes toward people

b) The "self-control" attitude:
—Belief that man is moral and that his sense of responsibility and his ideals will counterbalance all aggressive tendencies. To give people responsibility and to appeal to their sense of duty become the main principles of social operations

c) The "control by authority" attitude:
—Belief that man is weak and can be governed only by a few selected people. A rigid system of cultural and social institutions is necessary for implementing this attitude

d) The "steering by enlightenment" attitude:
—Belief that man is rational and that by means of education and reasoning people can be brought to do what is good for them and for society

e) The "people are social" attitude:
—Belief that people become disturbed when social needs are interfered with. To steer people in the right direction, an attitude of inclusion and provision for satisfactory group membership are needed.

AA-17. *Disturbances.* Some of the basic attitudes toward people can be exaggerated or distorted to the point of becoming caricatures. Such views, which in themselves contain a distorted blueprint of human relations, inevitably lead to a breakdown of communication.

a) The potentially or actively assaultive person:
—The excited catatonic

b) The person who is overwhelmed by an overbearing conscience and high-pitched ideals:
—The depressive

c) The person who advocates or practices tyranny:
—The cruel father
—The paranoid

d) The person who advocates or practices reasoning in places where action is called for:
—The mother who prematurely appeals to the rational understanding of children
—The person who explains technical matters that others cannot understand

e) The person who advocates or practices noninterference:
—The person who mistakes chaos for permissiveness
—The parent who cannot set limits for children

f) The "materialistic" attitude:
—Belief that people can be controlled by satisfying their bodily needs and providing them with material goods and an ever-rising standard of living

f) The person who supplies goods and money in place of affection:
—The parent who showers the child with presents instead of observing what he needs

A-18. Ways of appealing. When an individual's method of appealing is specially adapted to certain patterns of perception and evaluation of the other person, particular kinds of effects can be achieved (215). This procedure is based on subtle and intuitive appraisal of the other person's needs.

a) Appeal tuned primarily to tactile-thermal-pain-osmetic-gustatory reception. Tendency to emphasize small audience and short-lasting codification:
—Approach through perfumes, caress, and physical support

b) Appeal tuned primarily to visual-auditory perception of the other person. Tendency to emphasize large audience and durable codification:
—Approach through spoken or written word, pictures, playing of music

c) Appeal tuned primarily to intuitive understanding with emphasis upon nonverbal systems of codification:
—Approach to common sense and satisfaction of ubiquitous needs such as hunger or sleep

d) Appeal tuned principally to rational understanding with emphasis on verbal-digital systems of codification:
—Approach to analytic understanding and logic of the other person

e) Appeal tuned to the perception of social or physical context:
—Approach through employment of furniture arrangement or lighting to produce effects

f) Appeal tuned to perception of action:
—Approach geared to the other person's observation of gestural signals or silent action

AA-18. Disturbances. Exclusive emphasis on one kind of appeal and concomitant neglect of alternative approaches may lead to disturbances of communication. Individuals who do not possess diversified methods of appeal are able effectively to approach few people only; in all their other relationships they are liable to be misunderstood.

a) Overemphasis on other person's closeness receivers and disregard for his distance receivers:
—The person who warms up conversationally only following bodily contact with another person

b) Overemphasis on the other person's distance receivers and disregard for his closeness receivers:
—The mother who fails to stimulate her child through touch and movement and fails to respond to his action expression, while paying attention to what he says

c) Overemphasis on other person's intuitive understanding and disregard for his rational understanding:
—The infantile person's assumption that all people understand his particular needs without a detailed explanation

d) Overemphasis on the other person's rational understanding and disregard for his intuitive understanding:
—An obsessive's labored explanation of the obvious

e) Overemphasis on the other person's understanding of context in neglect of his appreciation of action signals:
—The parent who sends the child to school and neglects his need for nonverbal appreciation

f) Overemphasis on the other person's understanding of action signals and neglect of his understanding of context:
—The overprotective mother who gives too many directions

A-19. *Ways of replying.* Regardless of the topic of discourse or of the social situation involved, people tend to reply to the statements of others in certain systematic and often repetitive ways (208).

a) Replies openly, directly, and to the point:
—Commits himself when called upon

b) Replies indirectly and evasively:
—Avoids committing himself

c) Does not reply when such an option exists:
—Leaves people with the impression that he has not expressed himself

d) Replies tangentially:
—Ignores that component of the message which requires a reply and responds to another, bringing into play his own interests rather than considering those of the other person

e) Replies unrelatedly:
—Ignores the message of the other person completely and brings in an entirely new topic—a mother's cutting in on her child's story

AA-19. *Disturbances.* When patterns of reply become rigid and systematized and when the individual feels that he is not free to choose the most appropriate reply, then communication becomes restricted.

a) Replies exclusively to the latent content—that is, the unconscious intention of the other person:
—As in the case of some schizophrenics
—As in the case of people who want to demonstrate their superiority

b) Replies exclusively to the manifest content—that is, the overt statement of the other person:
—As in the case of certain compulsives
—As in the case of people who do not want to understand

c) Does not reply where a reply is called for:
—The catatonic
—The mute
—The person who locks himself in his room

d) Replies systematically to an incidental part and leaves the core of the message unanswered:
—The sadistic person

e) Replies at random; disregards content completely, but acknowledges the fact that the other person has made a statement by making another statement of his own:
—Dissociated reply and word salad

A-20. *Learning and correction.* Problem-solving—that is, learning by trial and error—and learning by imitation are the two fundamental ways of acquiring knowledge and skill. Self-correction and reward through mastery are operative in problem-solving; correction and reward by others are operative in learning through imitation. Careful observers can also learn by first observing and then avoiding the errors of others (169).

a) Prefers to find things out for himself, to correct by trial and error, and to solve problems alone:
—Goes out on his own without seeking instruction

b) Prefers to learn from interaction with other people:
—Exchanges information, is eager to be shown, and seeks instruction

c) Prefers to learn from the errors made by other people:
—Avoids being in the lead; watches others carefully and learns from their mistakes

d) Prefers to correct information primarily through logical and theoretical thinking:
—Figures out problems; trusts formulae; relies on probabilities; learns concepts of action rather than to master action itself

AA-20. *Disturbances.* A person's exclusive reliance upon one method of correction or his application of a learning method ill-suited to the situation may result in his acquiring incomplete or incorrect information. With his use of one-sided methods of correction, his already acquired information is not brought up to date and serious disturbances of communication may develop.

a) Disturbed learning and correction by trial and error:
—Does not heed warnings and has to make mistakes himself: the psychopath
—Cannot solve problems by himself: the overprotected child

b) Disturbed learning and correction through interaction with other people:
—Cannot take over cues from others
—Relies upon encouragement of others

c) Disturbed learning and correction by observation of other people:
—Cannot watch others; instead, has to try out things himself

d) Disturbed learning and correction through logic and speculation:
—Armchair strategist who does not check his speculations against reality but controls them with his own erroneous logic

A-21. *Social conflict.* Almost all individuals tend to devise two or three special methods to resolve conflicts and rarely does any one person have at his disposal the whole range of possible techniques. Depending upon the person's skill and the method chosen, more or less conflict will be apparent in a person's life.

a) Acknowledges conflict without attempt at resolution

b) Takes overt action to resolve conflict

c) Makes verbal suggestions to reduce conflict

d) Seeks support from others for action designed to reduce conflict

e) Appeals to proper authorities for handling of conflict

f) Pins down responsibility for conflict

g) Fails to acknowledge conflict

h) Undertakes to increase conflict

AA-21. *Disturbances.* While the healthy individual occasionally gets away with not handling a conflict at all, leaving its resolution to other participants and to time, the sick individual usually is unsuccessful in this method. In contrast, he tends to reassure himself or asks to be reassured that he is doing something to handle the situation. But these assurances are often empty gestures which leave the conflict unresolved or make it even worse.

a) Allows conflict to exist and assumes it will take care of itself

b) Undertakes action which does not influence the conflict

c) Makes verbal comments about the conflict without undertaking action to change the situation

d) Induces others to handle the conflict and to make the necessary decisions

e) Seeks "canned" solutions offered by authorities, but does not apply them in action

f) Accuses and blames self or others but does not tackle conflict

g) Is oblivious to conflict; ignores early storm signals

h) Gleefully promotes more conflict to the point of having most people turn against him

A-22. *Adaptation and control.* Whenever a person makes a statement, he intends either to induce action or to foster general enlightenment. Thus, depending upon his purpose, an individual will prefer social situations which implement his intentions. The physical and social contexts so chosen not only serve as interpretative devices for others but also significantly characterize the communicative behavior of an individual.

a) Maximizes fantasy and tends to disregard the actual structure of social situations; therefore, seeks situations in which a minimum of adaptation is required and in which he can pursue his ideas:
—The theorist
—The philosopher
—The artist

b) Attempts to impose preconceived plans upon surroundings; manages, structures, and changes the physical and social environment; therefore, seeks situations in which control is successful:
—The engineer
—The advertising man
—The executive

c) Adapts internal codifications to actually existing social situations; therefore, seeks contexts which require a maximum of adaptation:
—The naturalist
—The trouble-shooter
—The middleman

AA-22. *Disturbances.* Selective adherence to or avoidance of certain contexts may lead to disturbances of communication.

a) Oblivious to social reality; concerned with internal events:
—The schizophrenic
—The manic
—The pseudological person
—The hysterical person

b) Oblivious to limitations of power and talent: the under- or overcontroller:
—The disorderly person
—The compulsive person
—The duty-bound person
—The pathological manipulator

c) Oblivious to limitations of adaptation: the under- or overadapter:
—The person who reacts with anxiety to demands for adaptation
—The person who adapts to other people's pathology
—The exercise and vitamin addict

INTERACTION PROFILE
or
The Individual's Communicative Behavior
in Two-Person Situations

B-1. *Structure of two-person systems.* In two-person systems, the role distributions seem to be more time-enduring than those in group situations primarily because the mutual adaptability of the two participants tends to maximize or minimize certain aspects of the relationship. In spite of such specialization, the growth and development of the participants can progress as long as the individuals do not limit themselves to one kind of system.

a) Prefers systems in which other members are duplicates of self; system has no permanent differentiation of functions:
—Playmates of the same sex

b) Prefers systems characterized by complementarity and specialization of functions:
—The introspective and shy brother doing the planning; the brash and active brother carrying out the actions
—The composer and the song writer

c) Prefers systems with hierarchical, patriarchal, or matriarchal structure:
—Young man passing through apprenticeship with experienced older person

d) Prefers random, short-lasting systems with no long-term structure:
—The migratory worker

BB-1. *Disturbances.* Disturbances in two-person systems arise if the individual does not get along with the other person when together and feels frustrated when separated. The existence of this kind of conflict precludes social and psychological growth for one or both participants.

a) Participates in two-person systems in which his own pathological features are reinforced:
—The delinquent
—The homosexual

b) Participates in symbiotic system where the pathology consists of inability to assume certain functions which then are taken over by the other:
—One person makes decisions and the other carries them out
—One person thinks and the other acts
—The blind person and his guide
—The phobic person and her companion

c) Participates in two-person systems in which one person has usurped significant controlling or exploiting functions, leaving the other person helpless:
—The domineering mother and the overprotected child

d) Does not voluntarily enter into two-person systems, and when forced to do so withdraws:
—The aloof schizophrenic
—The spinster who withdraws from close contact with others

B-2. *Concurrent participation in several two-person systems.* An individual's participation in two-person systems shows distinct characteristics, particularly with regard to the number of systems involved, the nature of the activity, and the duration of the relationships. These factors vary with the individual's complexity, specialization, and emotional needs.

a) Long-term participation in several two-person systems and in groups; the various systems are coordinated and do not collide:

—Married man has friend with whom he goes fishing; in the meanwhile, his wife sees girl-friend with whom she goes shopping

b) Long-term participation in one two-person system only. All other relationships are in groups. Partner does likewise:

—Husband attends professional meetings and wife is active in social organizations

c) Long-term participation in one two-person system only; no group relations:

—Teen-ager who lives with mother; does not attempt to date a girl or to play with age-mates

BB-2. *Disturbances.* Adherence to two-person systems because of inability to function in a group or avoidance of multiple two-person systems because of inability to function in an intimate setting leads to disturbances of communication.

a) Participation in several two-person and group systems, but systems are not coordinated and collide with each other:

—Instead of specializing, establishes several parallel two-person systems such as the man who hires several doctors or lawyers to do the same job or the boy who dates several girls for the same evening

b) Participates in one two-person system only; restrains partner from participating in other two-person systems. Group relations not coordinated with individual functioning:

—Prevents the other or is prevented from entering any other two-person relationship regardless of scope, purpose, or situation; suspects that all group gatherings are subterfuges— for example, the jealous wife or husband

c) Participates in only one two-person system which functions poorly; no other relations of any kind:

—The phobic or paranoid person who prevents his companion from leaving the room; however, when the other stays, makes life miserable for him

B-3. *Successive participation in various two-person systems.* In considering the systems in which a person has participated in the past, one can detect certain consistencies in the choice of partners.

BB-3. *Disturbances.* Disturbed people frequently yearn for some imaginary figure which they believe to find in a certain person. When they discover that this person does not match the image, they look for a substitute. Such relationships are usually based on some characteristic of social role, which factor tends to become the pivot around which the interaction revolves.

a) Chooses persons of a certain age and sex:
—Associates with younger mates
—Seeks either boys or girls

a) Maximizes, minimizes, or distorts features of age, sex, or family role in the other person
—The other person is treated as if she were a mother or a sister

b) Chooses persons who are members of prominent families:
—Associates with aristocrats

b) Maximizes, minimizes, or distorts the other person's family reputation:
—The other person's family suddenly acquires ancestors it never possessed before

c) Chooses persons characterized by personal distinction:
—Associates with famous or notorious persons

c) Maximizes, minimizes, or distorts the other person's personal distinction:
—The other person is talked about as if he were a hero or a villain

d) Chooses persons characterized by mediocrity:
—Associates with persons who are not outstanding in any way

d) Maximizes, minimizes, or distorts the other person's mediocrity:
—The other person is viewed as average in spite of previous notoriety

e) Chooses persons who are pursued by hard luck and ill fate:
—Associates with invalids or unsuccessful persons

e) Maximizes, minimizes, or distorts the other person's hard luck and ill fate:
—The other person is treated as an invalid although not seriously sick

f) Chooses persons in certain occupations:
—Associates with professional people, with artists, with businessmen

f) Maximizes, minimizes, or distorts the other person's occupational characteristics:
—The other person is thought of as an expert, although he does not possess any qualifications

B-4. *Specialization in two-person situations.* An individual's preference for certain functions in a network of communication is clearly reflected in two-person situations. In spite of specialization of roles, the healthy person retains his ability to carry out other functions.

a) Participation in a two-person team where perception characterizes the role:
—The blind man's companion
—The interpreter

b) Participation in a two-person team where evaluation characterizes the role:
—The decision-maker: the mother
—The critic: the perfectionistic husband

c) Participation in a two-person team where transmission characterizes the role:
—The errand boy
—The strong man

BB-4. *Disturbances.* If certain functions of communication are not delegated but are successfully usurped by one of the partners or are forced upon him by unavoidable circumstances, pathological interdependence is the result. In such a system, the partners usually are incapable of assuming the other person's functions, which situation seems to arise frequently when wealthy, famous, or sick people are involved.

a) Participation in a symbiotic team in which one individual becomes the perceiver for the other person:
—The permanent spectator of an exhibitionistic person
—The companion who reports about events which the invalid cannot attend

b) Participation in a symbiotic team in which one individual becomes decision-maker for the other person:
—The overbearing mother who decides whom her son is to marry
—The "brains" of a two-person burglar team
—The "agent-manager" of a talented but indecisive artist

c) Participation in a symbiotic team in which one individual becomes the motor extension of the other:
—The gangster's devoted bodyguard
—The pander's prostitute

B-5. *Facilitation and inhibition of functions in two-person systems.* The presence of another person frequently changes an individual's habits in perception, evaluation, and transmission. It may either facilitate or inhibit one or more functions, and it may change sequence and timing.

a) Observation facilitated:
—With other person, is stimulated to perceive, look, and listen, being constantly on the alert

b) Observation inhibited:
—With other person, becomes blinded to facts, as in the case of lovers

c) Evaluation facilitated:
—With other person, behaves critically and reaches verdicts as if he were asked to be a judge

d) Evaluation inhibited:
—Postpones any decision-making and utterances of opinion as if to safeguard himself

e) Action facilitated:
—With other person as audience, shows off skill

f) Action inhibited:
—With other person, tends to be shy and to postpone activity

BB-5. *Disturbances.* Quantitative exaggeration of the normally occurring facilitation or inhibition of functions in the presence of another person can lead to serious disturbances of communication resulting in frustration for both participants.

a) Mandatory observation:
—The peeping Tom who, regardless of conventions and feelings, invades the other person's privacy

b) Blocking of observation:
—The inattentive driver who converses rather than watch the road

c) Mandatory evaluation:
—Destructive criticism and prejudice directed at the other person

d) Blocking of evaluation:
—Is ambivalent, postpones decisions

e) Mandatory engagement in action:
—The manic patient
—Impulsive reactions of rage

f) Blocking of action:
—The catatonic person

B-6. *Language in two-person systems.*
The two-person situation lends itself to the development of special combinations of codifications. New words may be invented, actions and gestures may be combined with words in rather unique ways, inasmuch as only two people have to agree as to their significance (182).

a) Circumvents use of interpersonal language and refers to experiences in common: communizing:
—Couple knowing each other's concern about the sickness of their child casually allude to the illness

b) Develops language characteristic for two-person situations:
—Baby talk
—Secret sign language of children
—The private language of lovers

c) Language not optimally adapted to two-person situations, leaning either toward the self-centered side or toward official lingo:
—Man who thinks out loud
—Man who lectures his wife to whom he has been married for twenty years

BB-6. *Disturbances.* Disturbances of communication arise when language applicable to a given two-person system is mistakenly used in another, or when under- or overspecialization prevents the full deployment of the vocabulary.

a) Inability to communize or excessive reliance upon communization:
—Inability to cooperate and therefore to experience in common, as in the case of certain schizophrenics
—Excessive reliance upon communization as in the case of dependent, inarticulate people

b) Over- or underspecialization of two-person codifications:
—Exclusive baby talk preventing any serious discussion

c) Displacement of specific two-person codifications to other two-person systems or to group systems:
—Names and pet names of one girlfriend applied to another

B-7. *Switch of language system in two-person situations.* A change in codification systems is necessary if different aspects of events are to be discussed. In two-person relations, a subject may be satisfactorily treated when one of the partners assumes responsibility for one aspect—that is, one kind of language—and the other partner for another.

a) Associates with people who can operate within the same language dimension:

—*First Person*	*Second Person*
Analogic-digital	Analogic-digital
Affective-intellec-tual	Affective-intellec-tual

b) Associates with people who can operate at the other end of the same dimension:

—*First Person*	*Second Person*
Concrete	Abstract
Analogic	Digital
Denotative	Connotative
Affective	Intellectual
Lowbrow	Highbrow

c) Associates with people who operate with other dimensions:

—*First Person*	*Second Person*
Analogic-digital	Lowbrow-high-brow
Denotative-con-notative	Affective intellec-tual

BB-7. *Disturbances.* When in the course of a discussion one person switches codifications, the other person must follow suit. Skillful persons eventually adapt their codifications to the rhythmical changes in style of the other person; but insensitive or rigid people cannot follow such changes, and serious disturbances of communication will arise.

a) When first person switches, second person perseverates in the same codification system:

—*First Person*	*Second Person*
Concrete	Concrete
—s w i t c h—	
Abstract	Concrete

b) When first person switches system of codification, second person also switches, but into a different system:

—*First Person*	*Second Person*
Concrete	Concrete
—s w i t c h—	
Highbrow	Abstract

c) When first person switches system of codification, second person also switches, but the participants do not come together:

—*First Person*	*Second Person*
Lowbrow	Concrete
—s w i t c h—	
Highbrow	Abstract

B-8. *The individual's view of two-person situations.* Ideas and attitudes toward two-person relations are communicated through word and action and hence imperceptibly structure the interaction.

a) Views two-person situations essentially as an opportunity to engage in body-to-body contact and cooperate in action:
—Intercourse, petting, caress, boxing, roughhousing

b) Views two-person situations essentially as an opportunity for high-level, bilateral exchange of information, for spirited conversation, and for mutual understanding

c) Views two-person situations essentially as an opportunity for competition; to outdo, outwit, or outperform the other person

d) Views two-person situations essentially as an opportunity to learn, to grow, and to acquire skill and experience

e) Views two-person situations essentially as an opportunity to exploit and utilize the other person

BB-8. *Disturbances.* An individual's distorted views of two-person situations reflect themselves in word and action; these expressions are experienced by others as coercive. This unfavorable reaction of course has a feedback effect upon the individual, who, because of his psychopathology, is unable to correct his performance. Eventually such a two-person system breaks down.

a) The two-person system as an opportunity for carnality:
—The sexual criminal

b) The two-person situation as a mystic or metaphysical experience:
—The eternal search for the soul-mate

c) The two-person situation as a rivalry situation:
—The competitive mother

d) The two-person situation as a teacher-pupil or parent-child relation:
—The eternal student

e) The two-person situation as an extension of self:
—The spiritualist and his medium

B-9. *Concern for internal or external affairs in two-person situations.* Confining operations to an established two-person situation with relative disregard for other people and, conversely, interest in other people's affairs with relative disregard for own two-person relationships are complementary orientations.

a) Preference for maintaining two-person team in most situations:
—Two people who work, play, and live together

b) Preference for pairing with other two-person teams:
—Two couples playing bridge together
—Two teen-aged pairs petting on lovers' lane

c) Preference for operating outside of an established two-person situation:
—Husband who prefers cronies to wife
—Wife who prefers social gatherings to company of husband

d) Preference for crisscrossing established two-person situations:
—Bachelor who is attached to married woman

BB-9. *Disturbances.* If a person disregards the complementarity of in- and outgroup orientation and is exclusively concerned with either "domestic" or "foreign" affairs, disturbances of communication will arise. These are brought on by the fact that every individual needs and is forced to consider both orientations.

a) The inseparable couple:
—Twins who never play with other children
—Homosexual lovers
—The phobic person and his protector
—The sadistic-masochistic involvement

b) The paired couples:
Those who have not mastered group communication and can function only in two-person or multiple two-person situations:
—Invalids with their caretakers

c) The lonely person who dreams about a partner:
—The impotent person
—The fearful homosexual
—The wife whose husband has disappeared
—The abandoned child

d) Breaking up two-person situations:
—Mistress who attempts to break up a marriage
—Daughter who is jealous of mother's affection for her brother

B-10. *Preference for certain universes of discourse.* In two-person situations, the universe of discourse is intimately linked to certain ways of talking, arguing, and gesticulating, so that each topic is characterized by a somewhat different procedure (167).

BB-10. *Disturbances.* Over- or under-emphasis on one universe of discourse or application of an approach to an unsuitable situation influences the participants unfavorably, particularly if they are young. If children are not exposed to a variety of universes, they will encounter difficulties when they wish to enter into other two-person relations (14).

a) Mythological discourse

a) Distortions, over- or underemphasis, of mythological discourse:
—The parent who rewards the child for fantasy elaborations about heroes

b) Cosmological discourse

b) Distortions, over- or underemphasis, of cosmological discourse:
—The parent who teaches the child to make generalizations about the nature of the universe

c) Religious discourse

c) Distortions, over- or underemphasis, of religious discourse:
—The parent who teaches his child to accept religious figures as if they were contemporary human beings

d) Moral discourse

d) Distortions, over- or underemphasis, of moral discourse:
—The parent who constantly reminds the child of the moral value of his actions

e) Fictive discourse

e) Distortions, over- or underemphasis, of fictive discourse:
—The parent who encourages his child to invent stories; science-fiction

f) Poetic discourse

f) Distortions, over- or underemphasis, of poetic discourse:
—The parent who rewards his child for talking in rhymes and saying things poetically, although they may not be true

g) Critical discourse

g) Distortions, over- or underemphasis, of critical discourse:
—The parent who teaches his child to be critical and through criticism teaches him to emphasize the negative features

h) Legal discourse

h) Distortions, over- or underemphasis, of legal discourse:
—The parent who teaches his child to observe rules rigorously and to talk about the legality of action

i) Linguistic-semantic discourse

i) Distortions, over- or underemphasis, of linguistic-semantic discourse:
—The parent who teaches his child to emphasize grammar and the dictionary meaning of words rather than what words stand for in a given situation

j) Logical discourse

j) Distortions, over- or underemphasis, of logical discourse:
—The parent who teaches his child to be verbal, to emphasize thought; for example, in teaching him prematurely to play chess

k) Scientific discourse

k) Distortions, over- or underemphasis, of scientific discourse:
—The parent who teaches his child to analyze problems in a scientific, impersonal, objective manner and to disregard his feelings

l) Technological discourse

l) Distortions, over- or underemphasis, of technological discourse:
—The parent who teaches his child to look at the engineering aspects of things regardless of their social impact

m) Political discourse

m) Distortions, over- or underemphasis, of political discourse:
—The parent who teaches his child to consider the effects of personal management, publicity, and success to the detriment of other considerations

n) Propagandistic discourse

n) Distortions, over- or underemphasis, of propagandistic discourse:
—The parent who teaches his child to consider actions in terms of popularity, slogans, and the salesmanship he brought into play

o) Rhetorical discourse

o) Distortions, over- or underemphasis, of rhetorical discourse:
—The parent who teaches his child to say things clearly at the expense of action

B-11. *Congruity and ambiguity in expression.* When all elements of a message blend, then attention is drawn to its face value. When one or another element does not blend, then the listener's attention is drawn to the discrepancy. Such contradictions, if judiciously played upon, frequently can be used to create certain effects which cannot be achieved by direct expression (186).

a) Contradiction between what is said and what is done:
—Unfulfillable promise as a sign of good will

b) Contradiction between verbally stated and nonverbally stated information:
—The mother who says "Good boy" and gives him a playful slap on the behind to remind him that there are exceptions

c) Contradiction between past behavior and planned future behavior:
—"I will take you out someday" to compensate for the fact that he never has in the past, creating the effect that things still may change one day

d) Contradiction between behavior for home consumption and behavior for foreign consumption:
—Dresses sloppily at home but dresses up when going out, to indicate the value placed on the reaction of other people

e) Contradiction between feeling and action:
—Shakes hands but makes a grim face to reduce the effect of the handshake

f) Contradiction between stated values and observed values:
—Explains rules and then goes about to circumvent them to indicate individualism as well as resourcefulness

the future
g) Contradiction between prediction and outcome:

BB-11. *Disturbances.* When a person consistently communicates by means of contradictions, others learn to disregard either one or all of his modes of expression. Reactions under these circumstances become rather unspecific, and people respond not to the content of the message but to the frustration it imposes.

a) Word and action do not match:
—Outright lies

b) Verbal and nonverbal statements do not match:
—The harsh movements of the schizophrenic and his polite words

c) Past and present behavior do not match:
—The prostitute who suddenly leads a respectable life

d) Home and outside behavior do not match:
—The angry psychopath who smiles "pleasantly" when going out

e) Feeling and action do not match:
—The person who does not act upon his feelings of hatred

f) Stated and observed values do not match:
—The polygamist who is "ideal husband" to four wives

g) Prediction and outcome do not match:
—The unsuccessful gambler who indicates his belief in better luck in
—Consistently faulty judgment

B-11.1. *Subject matter, role, and personal consideration.* In group situations, opinion and person can be adequately separated because multiple views by different people crystallize and illuminate the problem. In interpersonal relations, in contrast, it is difficult to separate the topic of discourse from the personality that discusses it. But if such distinctions are made, they may clarify an ambiguous situation.

BB-11.1. *Disturbances.* When in two-person situations personal considerations and subject matter are strictly separated, disturbances of communication are likely to arise.

a) Personal support:
—With understanding consideration, lavishes praise and reward upon other person, makes him feel included, and raises his self-respect. He responds to the person rather than to subject matter or role, and he conveys this attitude to the other person

a) Exclusive personal support, or inability to give support:
—The man who hires a secretary exclusively from the viewpoint of sex appeal
—The man who is incapable of consoling his grief-stricken wife

b) Personal rejection:
—By not understanding and through hostile response, deflates other person, lowers the latter's self-respect, and lets it be known that he responds to person rather than to subject matter or role

b) Exclusive personal rejection, or inability to reject:
—The scientist who is interested only in refuting another person's opinion
—The person who is incapable of rejecting a mother who interferes with his time and work

c) Support of subject matter or action:
—Supports view presented or action suggested, but lets it be known that he does not include personal support of the bearer

c) Exclusive support of subject matter or inability to support it:
—Disregards personal considerations entirely and rigidly sticks to the subject matter, or, conversely, is incapable of concentrating on topic or goal

d) Rejection of subject matter or action:
—Rejects view presented or action suggested, but lets it be known that he is not prejudiced vis-à-vis the bearer of the opinion

d) Exclusive rejection of subject matter or inability to reject it:
—Disregards any viewpoint other than his own or, conversely, is incapable of discarding a view he does not agree with

e) Role support:
—By deferring to role of bearer, omits consideration of person as well as of topic. Responds to status, prestige, and official function

e) Exclusive support of role or inability to support role:
—Defers to authority of officialdom or, conversely, is incapable of doing so

f) Role rejection:
—By rejecting role assumed by other person, disregards official function and emphasizes the human aspects of the situation

f) Exclusive rejection of role or inability to reject role:
—Does not want to be associated with a person of dubious reputation regardless of situation

B-11.2. *Personal reference in the exchange of information.* A variety of personal references can be made in the exchange of messages, either explicitly or implicitly, which tend to attenuate, alter, or radically change the topic of discourse.

a) Makes reference to material security of self or other person

b) Makes reference to social position, status, or prestige of self or other

c) Makes reference to power or weakness of self or other

d) Makes reference to aspirations, hopes, wishes of self or other

e) Makes reference to assumptions and beliefs of self or other

f) Makes reference to past behavior of self or other

g) Makes reference to racial or cultural background of self or other

h) Makes reference to experiential background and skills of self or other

i) Makes reference to health of self or other

BB-11.2. *Disturbances.* Statements may be formulated in such a way that they bear too much on the interests of one and disregard the interests of the other person. Such a procedure alters the gain that both people may have from an interchange, often to the point that one person loses interest altogether.

Exclusively emphasizes, isolates, or threatens:

a) Material security of self or other

b) Social position of self or other

c) Power or weakness of self or other

d) Aspirations of self or other

e) Assumptions and beliefs of self or other

f) Past behavior of self or other

g) Racial or cultural background of self or other

h) Experiential background and skills of self or other

i) Health of self or other

B-12. *Social techniques.* Social techniques can be conceived of as goal-seeking or goal-changing activities; they are defined in terms of the effect they achieve; they may be verbal or nonverbal, explicit or implicit. Each individual seems to develop fairly time-enduring, personal preferences in choosing and applying certain social techniques (74, 200).

BB-12. *Disturbances.* Inability to use a modality, consistent dominant use of one and the same modality, or use of modalities where they are out of place may result in disturbances of communication.

Perception and action geared to:
a) Taking in—demanding:
—The child or the pupil in a learning situation

b) Interference reduction—fighting:
—The competitive person

c) Possession—retention:
—The possessive wife

d) Riddance—elimination:
—The spendthrift

e) Marketing—exchange:
—The salesman

f) Attraction — recognition — exhibition:
—The belle

g) Play, pretend—impersonating:
—The playboy, the actress

h) Exploration—searching:
—The adventurer

i) Intrusion—trespassing:
—The conqueror

j) Inception—receiving:
—The receptive woman

k) Creation—conceiving:
—The designer

l) Raising, letting grow—encouraging:
—The benefactor

m) Avoidance—flight:
—The shy, retiring person

Displaced, exaggerated, or restricted perception and action geared to:
a) Taking in—demanding:
—The dependent person

b) Interference reduction—fighting:
—The hostile person

c) Possession—retention:
—The miser, the constipated person

d) Riddance—elimination:
—The losing gambler, the colitis patient

e) Marketing—exchange:
—The prostitute

f) Attraction — recognition — exhibition:
—The exhibitionist

g) Play, pretend—impersonating:
—The impostor, the phony

h) Exploration—searching:
—The burglar

i) Intrusion—trespassing:
—The rapist, the murderer

j) Inception—receiving:
—The rape victim

k) Creation—conceiving:
—The "crackpot" inventor

l) Raising, letting grow—encouraging:
—The mother of a delinquent

m) Avoidance—flight:
—The phobic

B-13. *The frame of reference in two-person situations.* In two-person situations, either one person imposes or both persons agree to a certain frame of reference for discourse and action. But such a frame of reference is likely to change or to be modified as time passes on.

a) Tends to respect and maintain one frame of reference:
—Does not mix business with pleasure

b) Tends to change frames of reference, and indicates this change at once:
—While dictating, employer makes pass at secretary

c) Tends to change frames of reference, but indicates such change belatedly, thus winning temporarily an advantage or a disadvantage:
—Is tired or bored but professes interest

BB-13. *Disturbances.*   Disturbances can be avoided if both partners flexibly agree upon the frame of reference as they go along. Excessive rigidity or flexibility and failure to notify the partner of a change in the frame of reference are frequent reasons for breakdown of communication.

a) Is rigid and cannot step outside the given frame of reference:
—The person who has no sense of humor

b) Tends constantly to change frames of reference:
—The scatterbrain

c) Tends purposely to change frame of reference without notifying partner:
—The sadistic conversationalist who is always one jump ahead
—The man who engages in double talk

B-14. *Observation of rules in two-person situations.* Rules in two-person situations are usually flexible, unless people feel insecure and prefer to adhere to a cliché with set and inflexible rules. Also those whose major interests lie in group relations may prefer not to elaborate rules in two-person situations (217).

a) Enters into standardized two-person relations and utilizes stereotyped rules:
—The model husband
—The ideal boss

b) Enters particularistic two-person situations and makes rules which for long periods of time apply to this special relationship:
—Man with butler who is also his fishing companion

c) Changes relationship and rules as time goes on:
—Switches from boss-secretary to lover-lover to husband-wife relationship

BB-14. *Disturbances.* Pathology in the observation of rules occurs when these are either compulsively followed or compulsively disregarded or when the partner is not informed about changes in rules.

a) Cannot enter standardized two-person situations; rebels against marriage or any other traditional relationship

b) Cannot enter particularistic two-person situations; cannot adapt rules; functions only in cliché situations

c) Constantly switches rules and changes nature of the relationship to confuse partner and to assume control

B-15. *The choice of roles in two-person situations.* The nature of roles can be indicated by uniforms, implements, posture, movements, or position with regard to others. They are the foremost keys to the correct interpretation of messages. Although people tend to show certain consistencies in their choice of roles, these preferences do not prevent a person from efficiently operating within the framework of another role or from adapting successfully to role systems chosen by other people (217).

Principal factors determining choice of roles—

a) Status: Preference for being status superior, equal, or inferior; perception of status differences

b) Intimacy: Preference for being in role of intimate, indifferent, or distant person; perception of cues referring to intimacy

c) Similarity: Preference for identical, similar, or dissimilar roles; perception of cues bearing on similarity or dissimilarity

d) Activity: Preference for active or passive roles; perception of details referring to amount of activity

e) Duration: Preference for short- or long-term roles; perception of role problems in terms of duration

f) Contact: Preference for roles with numerous or few social contacts; perception of contact possibilities

g) Marginality: Preference for clear-cut or marginal roles; perception of relevant details

h) Responsibility: Preference for roles of responsibility or dependency; perception of such possibilities

BB-15. *Disturbances.* Disturbances of communication may arise when human relations in perception and action are exclusively structured through one predominant set of roles with inability to assume other roles or to adapt to role systems chosen by other people (120).

Displaced, dominant, or restricted emphasis upon—

a) Status:
—The self-effacing person
—The person with ideas of grandeur

b) Intimacy:
—The aloof, distant schizophrenic
—The confidence vulture

c) Similarity:
—The overidentified, hysterical person
—The unidentified person

d) Activity:
—The passive, receptive person
—The hyperactive psychopath

e) Duration:
—The security-seeker
—The one-night stand

f) Contact:
—The social butterfly
—The recluse

g) Marginality:
—The bohemian
—The "rolling stone"

h) Responsibility:
—The overburdened ulcer bearer
—The dependent person

B-16. *Responses to quantitative variations in two-person situations.* In order to grow, any child or person who learns must be exposed to progressively more difficult tasks as time goes on. Proper timing and repetition are fundamental to any learning or conditioning process.

a) Is exposed to or exposes another to well-timed and quantified stimuli:
—The successful educator

b) Is exposed to or sets for another reasonable limitations of activities, tasks, aspirations:
—The warm but firm mother

c) Is exposed or exposes another to flexible timing and rhythm:
—Military training

d) Is exposed to demands for or demands of another repetition of activity which has not been mastered completely:
—After-school drill

e) Is exposed to or exposes another to one thing at a time:
—The considerate physician

BB-16. *Disturbances.* Distortions arise when the intensity of stimuli exceeds the tolerance limits of the individual, when stimuli are improperly timed, or when the individual is asked to perform beyond the limits of his resources.

a) Exposed to or exposes another to stimulus barrage:
—The person who is excessively exposed to radio, television, and other audio-visual stimuli
or stimulus dearth:
—The prisoner in solitary confinement
—The institutionalized child

b) Pushed into or pushes another into tasks for which he is biologically or psychologically unprepared:
—Premature toilet training, eating with spoon, walking, or learning by rote
—Parent who sets limits verbally but never enforces them

c) Pushed into or pushes another into tempo, rhythm, or timing which is not his own:
—Imposition of fast acting upon slow person
—Imposition of arbitrary feeding schedule upon biological intestinal rhythm

d) Pushed into or pushes another into repetition of activities which he is struggling to leave behind:
—Treating a child like a baby

e) Pushed into or pushes another into mastery of several activities at once:
—Forced toilet training while child is teething and is afflicted with flu

B-17. *The selection of communication partners in two-person situations.* The smaller the system of communication, the more its functioning is dependent upon each human participant. Although children do not select their parents and thus have no choice as to the family into which they are born, they nonetheless are selective with regard to their choice of playmates. As people grow older, they become more and more selective with regard to their communication partners. Their interests, values, and skills and the way they communicate make many small communication networks rather unique.

a) Selection based on other person's characteristics of perception: observation of details or whole structures; of movement or more static elements; of color or shape

b) Selection based on other person's characteristics of evaluation: decision-making, principles of evaluation, value systems, and code of ethics

c) Selection based on other person's characteristics of transmission: activity rate, skills, efficiency of expression

d) Selection based on other person's characteristics of language: choice according to verbal or nonverbal emphasis; organ, action, or verbal-gestural language

e) Selection based on the nature of the information exchanged: technical aspects, goals, humanistic aspects, manipulative aspects

f) Selection based on other person's assumption of family or family-like roles: parental, filial, mate

BB-17. *Disturbances.* When partners are selected not on the basis of opportunity for further growth but because of certain isolated features, the relationship may operate with regard to casual contacts but proves disturbing in long-term associations. A man cannot live successfully with a woman who has beauty and no skills or warmth, and a woman cannot live without frustration with a man who offers only mathematical talent and is ignorant of ordinary human considerations.

a) Selection of partners based on outspoken emphasis on perception:
—A husband selected on the basis of his painting skills

b) Selection of partners based exclusively on ability to make decisions:
—The woman who marries a man because he can make decisions that she can't make

c) Selection of partners based exclusively on ability to express:
—A man who marries a woman exclusively because she is an actress

d) Selection of partners based on outspoken emphasis on or deficiencies in language:
—The psychopath who chooses people who use primarily action language

e) Selection of partners based exclusively on skills, knowledge, or interests, with disregard of other features:
—The young teen-ager who admires the older teen-ager for his skill in stealing automobiles

f) Selection of partners based exclusively on their assumption of family roles:
—The dependent male who marries a mother substitute twenty years older

g) Selection based on other person's assumption of wider social roles and status: leader, follower, rebel

g) Selection of partners based exclusively on the assumption of wider social roles:
—The servant of an autocratic tyrant

h) Selection based on other person's emotional reactions: restrained, demonstrative, serious

h) Selection of partners based exclusively on their emotional reactions:
—The fearful girl's choice of a soft-spoken male who turns out to be impotent

i) Selection based on other person's particularistic personality traits: reliable, understanding, promising

i) Selection of partners based exclusively on an overvalued trait:
—Rugged individualism, which in turn interferes with all human relations

j) Selection based on other person's correction and feedback methods: helpful, supportive, noncoercive, dominating

j) Selection of partners based exclusively on feedback methods:
—Selection of overcritical partners who through destructive criticism nullify their own usefulness

k) Selection based on other person's racial and cultural characteristics: white, Anglo-Saxon, Southern

k) Selection of partners based exclusively on racial or cultural characteristics:
—The wealthy infantile girl who marries a psychopathic aristocrat

B-18. *Preferences in appealing in two-person situations.* In appealing, an individual usually attempts to stimulate the anticipation of some future events or the recall of some past events or tries to mobilize forces in the other person which are temporarily repressed or subdued. Appeal thus revolves around future reward, precedent, conscience, good will, or greed, whereby the immediate approval and thanks of the appealing person exert considerable leverage upon the addressee.

a) Appeal to postpone immediate reward for some future reward:
—"Could you not wait a little longer?"

b) Appeal to sense of opportunity:
—"In three years you will get your money back plus a sizable profit"

c) Appeal to act in the name of tradition and precedent:
—"Our families have always been close"

d) Appeal to declare exception or emergency:
—"Could you not for once make an exception?"

e) Appeal to self-control:
—"Pull yourself together"
—"You ought to . . ."

f) Appeal for clarification:
—"I am not quite clear about . . ."

g) Appeal for help:
—"S.O.S."

BB-18. *Disturbances.* When appeal becomes routine and its implementation stereotyped, appeal as a method of approach may be used in situations where it is ineffective. Under such circumstances, appeal tends to be used as a substitute for more appropriate ways of communication.

a) Consistent appeal to renunciation:
—The excessively puritanical parent

b) Consistent appeal to sense of opportunity:
—The parent who induces his children to take unfair advantage of others

c) Consistent appeal to tradition and precedent:
—The aristocrat who prevents his daughter from marrying a commoner

d) Consistent appeal to emergency:
—The alcoholic who appeals to the appreciation of the special in order to celebrate

e) Consistent appeal to self-control and responsibility:
—The mother who shames the child

f) Consistent appeal for clarification:
—The student who always asks for additional information

g) Consistent appeal for help:
—The ineffectual, dependent person
—The feeble-minded

B-18.1. *Personal leverage*. Every individual tends to be aware of his or her own leverage upon particular persons. Special techniques are brought into play on occasions when the other person must be influenced, swayed, or controlled.

a) Uses bodily functions for leverage:
—Girl exhibits beauty; boy, strength, agility

b) Uses personality traits:
—Reliability, temper

c) Uses material objects:
—Wealth, poverty

d) Uses reputation:
—Points to past record

e) Uses life and health:
—Points to ill effects it would have upon him

BB-18.1. *Disturbances*. Coercion of others may be achieved by selecting oneself as the target of manipulation. Violation of certain rules, destruction, or assumption of certain unpleasant roles can embarrass, threaten, or irk the other person to such an extent that he might yield.

a) Predominantly uses his body functions to coerce:
—Girl threatens to scream and walk nude into the hall

b) Predominantly threatens or rewards with his own good or bad behavior, which might please or embarrass the other person:
—The psychopath who misbehaves to embarrass his parents

c) Predominantly threatens or rewards with accumulating or throwing away his property:
—The child who destroys his toys

d) Predominantly uses his own reputation and status in order to be heard:
—The "big shot" who demands special treatment in court

e) Predominantly uses effects upon his health and life to force compliance:
—Threatens to kill himself

B-18.2. *Leverage through manipulation of needs of other person.* Many people are aware of the "soft underbelly" of the other person; of his needs for status, money, sex, or acceptance. When the other person has to be influenced, such people tend to manipulate his weaknesses to achieve their own personal ends.

BB-18.2. *Disturbances.* When an individual assumes that others can be influenced through the manipulation of a particular need, disturbances of communication may arise. The manipulative attitude is particularly pernicious when parents consistently approach their children in this manner without interposing periods of primarily enlightening communication. The manipulative approach, when dominant and prevailing most of the time, forces the child to develop inappropriate replies which are geared to cope with coercion rather than with information.

a) Satisfies or frustrates other person's material needs:
—Offers to increase pay or threatens to withhold payment

a) Manipulates others predominantly by means of pay-offs, bribes, or cuts in support:
—The father who bribes his son to go to college in his home town

b) Satisfies or frustrates other person's need for group membership:
—Proposes other person for club membership, or threatens to blackball applicant

b) Manipulates others predominantly by the inclusion-exclusion method:
—The parent who says "I will not take you with me because you have not been a good boy"

c) Satisfies or frustrates other person's curiosity and desire for knowledge:
—Offers to share or withholds a secret

c) Manipulates others predominantly by sharing or not sharing secrets:
—The parent who consistently asks the child to leave the room because the topic is not destined for his ears

d) Satisfies or frustrates other person's need for sex:
—Offers or withholds herself as a sex object, "if . . ."

d) Manipulates others by offering or withdrawing sex:
—The wife who handles sex as a commodity and admits her husband after "good behavior"

e) Satisfies or frustrates other person's need for affection:
—Offers encouragement or is critical

e) Manipulates others predominantly by offering or withholding affection:
—The mother who punishes by not talking to the child

f) Satisfies or frustrates other person's need for exhibitionism, limelight, or fame:
—Producer who offers star a big role or threatens to keep her out of the limelight

f) Manipulates the other predominantly by being the audience:
—The mother who watches her child exhibit a temper tantrum

g) Satisfies or frustrates other person's need for abasement or penitence:
—The person who drags the wall-flower into the limelight

h) Satisfies or frustrates the other person's need for fight:
—The challenger or the avoider

i) Satisfies or frustrates the other person's anxiety and need for flight:
—The person who enables the other to escape or, conversely, who admonishes him to stay

g) Manipulates others predominantly by allowing or preventing abasement:
—The mother who fosters apology and abasement

h) Manipulates the other predominantly by allowing or preventing anger:
—The mother who does not allow expression of anger

i) Manipulates others predominantly by allowing or preventing withdrawal:
—The father who forces the child to witness the beating of another child

B-19. *Ways of responding in two-person situations.* There are essentially four ways of relating: informing the other; acknowledging the other's statement; appealing to him; and making mandatory statements which control the other person's actions. While acknowledgment is sought by most people and is appreciated when received, appeal is more coercive, and control, of course, leaves no freedom.

BB-19. *Disturbances.* In two-person situations, the four basic ways of relating—informing, acknowledging, appealing, and commanding—can be qualitatively or quantitatively disturbed.

a) Informing the other:
—You have mail
—The road is blocked
—Johnny is looking for you

a) Absent, distorted, or exaggerated relaying of information:
—Failure of son to inform mother of his stay with a friend
—Telling lies about the origin of a present
—Confabulatory tale of past experiences
—Sending somebody on a wild-goose chase

b) Acknowledgment of the other person's statements:
—Thank you
—I understand
—Yes; no
—There you are!

b) Selective, partial, or absent acknowledgment:
—The selective response: picking up a detail
—The tangential response; response to the unintended part of the statement
—No response: the person who does not answer the door bell

c) Appeal to the other person's needs:
—Would you like to participate?
—Do you want to go to the theater?
—What about lunch?

c) Insistence in or absence of appeal:
—Insistent appeal: the desperate salesman
—The tangential appeal: the student who pesters the teacher with questions when he really wants a job
—Absence of appeal: the person who never wants anything and therefore frustrates the other

d) Control and command of the other person's actions:
—Call me at three o'clock
—Be on time
—Wash your hands
—Will you pass the sugar, please

d) Exaggerated or absent control and command of other:
—Tyranny or complete control
—Control of thought and feeling: attempt to prescribe the other person's feelings
—Lack of limitations; inability to limit plans for possible action or action itself

B-19.1. *The selective response.* Selectivity of reply shapes the exchange of messages inasmuch as each person tends to respond in ways which are individually characteristic. A person's selectivity is in part determined by the nature of the encounter and the type of situation; however, any conversation is subject to continuous change, although in ordinary circumstances the changes are so gradual that the partner is usually quite able to follow. Through such changes, the subject of discourse can be illuminated from various viewpoints, a process which undoubtedly is the greatest asset of interpersonal communication. Depending upon his interests and personality structure, an individual tends to emphasize various aspects of communication.

Selective acknowledgment of:

a) System of codification used:
—Organ language, action language, verbal language

b) Function of communication emphasized:
—Perception, evaluation, transmission

c) Level of abstraction

d) Roles assumed and rules abided by

BB-19.1. *Disturbances.* Although the content of a statement can have a disruptive influence upon communication, more often the formal characteristics of a response and its lack of fit with the initial statement are responsible for disturbances of communication.

a) Exclusive emphasis on or avoidance of a particular system of codification:
—Avoids nonverbal codification

b) Arbitrary emphasis on perception, evaluation, or transmission, regardless of the situation:
—The parent who teaches the child to recite and memorize verses that he does not understand

c) Responds on an entirely different level of abstraction:
—The vague hebephrenic who answers with a fuzzy abstraction the question of where the bus stops
—The organic or confused patient

d) Responds by disobeying rules or not matching roles and thereby changes the existing situation:
—Breaks up conversation by making jokes
—Participates in a game but delights in breaking the rules

e) Emotions:
—Pleasure, anger, anxiety, remorse

e) Responds by not displaying emotions:
—Replies with a logically formulated statement to the other person's display of affection
—The parent who responds with marked detachment to the child's alarm

f) Tempo and rhythm:
—Speed of talking or thinking

f) Responds by unduly or indefinitely delaying answer:
—The catatonic
—The mute

g) Performance, skill

g) Responds with exaggerated emphasis on performance or with disregard for skill:
—The parent who teaches the child to swim at the age of two years
—The parent who does not teach the child any skills

h) Effort, intention, and good will

h) Responds with over- or underemphasis on effort, intention, and good will:
—The parent who responds to the child's good intentions without regard for effect and achievement

i) Effect achieved, accomplishment, success or failure

i) Responds by over- or underemphasis on accomplishment, success, or failure:
—The parent who criticizes the failures of his child but does not reward success
—The parent who rewards the child for selling something worthless to the neighbors

j) Social approach, conformance, and manipulative endeavor

j) Responds with over- or underemphasis on social approaches and manipulative skills:
—The parent who teaches his child to gauge his actions in terms of popularity

k) Appropriacy, fit, and esthetic aspects

k) Responds by stating something that does not correspond to reality:
—The parent who tells the tale of the stork at a time when the child is already informed about childbirth

B-19.2. *Reactions to the other person's way of perceiving-evaluating.* Children are exposed to their parents' methods of perception and evaluation and they tend either to take over these patterns or to react against them. In daily interaction, adults may warm up to each other or become defensive, depending upon the way they react to each other's methods of perception and evaluation.

a) Reacts to the other person's perception-evaluation of esthetic aspects:
—"Isn't this a gorgeous green"

b) Reacts to the other person's perception-evaluation of the "I know how it works":
—"You have to turn this valve . . ."

c) Reacts to the other person's perception-evaluation of emotions:
—"You look tired"

d) Reacts to the other person's perception-evaluation of intellect:
—Reacts to a remark that hits the nail on the head

e) Reacts to the other person's perception-evaluation of social standing, success:
—"He certainly knows how to get elected"

f) Reacts to the other person's perception-evaluation of value judgments:
—"This picture offends a woman's sense of chastity"

g) Reacts to the other person's perception-evaluation of events which might have but did not take place:
—"It could have been better"

BB-19.2. *Disturbances.* When a person not only reacts to the other individual's way of perceiving and evaluating but is actually dependent upon it or violently rebels against it, two-person communication is unlikely to function. Under such circumstances, the individual who rebels becomes dependent upon the person against whom his performance is directed and he may break down when the other person is not around.

a) Is dependent upon or rebels against the other's esthetic sense:
—"You with your eternal interior decoration"

b) Is dependent upon or rebels against the other's evaluation of know-how:
—"You always know better"

c) Is dependent upon or rebels against the other's evaluation of people's emotions:
—"You only care for people's feelings"

d) Is dependent upon or rebels against the other's intellectual interpretations:
—"You may be bright and logical but it doesn't make sense to me"

e) Is dependent upon or rebels against the other's social sense:
—"You and your family prejudices"

f) Is dependent upon or rebels against the other's morality and value judgments:
—"Your sanctimonious judgments"

g) Is dependent upon or rebels against the other's listing of alternatives:
—"What's done is done"

B-19.3. *Reactions to the other person's decision-making and exertion of control.* An individual may show a particular kind of reaction upon observing that the other person has made a decision, implemented it by decisive action, or assumed control of the situation.

a) Reacts with a "yes" or a "no" to the other person's clear-cut, short-term decisions:
—A: "I shall have to leave"
  B: "Okay"

b) Reacts with tolerance and patience to the other person's short-term hesitancy and long-term planning:
—A: "I don't know how to proceed, but I should like to build my own house"
  B: "I will show you the plans of my house"

c) Reacts with identification and submission to the assumption of control by the other person:
—A: "We've got to get out of here—come"
  B: Follows the instructions given by the other person

d) Reacts by making decisions and assuming control in view of failure of the other person:
—A: Yawns, stretches, closes eyes
  B: "I think you had better go to bed now; you are all worn out and tired"

BB-19.3. *Disturbances.* Subtle is the art of opposing, attenuating, or altering the other person's decisions. Those who have not mastered this skill and merely oppose the other person usually aggravate the existing difficulties.

a) Reacts with passive resistance or halfhearted replies to the other person's clear-cut decisions:
—A: "I shall have to leave"
  B: "You should stay longer"

b) Reacts with intolerance or confusion to the other person's hesitancy:
—A: "I don't know how to proceed, but I should like to build my own house"
  B: "You never know anything"

c) Reacts with rebellion to the other person's assumption of control:
—A: "We've got to get out of here—come"
  B: "Go to hell"

d) Reacts with resentment, does not pitch in, and does not compensate for other person's failure:
—A: Yawns, stretches, closes eyes
  B: "Why are you always so tired and worn out when you come to see me?"

B-19.4. *Reactions to the other person's modality of action.* The nonverbal ways of responding to other people's actions can be complementary, identical, opposite, or poorly matched (59).

a) Responds to the other person's activity by complementation:
—Intrusion-inception: the one who bursts in is graciously received
—Marketing: neighbors exchange garden fruits; one gives apples, the other pears

b) Responds to the other person's activity by doing the same:
—Intrusion-intrusion: where he examines her purse, she examines his pockets
—Retention-retention: both wife and husband are tight with money and do not give each other presents

c) Responds to the other person's activity by doing the opposite:
—Retention-riddance: whenever the husband saves, the wife spends lavishly
—Withdrawal-approach: whenever mother lies down for a rest the son plays the trumpet

d) Responds to the other person's ways of acting by doing something that fits halfway:
—Fighting-avoidance: the wife avoids the angry husband
—Output-storage: the birthday present is received and immediately stored away

BB-19.4. *Disturbances.* Disturbances arise when the actions of people clash or when they remain entirely unrelated.

a) Responds to the other person's activity with another activity that produces social conflict:
—Intrusion-elimination: the one who bursts in is thrown out

b) Responds to the other person's activity with duplication, thus setting up destructive competition:
—Intrusion-intrusion: "You barge in on me, I barge in on you."

c) Responds to the other person's activity by doing the opposite:
—Intrusion-avoidance: when a visitor appears at an unexpected hour, goes out the back door

d) Responds to other person's activity by doing something that does not fit:
—Inception-exhibition: the one who is hired and accepted as a janitor proceeds to give a demonstration of his theatrical talents

B-19.5. *Emotional gratification given by replying in different ways.* In two-person situations, replies received are judged not only in terms of the information received but also in terms of the gratification which the acknowledgment provides. The more specific Person B's acknowledgment is and the more it coincides with the anticipations of Person A, the greater is the latter's emotional satisfaction.

a) Fully acknowledges the intent of the sender in terms which are qualitatively and quantitatively satisfactory to him:
—"I do understand" (said with all the necessary nonverbal concomitants)

b) Acknowledges but part of the other person's message, as in a tangential reply; gives the other person partial satisfaction:
—Talking about the sensation of flying: "I have never been in the air myself, but I have some experience with elevators"

c) Acknowledges agreement and disagreement existing between self and other person in terms which are qualitatively and quantitatively satisfactory:
—"I fully support your view, except for one minor point"

d) Postpones reply, but indicates that such will be forthcoming:
—"I cannot give you an answer right now, but I'll write you in the next few weeks"

e) Fully or partially withholds reply, thereby frustrating the other person:
—When asked a question, does not answer at all or answers in an evasive way

BB-19.5. *Disturbances.* Disturbances arise when Person B's way of replying increases the dissatisfaction or anxiety of Person A. This occurs when A is given to understand that what he had in mind has not been understood by B. Under these circumstances, A should disregard what he had in mind and reply to B's new statement. If he does not, but rather persists in pursuing his first intention, communication is likely to be disrupted.

a) Does not acknowledge intent of sender:
—When listening, does not indicate whether he has understood or not

b) Replies in tangential way, without giving any partial acknowledgment:
—Child comes running in from garden after digging for worms and says: "Mommy, I found a worm!" Mother's reply: "Go wash your dirty hands"

c) Does not outline areas of agreement and disagreement:
—"Do you agree with my proposal?" "Yes and no. Let's not waste any more time"

d) Postpones reply indefinitely:
—Does not answer a letter

e) Withholds reply, but lets the other person know he could reply if he wanted to:
—"I'll let you know when the time has come"

B-19.6. *Agreement and disagreement in two-person situations.* Two-person discussions are particularly useful in defining the areas of agreement and disagreement and in exposing and resolving ambiguities.

a) Declaration and question regarding commitment:
—"I am game; what about you?"

b) Statement of ambiguity and outlining of alternatives:
—"There are several routes; which one is the shortest?"

c) Resolution of ambiguity:
—"We have eliminated all alternatives but one"

d) Partial contradiction, forcing the other person to elaborate and interpret further:
—"I agree with your findings but not with your conclusions"

e) Full contradiction, forcing a decision in the other person's mind:
—"Your proposal is not acceptable to me; your plans are contrary to what is considered safe"

f) Counterproposal:
—"I suggest staying home on Sunday and taking off on Monday"

g) Termination:
—"I have had enough; let's go"

h) Postponement:
—"Let me think about it; I will let you know in a few days"

BB-19.6. *Disturbances.* Whenever a discussion increases the existing ambiguity without contributing toward its resolution, disturbances of communication may arise.

a) Declaration increasing ambiguity:
—"I told you what I want, but you seem to avoid the issue"

b) Omission of alternatives, fixating ambiguity:
—"There is nothing you can do but remain at your present job"

c) Ambiguity retained:
—"There is nothing we can do but wait and see"

d) Partial contradiction which increases ambiguity:
—"You have included some incorrect measurements that invalidate your conclusions"

e) Full contradiction which increases ambiguity:
—"I do not believe a word of what you say"

f) Counterproposal that increases ambiguity:
—"What about returning home and starting out anew?"

g) Termination that increases ambiguity:
—"There is no sense in entering this discussion; we will not be able to reach an agreement"

h) Postponement that increases ambiguity:
—"Some other time, please"

B-20. *Learning, teaching, and correction in two-person situations.* The successful teacher is able to perceive cues, to give emotional rewards, to learn from failure, and to express himself in word and action. The personal transmission of cues and the management of rewards determine the outcome of learning by imitation.

a) Prefers to learn from or teach a person who needs arbitrary, simplified cues

b) Prefers to learn from or teach a person who needs complex and subtle cues

c) Prefers to learn from and teach a person who gives and takes personalized attention and emotional reward

d) Prefers to learn from and teach a person who wants only technical guidance without personalized attention

e) Prefers to learn from or teach a person who allows errors and failures, thus emphasizing experience

f) Prefers to learn from or teach a person who is gentle, foresees failures, and avoids painful action

BB-20. *Disturbances.* The pathology encountered in the process of learning and correction is related to the attitude of both the pupil and the teacher. Transmission of erroneous cues, ill-timed rewards, inappropriate setting of limitations, and mismanagement of the personal factor may contribute toward breakdown of interpersonal communication.

a) Inability to use simplified cues in the processes of learning and correction:
—Some schizophrenics

b) Inability to use complex cues in the process of learning and correction:
—Some psychopaths

c) Inability to give or accept emotional rewards:
—Some schizophrenics

d) Inability to give or accept technical guidance:
—Some dependent personalities

e) Inability to learn from or teach a person who is skilled:
—The unintelligent person

f) Inability to learn from or teach a person who is protective of self or others:
—The overprotected child

B-21. *Management of conflicts in two-person situations.* The art of pursuing one end overtly and another covertly is intentionally practiced in politics, but the issue also arises in daily life when an individual's emotional attitudes do not jibe with his actions and his convictions are not expressed in words.

a) Openly supports the person whom he covertly despises and resents

b) Openly opposes the person whom he covertly respects and supports

c) Accepts support from the person whom he covertly despises and resents

d) Accepts rebuff and criticism from the person whom he covertly appreciates and respects

BB-21. *Disturbances.* If an individual's sentiments and emotions do not jibe with his verbal and nonverbal actions, a paradoxical effect is achieved which is perceivable by the other person. Occasional discrepancies per se are not pathological, but when the distortions become systematic, disturbances of communication will arise.

a) Openly supports the person who flatters him but whom he despises:
—The vain, infantile person who caters to human vultures who leave him when his power diminishes or his wealth is exhausted

b) Rebels against the person from whom he expects emotional support:
—The adolescent who returns late from a date but expects to be admired by his mother for his deliberate infraction of the rule to be home by 10 o'clock

c) Asks for and accepts support from the person he hates and despises:
—The juvenile delinquent who asks for protection from the veteran criminal
—The dependent son who accepts support from his frustrating mother

d) Invites cruel treatment and rejection from the person from whom he expects emotional support:
—Young man who tends to criticize his wife's appearance in public finds his pride of ownership hurt, his prestige vis-à-vis other men lowered, and his need for support from his wife frustrated

B-22. *Adaptation and control in two-person situations.* People can be manipulated through a variety of methods which range from complete adaptation to complete control. The effective operator knows exactly when and where to use any of these methods.

a) Exertion of direct power; commanding the other person:
—Officer and private

b) Manipulation of external circumstances; managing the other person diplomatically:
—Planned meeting rigged as a coincidental encounter

c) Stimulating the other person's anticipatory behavior with regard to sex, security, status, income, or approval:
—Making promises

d) Operating through the inhibiting forces inside the other person; mobilizing sense of responsibility, shame, guilt, fear, anxiety:
—Statements such as "You ought to . . ."

e) Seduction into violation of rules to gain control over the other person:
—Seducing a teen-ager to drink

f) Forcing response by initiating action which demands adaptation:
—The prankster

g) Yielding to the other person's desire for control and, through habituation, exerting a countercontrol:
—The person who makes himself indispensable

h) Opposing the other person's desire for control and therefore stimulating the other person's adaptive qualities:
—The domineering woman

BB-22. *Disturbances.* Adaptation or control employed in the wrong situation or at the wrong time can lead to a breakdown of communication. Poor timing and rigidity in switching from adaptation to control characterize the psychiatric patient.

a) Ill-timed command—when the other person is not ready to accept it

b) Ill-timed manipulation—when the other person is not sensitive to the kind of manipulation employed

c) Ill-timed support—when the other person needs independence

d) Ill-timed appeal to inhibitory forces—when there are none in the other person

e) Ill-timed seduction—when the other person is not in the mood

f) Ill-timed initiation of action—when the other person is incapable of responding

g) Ill-timed yielding to control—when adaptation to an ill-conceived plan will bring about failure for all

h) Ill-timed opposition—when cooperation is needed

GROUP PROFILE
or
The Individual's Communicative Behavior
in Group Situations

C-1. *The structure of group situations.*
Groups must have organized systems of
communication if they wish to function; but their organization may be
rigid or flexible, formal or informal.

CC-1. *Disturbances.* People who are
incapable of participating in certain
groups or who seek certain groups to
the exclusion of others are characterized by rigidities which may lead to a
breakdown of communication when
they have to function in those groups
which they have so carefully avoided.

a) Participates in informally organized family and neighborhood
groups:
—Occasionally drops in at neighbors'
for a drink

a) Participation in family group only:
—The feeble-minded child

b) Participates in transitory and spontaneously organized groups:
—The transitory groups developing on
beaches, in bus stations, in hotel lob-
bies, and at bars

b) Participation in transitory groups
only:
—The hobo
—The alcoholic

c) Participates in informal groups that
convene intermittently but over a
period of years:
—Sports groups convening for purposes of fishing or hunting
—Professional gatherings
—Class reunions

c) Participation in groups that seldom
or never convene:
—The hermit

d) Participates in so-called informal
groups which adhere to rigid un-
written rules:
—The debutantes, socialites, and playboys
—The habitués of a bar

d) Participation in social groups only:
—The unidentified, hollow person
whose identity depends on association

e) Participates in rigidly organized
groups:
—Football teams, executive groups,
lodges, professional organizations

e) Participation in rigidly organized
groups only:
—The professional criminal

f) Participates in involuntary groups:
—Prisoner of war, military service,
groups in hospitals and those
formed under the pressure of emergency conditions

f) Participation in groups only when
forced or arranged by others:
—Certain schizophrenics

C-2. *Concurrent participation in several group systems.* An individual may participate in few or many group systems at the same time. Duration of participation and the nature of the groups chosen constitute fairly time-enduring characteristics of the personality.

a) Participates in one group system consistently over a period of years:
—The family man and Jack-of-all-trades

b) Participates in several group systems consistently over a period of years:
—The man with memberships in family, occupational, lodge, and sports groups

c) Frequently changes the various groups in which he participates:
—The newspaper reporter or the anthropologist

d) Does not participate consistently in any group system over a period of years:
—The poet

CC-2. *Disturbances.* Nonparticipation in groups may be dictated by compulsive or phobic character features, while participation may represent an overcompensation for inability to function in two-person situations.

a) Dependent upon one group system:
—The feeble-minded or crippled child

b) Incapable of short-term participation or of change of groups:
—The rigid snob

c) Has to change continuously the various groups in which he participates:
—The hobo
—The social climber

d) Avoids crowds, the presence of which creates anxiety:
—The phobic person
—The catatonic

C-3. *Successive participation in various group systems.* An individual's associations reflect not only his occupation, interests, and ambitions but also those subtle features of his personality which deal with his attitudes toward power, magic, and property.

CC-3. *Disturbances.* Change of group membership, although sometimes a necessity, can become a smokescreen for individual psychopathology. The necessity to stick it out, to stay with the same people, to endure the same conditions can become an unbearable source of frustration; through change and search for participation in new groups, some people can manage their dissatisfaction; and by avoiding prolonged contact in the same setting, they can prevent the expression of hostility.

a) Seeks groups characterized by different status; social climber, social decliner:
—Associates with richer people and those superior in rank, avoiding those who have lesser status, or, conversely, associates with poorer people and those inferior in rank

a) Change of social class as a means of seeking new group identity; perpetual striving results in lack of mastery, and therefore the person frequently becomes marginal:
—Member of "café society"

b) Seeks groups characterized by different ethnic background:
—Associates with foreigners and people with backgrounds different from his own; travels and transcends cultural and racial barriers

b) Change of value system as a means of seeking new group identity in order to repudiate family tradition:
—Religious convert

c) Seeks groups characterized by different ideologies, interests, occupations, and skills:
—Associates with mixed occupational groups; joins associations the membership of which is composed of people from all walks of life

c) Change of interests and occupations in order to prolong the apprenticeship phase and student state, which results in avoidance of more permanent group membership:
—Ph.D., M.D., D.D.S.

d) Seeks groups characterized by purity of membership, ideology, purpose, and goal:
—Associates with exclusive clubs or exclusive professional, sports, or religious groups

d) Change of membership from mixed to pure groups and progressive adherence to dogma and orthodoxy as a means of practicing intolerance and prejudice in the name of a cause:
—The religious fanatic who hides paranoid schizophrenia behind his orthodoxy

e) Seeks groups which are determined by geographical location:
—Associates primarily with neighbors, and when moving to another place seeks new friends in the neighborhood

e) Change of membership in regional groups and change of residence as an expression of the inability to get along with unselected neighbors:
—The quarrelsome neighbor

C-4. *Specialization in group situations.* A person's preference for certain functions may be noticed particularly in group situations because in groups people have a chance to gravitate toward positions of their choice.

a) Participation devoted primarily to observation, and membership in that branch of the organization which deals with input:
—In military service—scouting, reconnaissance, and intelligence
—In warehousing—receiving station
—In radio network—monitor station
—In business—observer of competitors

b) Participation devoted primarily to evaluation, and membership in executive division of an organization:
—In military service—general staff and command
—In warehousing—office
—In radio network—executive, business office
—In business—director, president

c) Participation devoted primarily to transmission, and membership in that branch of the organization which deals with output:
—In military service—combat troops
—In warehousing—shipping department
—In radio network—broadcasting, showroom
—In business—worker

CC-4. *Disturbances.* In group situations, disturbances may arise when individuals are incapable of carrying out their assigned functions or when they do not keep the rest of the organization informed of what they are doing.

a) Inability to function as observer:
—Makes decisions or transmits instead of functioning as receiver
—Does not keep in contact with other parts of the organization that rely on his reports

b) Inability to function in evaluative capacity:
—Perceives or transmits instead of making decisions
—Cannot participate in a decision-making body
—Does not keep other branches of the organization informed of his decisions

c) Inability to function as transmitter:
—Perceives or evaluates instead of transmitting; cannot carry out orders
—Does not keep other branches of the organization informed of the effects of their activities

C-5. *Taking turns in group situations.* In many group situations, people have to take turns—in talking, entering through doors, drinking at a fountain, or waiting for a seat. Preferences develop for certain positions in the serial order.

a) When it is best:
—Perception—observes when there is a display of events
—Evaluation—makes decisions at the right moment
—Transmission—optimal timing of actions

b) First:
—Perception—comes early to get the best seats in movie; wants to be the first to inspect a new situation
—Evaluation—wants to be the first to pass judgment
—Transmission—tries to be the first speaker or the first one to have done something

c) Last:
—Perception—is the last to go and look or listen
—Evaluation—is the last to pass judgment
—Transmission—is the last to move

d) When others do:
—Perception—looks when others look
—Evaluation—when forced to, makes decisions
—Transmission—acts and speaks when others speak up

CC-5. *Disturbances.* Individuals who are incapable of timing their turns can seriously disrupt group communication. These individuals do not rely upon the feedback from the group, lack a sense of fit and closure, and seem to react to some inner sense of timing.

a) When it is worst:
—Perception—when there is nothing to see or when it is too late
—Evaluation—when information is incomplete or antiquated, or when the decision makes no difference
—Transmission—when the action comes too late or when others are not willing to listen

b) First:
—Perception—when his function is to be last, and he is first
—Evaluation—when his function is to wait, and through his premature decision he sets a bad precedent
—Transmission—when he is not supposed to act and fires prematurely

c) Last:
—Perception—when his function would have been to look first
—Evaluation—when his function would have been to set the pace
—Transmission—when he should have acted earlier

d) Out of step with others:
—Perception—he does not perceive when others give the signal
—Evaluation—when he should make decisions by consulting others, he does so alone
—Transmission—when he does not conform to what others do in spite of the fact that conformity might save his life

C-6. *Codification in group situations.*
The media of communication in groups are a function of distance reception—auditory, audio-visual, and visual. The signals thus must be heard or seen, and usually cannot be appreciated by means of the closeness receivers involving touch, smell, taste, vibration, temperature, or pain.

a) Face-to-face situations:
—Informal gatherings
—Planned meetings
—Organized conferences
—Demonstrations

b) Communication by intermediary of machines:
—Movies
—Television
—Radio
—Public-address system
—Telephone

c) Communication by means of pre-arranged signals:
—Smoke signals
—Semaphore, flag, and blinker systems

d) Written communication:
—Letters
—Circulars
—Manuals
—Books
—Announcements
—Pamphlets
—Signs

e) Pictorial and three-dimensional models:
—Paintings
—Drawings
—Photographs
—Maps
—Models
—Posters
—Cartoons

CC-6. *Disturbances.* When physical pathology interferes with the functioning of the distance receivers, the individual's participation in groups is severely restricted. Personality disturbances such as being prejudiced, lacking skills, or suffering from phobias may also interfere with participation in group situations.

a) Is incapable of functioning in or is entirely dependent upon face-to-face encounters:
—The phobic person who is afraid of crowds
—The abnormally shy person

b) Incapable of functioning with the intermediary of machines:
—Some paranoids

c) Incapable of using or dependent upon sign language:
—The blind
—The deaf and dumb

d) Incapable of using or dependent upon written communication:
—The illiterate
—Some aphasics
—Some deaf persons

e) Incapable of using or dependent upon pictorial communication:
—The blind
—The illiterate

C-6.1. *Downward, upward, and horizontal communication.* The channels of communication, the forms of codification, and the structure of the sentence or of the action vary with the direction of the flow of messages within the network.

a) Prefers downward, or centrifugal, flow of messages:
—Gives and takes orders
—Issues and observes directives
—Gives and receives instructions
—Can lead and follows leadership in action

b) Prefers upward, or centripetal, flow of messages:
—Reads and makes reports
—Relies on opinion polls
—Signs and accepts petitions
—Answers and puts questions
—Makes and accepts suggestions

c) Prefers horizontal flow of messages:
—Attends conferences
—Reads and distributes newsletters
—Engages in conversations
—Plays games

CC-6.1. *Disturbances.* Inability to participate in any one of the three fundamental ways of communication—downward, upward, or horizontal—necessarily leads to a disturbance of communication inasmuch as nobody is capable of avoiding these basic directions of communication.

a) Cannot participate in downward, or centrifugal, communication, either as transmitter or as receiver:
—The person with authority problems
—The person who cannot command

b) Cannot participate in upward, or centripetal, communication, either as receiver or as transmitter:
—The person who is incapable of reporting without making judgments
—The person who cannot rely upon someone else's observations

c) Cannot participate in horizontal communication, either as receiver or as transmitter:
—The person who cannot engage in informal discussions in group situations

C-7. *Switch of language in group situations.* During the phases of formation, consolidation, and dissolution of a group, the language used undergoes changes. Both at the beginning and at the end of group formations the language is more unspecific, while at the height of the group organization the language is often highly specialized. The language used has to be appropriate to the task of the moment, and switches in language employed by the participants signal a change in group process. Many groups remain stuck in a certain phase without going on to full development, or they may go through regular cycles in which certain developments are repeated.

As group meeting proceeds, an individual may appropriately introduce:

a) The language of introduction:
—Passes to the order of the day, introducing the major topic or getting ready for the discussion or action

b) The language of getting acquainted:
—In an attempt to strengthen bonds, stretches out feelers to other persons in order to explore their personalities

c) The language of warming up:
—Engages in small talk in order to draw others out and give them a chance to express themselves

d) The language of task orientation:
—After the preliminaries are over, becomes succinct, precise, to the point; avoids unnecessary ornamentation

CC-7. *Disturbances.* When the group changes from one phase of operation to another and an individual does not adapt to the concomitant language change, there can arise disturbances of communication which may interfere with the functioning not only of the individual but also of the group as a whole.

a) Persists in using or does not employ language of introduction:
—Cannot introduce or continuously introduces something new
—Cannot broach gently a delicate or painful subject

b) Persists in using or does not employ language of getting acquainted:
—At times of decision-making, recruits new members
—Upon joining a new group, barges in and behaves as if he had known the others all along

c) Persists in using or does not employ the language of warming up:
—During crucial moments, engages in small talk and delays group
—During warming-up period, presses toward major events

d) Persists in using or does not employ language of task orientation:
—Cannot pipe down; continues to talk about exciting phases of action
—Cannot be succinct, coordinated, brief, and to the point

e) The language of victory:
—After task completion, rejoices and casts off tension

f) The language of fatigue:
—After prolonged discussion or exercise, prepares for adjournment

g) The language of dissolution:
—After task completion, or because task was not accomplished, prepares for breaking up of the group organization

e) Persists in using or does not employ the language of victory:
—Twenty years out of college, behaves as if he had just made the decisive touchdown
—Behaves as if he never would reach the goal, in spite of the fact that the task has been accomplished

f) Persists in using or does not employ the language of fatigue:
—Sounds sleepy and looks tired during all phases of group activity
—Denies fatigue and keeps going in spite of the fact that he can hardly stay awake

g) Persists in using or does not employ the language of dissolution:
—Talks about giving up and leaving even though everything proceeds according to plan
—Cannot talk about giving up or cannot leave a group

C-8. *The individual's view of group relations.* Every leader and, as far as that goes, every member of a group tends to have some pet theories about the nature of group functioning; these may involve small groups or society as a whole.

CC-8. *Disturbances.* Belief in single causation, adherence to one dominant principle of organization, and isolated consideration of certain effects lead to distorted views of group relations which in turn severely handicap communication with people who have different beliefs, follow different principles, and observe different effects.

a) The institutional approach: in this approach, the individual lays primary emphasis on the significance of formal rules in the conduct of group relations:
—Makes regulations, draws organizational charts, establishes procedures. Handles difficulties by conference method

a) The "compulsive, abiding-by-rules" approach:
—Complete faith in the institutional solution of conflicts

b) The personal approach: the person matters; believes that the problem of group relations is bound to the selection of the "best man"
—Handles difficulties in face-to-face talks. Replaces persons in key positions when organization does not function; minimizes rules and regulations

b) The "selling the personality" approach:
—Complete faith in personal factors as determining events

c) The operational approach: in this approach, people's ability to get along with each other is maximized; their personal talents are minimized. Rules and red tape are discarded when they prove to be inefficient

c) The "gimmick" approach:
—Complete faith in operational tricks for the solution of conflicts

d) The marketing approach: here the problem of group relations is viewed as a function of the standard of living: "If you pay enough, you will get a good man"

d) The "money buys anything" approach:
—Dominant belief in man's greed

e) The nondirective approach: "Let things develop and do not interfere. Things will arrange themselves"

e) The "do nothing" approach:
—Belief in man's absolute inability to control anything

f) The efficiency approach: with a means-ends analysis, an attempt is made to treat groups like machines

f) The "production" approach:
—Complete faith that production and quantity of output solve human problems

g) The value-theoretical approach: here the belief prevails that a group will function well provided that it adheres to the "right" kind of values and fights for a "just" cause

h) The equipment and opportunity approach: in this approach, it is believed that if all members are properly equipped and if they take advantage of the strategic moment and of the opportunities offered, nothing can stand in their way

g) The moralistic approach:
—Dominant belief in the dichotomous labeling of events in terms of good and bad

h) The materialistic approach:
—Complete faith in the solution of human problems through material things

C-9. *Preferences for in- or outgroups.*
Participation with outgroups is largely dependent upon a person's mastery of value systems different from those of his own group, while operation with ingroups is a function of the skill in manipulation and control of people (9).

a) Operates primarily with ingroups, thus relying upon implicit rules, knowledge of contexts, and distribution of roles:
—Member of an exclusive club
—Administrator of an organization
—The labor leader

b) Operates primarily with outgroups, thus relying upon explicit rules, explanations, instructions, and roles:
—The career diplomat
—The police officer
—The public relations man

c) Operates primarily with mixed and transitional groups, thus relying either upon cultural provisions for dealing with strangers or upon individualistic arrangements:
—The innkeeper
—The priest
—The artist
—The psychiatrist

CC-9. *Disturbances.* Inability to operate either with the ingroup or with the outgroup manifests itself in anxiety when participation is required. In order to avoid these unpleasant reactions, such people usually restrict themselves to groups with which they feel at ease or avoid groups altogether.

a) Cannot operate with ingroups because of intolerance of similarities:
—The person with hostility against self and anybody who resembles self
—The unidentified person who does not know where he belongs
—The person who always has to be different in order to maintain self-respect

b) Cannot operate with outgroups because of intolerance of differences:
—The racially, religiously, or politically prejudiced person
—The person who never came in contact with strangers
—The person who always has to be like others

c) Cannot operate with mixed groups because of inability to deal with general human features:
—The person who cannot be simple
—The person who cannot recognize common denominators

C-10. *Task orientation in group situations.* The task of an action group or the topic of a discussion group can be conceived of in a variety of terms.

a) Problem orientation: defines the problem, formulates principles, specifies implementations; takes a long-term view and is not easily distracted from his problem. Whatever furthers the mastery of his task he accepts; whatever interferes, he rejects:
—Discusses and works on problems of immunity against poliomyelitis virus

b) Program orientation: concerned with the program that will implement his chosen goal:
—Promotes inoculation of children with Salk vaccine

c) Project orientation: concerned with a concrete, short-term detail which fits into either problem or program orientation
—Tests virulence of a particular virus

d) Organization orientation: interested in establishing, maintaining, and controlling organization that is dedicated to a program or project:
—Administers a scientific organization

e) Terminal orientation: concerned with finishing the job quickly in order to cash in on success in terms of money, honor, or popularity, or just to get it over with:
—Finishes the project quickly

CC-10. *Disturbances.* Task orientation can be distorted in several ways: by too-rigid pursuit; by a lack of application; or by disturbing the equilibrium of the group.

a) The distortion of problems:
Disregards all other problems or is incapable of pursuing the task for any length of time:
—The political screwball
—The scatterbrain
—The monomanic theorist

b) The programmatic distortion:
Overevaluates or disregards the impact of the program in question:
—The hygiene fanatic

c) The distortion of projects:
Overemphasizes a particular project:
—The "Rube Goldberg" inventor

d) The organizational distortion:
Reduces all problems to questions of human organization:
—The narrow-minded organizer
—Some hypomanic patients

e) The attitude of liquidation:
Reduces all issues to the problem of how to liquidate them:
—The tyrant executioner

C-10.1. *The change of tasks in group situations.* The task of an action group or the topic of a discussion group can be pursued, changed, or interfered with. Most individuals develop characteristic habits in changing their own and other people's goals.

a) Sticks to stated task or topic: personal interests, private considerations and undercurrents are disregarded:
—The dedicated person

b) Changes stated task or topic: personal interests, private considerations, and undercurrents are disregarded:
—The reformer

c) Disregards stated task or topic: introduces private considerations; undercurrents become dominant:
—The self-centered person
—The seeker of personal power

d) Does not have a task or topic of his own: relies upon its emergence in the group gathering:
—The collectively oriented person
—The passive administrator

e) Has secret task or topic and prevents emergence and crystallization of publicly stated task or topic:
—The politician

CC-10.1. *Disturbances.* Both goal-seeking and goal-changing behavior ensure survival, but for a given situation the appropriacy of each is often difficult to assess. People who are too rigid or too flexible and those who do not know when to be stubborn and when to be adaptive are likely to contribute to disturbances of group communication.

a) The fanatic orientation: sticks to stated task, even at the risk of losing his life

b) The overfacile orientation: in circumstances that require goal-changing behavior, is so versatile that others are unable to follow him:
—The irresponsible psychopath

c) The self-centered orientation: instead of sticking to task, maximizes secondary issues which are of personal concern to him:
—The autistic person

d) Dependent orientation: relies upon group guidance and support; not attached to any particular person; adheres to group dogma and techniques:
—The political radical

e) Subversive orientation: distracts people from what they set out to accomplish; eventually introduces new goals to replace established goals:
—The troublemaker

C-11. *The management of discourse in group situations.* Asking for, agreeing to, disagreeing with, giving, and withholding information constitute the principal methods of management of discourse in a group.

CC-11. *Disturbances.* An individual's inability to engage in satisfactory discourse in group situations is characterized by rigid adherence to one kind of procedure, its use at an inappropriate moment, undue persistence, or absence of participation.

a) Orientation:
—Either gives orientation and information through repeating, clarifying, and confirming or asks for orientation, information, repetition, and confirmation

a) Disturbances in orientation: cannot appropriately give or ask for orientation

b) Evaluation:
—Gives opinion, evaluates, analyzes, and expresses feelings and wishes or asks for opinion, evaluation, analysis, or expression of feeling

b) Disturbances in evaluation: cannot appropriately express opinions or ask for opinions

c) Instruction:
—Gives or asks for direct suggestions, directions, and possible ways of action

c) Disturbances in instruction: cannot appropriately give or ask for precise instructions

d) Clarification:
—Asks for amplification, deletion, or repetition

d) Disturbances in clarification: cannot appropriately give or ask for additional information

e) Correction:
—Asks for modification of report or corrects erroneous information

e) Disturbances in correction: cannot appropriately correct others or ask to be corrected

f) Closure:
—Prepares, ramifies, or summarizes comments made so far and brings episode to an end

f) Disturbances in closure: cannot terminate, summarize, or bring to an end a conversation or action; cannot ask others to do so; or does so at an inappropriate moment

g) Agreement:
—Either agrees, shows passive acceptance, understands, and concurs; or disagrees, shows passive disagreement, formally rejects, or withholds information

g) Disturbances in agreement: cannot reach active or passive agreement or reaches agreements when they are against his interests and the interests of the group

h) Disruption:
—Dominates by introducing a new and unrelated topic, changing the subject, going off on a tangent

h) Disturbances in disruption: cannot appropriately disrupt discussions or introduce new topic

i) Illustration:
—Relates own experience and tells anecdotes

i) Disturbances in illustration: does not cite appropriate examples

j) Interpretation:
—Defines topic of discourse and connects it with other information

k) Exchange:
—Considers group as a forum for give-and-take, deliberation, practice, and exercise

l) Service:
—Puts himself at the disposal of the group, offering his active services without concern for whether or not he is going to be in control

m) Orders:
—Gives or asks for mandatory or discretionary orders

n) Warnings:
—Gives or asks for warnings. Goes on record to have said . . .

j) Disturbances in interpretation: cannot appropriately connect several apparently independent pieces of information

k) Disturbances in exchange: does not enter into an exchange of views; is afraid to reveal himself

l) Disturbances in rendering service: cannot make himself available for group purposes

m) Disturbances in giving or taking orders: cannot assume command or cannot submit to orders

n) Disturbances in warning: cannot heed warnings or warn others

C-12. *Interpretative devices in group situations.* Correct use of metacommunicative instructions is of importance in group situations because correction of erroneous interpretations through interpersonal feedback cannot be relied upon. The speaker or actor must express himself in such a way that he is understood right away if he wishes to prevent a breakdown of communication.

Instructions given through:
a) Location and physical props:
—Uniforms and lapel buttons
—Position at speakers' table

b) Atmosphere:
—When everybody is primed through circumstances as to what to expect; the emergency

c) Rules:
—Announcement of explicit rules
—Banking on knowledge of implicit rules

d) Roles:
—The speaker
—The chairman
—The host

e) Explicit instructions:
—Briefing of a crew

f) Implicit instructions:
—Through formality of gathering, informal talk may be banned

CC-12. *Disturbances.* Messages have to be interpreted if they are to be understood. Thus, upon receipt of a message, most people look for metacommunicative clues and, when these are missing or are misleading, disturbances of communication must arise.

Misinterpretation in group situations can occur through:
a) Misleading physical props:
—The prankster who turns street signs
—Camouflage in warfare
—The impostor

b) Misleading atmosphere:
—When the tone is not set

c) Inappropriate rules:
—When rules are made that cannot be kept
—When rules are such as to interfere with the correction of information

d) Misleading roles:
—Criminals, spies

e) Misleading explicit instructions:
—When rules are not made explicit
—When false instructions are given

f) Misleading implicit instructions:
—When implications are made that are not backed up by subsequent action

C-13. *Preferred atmospheres in group situations.* The general tone and spirit that govern group situations largely determine the communicative exchange. Therefore, people seek and react to certain atmospheres more than to others.

a) The dedicated atmosphere as it exists in religious orders or athletic teams

b) The exploratory atmosphere as it exists on expeditions or in scientific teams

c) The existential atmosphere as it exists in groups that accept what the moment brings

d) The recreational atmosphere as it exists at a picnic

e) The defiant atmosphere as it exists at fraternity hazings

f) The apprehensive atmosphere as it exists in the waiting room of a hospital or in a landing barge before an attack

g) The stifled atmosphere as it exists in groups where nothing happens

h) The factional atmosphere as it exists in groups that are sharply split

i) The cozy atmosphere as it exists in certain inns, clubs, ski huts, or boat cabins

j) The emergency atmosphere as it exists at the site of a train wreck

CC-13. *Disturbances.* A disturbing atmosphere develops when several people with similar psychopathology convene; when the spirit of the participants induces them to go beyond the tolerance limits; or when frustrating circumstances are brought about which were not foreseen. Under all these conditions, the communicative exchange with the outgroup is interrupted and the communication within the group is severely impaired.

a) The fanatic atmosphere:
—When several paranoids convene

b) The temporary atmosphere:
—When adventurers convene

c) The atmosphere of resignation:
—When defeatists spread their attitude

d) The "festival out of hand" atmosphere:
—When stimulated people become destructive

e) The subversive atmosphere:
—When rebels convene

f) The "expect the worst" atmosphere:
—When pessimists and nihilists convene

g) The atmosphere of hopelessness:
—When disillusioned and depressed people cease to struggle

h) The hostile atmosphere:
—When resentful people convene

i) The overprotective atmosphere:
—When fearful people convene

j) The catastrophic atmosphere:
—When exhausted, sick, wounded, and anxious people are thrown together

C-14. *Observation of rules in group situations.* In group situations there exist two sets of rules: the printed rules and the unprinted rules. People who function well are informed about both; but there are others who rely more on one kind of rules than upon another, and some are altogether oblivious to the existence of certain rules.

a) Meticulously observes and supports all rules, traditions, and procedures:
—The full-fledged participant at the peak of his group interest

b) Meticulously observes and supports the explicit rules and neglects the implicit ones:
—The one unfamiliar with tradition
—The newly arrived person

c) Meticulously observes and reacts to the implicit rules and neglects the explicit ones:
—The one who is overconcerned with tradition
—The aristocrat who neglects the literal and explicitly stated

d) Does not pay special attention to either explicit or implicit rules:
—Is unconcerned with rules, tradition, procedure, and precedent

CC-14. *Disturbances.* Disturbances of communication arise when one or more participants use rules which differ from those applied by the remaining participants. Variant usage of explicit rules brings about controversy; variant usage of implicit rules results in misinterpretation of messages because of change in the metacommunicative context.

a) Introduces radical changes in rules that seriously upset group organization:
—Criminals
—Invaders

b) Introduces radical changes in explicit rules:
—Uses new rules while others are adhering to old ones
—Creates opposition on the level of ideological discourse

c) Introduces radical changes in implicit rules:
—Violates tradition
—Creates confusion through misunderstanding

d) Does not care for either implicit or explicit rules:
—The self-centered, autistic person

C-15. *The choice of roles in group situations.* Not every person is free to choose situations for which he is best suited. This is particularly true of group situations where people have to adapt to roles that are assigned to them or into which they are pushed by force of circumstance. An individual's personal choice of certain roles thus is dependent upon the kind of roles others assume. The greater the number of participants the greater the variety of roles into which an individual can fit, but the smaller the chance to play a prominent role.

a) Spectator: the role of observer without active participation

b) Chronicler: the role of historian

c) Interpreter: the role of translator and clarifier of statements made by the leader or other members

d) Leader: the role of decision-maker, initiator, and guide

e) Reinforcer: the role of watchdog, controller, and reminder of rules

f) Arbitrator: the role of peacemaker who gives "to each his own," who favors compromises, and who emphasizes the features in common

g) Devil's advocate: the role of agent citing the worst, the opposite, the extreme eventuality

h) Spokesman: the role of speaker formulating the majority or minority opinion, expressing what "some of us feel"

i) Rebel: the role of leader of a revolt against the "powers that be"

CC-15. *Disturbances.* When people assume roles which interfere with the task orientation of the group, the distribution of complementary roles, and the equilibrium of the group, they disturb the corrective feedback and therefore contribute to the breakdown of communication.

a) Voyeur: passive spectatorship where active participation is called for

b) The archreactionary: cites prudence and invokes tradition to explain the present situation

c) Simplifier: in order to make information available to many, obliterates discriminatory cues and reduces complex problem to simple alternatives

d) The tyrant: with his ideas of grandeur, believes himself able to control others but actually leads himself and others to destruction

e) The obstructionist: regardless of the situation, interferes with the actions of self and others

f) The equalizer: promises each participant whatever he wants

g) The prophet of evil: forecasts failure

h) The self-appointed spokesman: believes to speak for the others

i) The activator: regardless of appropriacy, prematurely triggers the group into action

j) Objector: the role of passive opponent (nonverbal) or active critic

j) The satirist and sarcast: makes caricatures out of serious problems

k) Protector: the role of helper who comes to the aid of the leader or any other member who is threatened

k) The overprotector: does not believe in other people's stamina

l) Handyman: the role of assistant, doing the dirty work and assuming disagreeable tasks

l) The slave and scapegoat: assumes blame and accuses himself of wrongdoing

m) Worker: the role of working bee; getting things done and exerting himself for the benefit of the group

m) The martyr: exposes himself unnecessarily

n) Loyalist: the role of conservative sticking to the aims of the group, collaborating, and occasionally opposing, depending upon the situation

n) The blind follower: dependent upon group membership, does not dare to assert himself

o) Trouble-shooter: the role of expediter, filling gaps and assuming other roles where necessary

o) The chameleon: can assume any function and subscribe to any opinion, but has no "color" of his own

p) Usurper: the role of active contender for leadership

p) The assassin: to achieve, engages in character and political assassination

q) Prosecutor: the role of investigator and prosecuting attorney

q) The inquisitor: accuses without evidence and probes into problems without proper jurisdiction

C-15.1. *Preferences for family roles.*
On many occasions, people's roles can best be described in terms of membership in an actual or hypothetical family. These roles depict actual practices existing in a given family or connote communicative behavior of a particular individual in family-like situations.
Prefers roles of:

a) Father — Mother

b) Brother — Sister

c) Son — Daughter

d) Husband — Wife

e) Grandfather — Grandmother

f) Uncle — Aunt

CC-15.1. *Disturbances.* Whenever people assume roles which do not fit the actual circumstances, such as married people behaving like mother and son or brother and sister behaving like lovers, a breakdown in communication is liable to occur.

a) Distorted father or mother roles:
—The father who is not fatherly
—The paternal employer
—The overprotective mother
—The maternal wife

b) Distorted brother or sister roles:
—The sibling who behaves like a parent
—The competitive sibling

c) Distorted son or daughter roles:
—The self-sacrificing daughter
—The son who abandons his parents

d) Distorted mate roles:
—The mate as sibling
—The mate as rival

e) Distorted grandparent roles:
—The grandparent who assumes parental role

f) Distorted aunt or uncle roles:
—The avuncular role conceived as role of clown

C-15.2. *Roles of decision-makers.* The leaders of groups can be characterized by the way in which they make decisions (234).

a) The integrator: he has the skill to recognize common denominators in conflicting approaches and to organize intellectually

b) The innovator: he may be variously, a rebel, a risk-taker, or an original thinker; he is likely to press toward the limits of his competence; he may also seek to redefine situations or to focus the activities of the group

c) The traditionalist: he is the conservative counterpart of the innovator and a saver of long-standing habits of procedure and thought; his actions contribute to a slowing up of change and to perpetuation of approaches

d) The literalist: he insists on a strict and narrow interpretation of rules; in perceiving only the major essentials of situations or problems, he usually has a passion for unadorned facts. He is willing to deal only with specific problems rather than with generalities

e) The power-seeker: the upward-mobile official may violate procedural norms and take public stands on policy issues if these serve his purpose. He is likely to overestimate his competence and to personalize his official relationships, even if it means to depart from customary procedure

f) The career servant: he maintains a conscientious attitude with respect to his role limitations. He is likely to identify himself with a concrete group, and he has a strong sense of his mission

CC-15.2. *Disturbances.* People who work in the communication center of a system and act as decision-makers have more influence upon the system than people who work at the periphery of the network. Distortions in decision-making—either willful or due to psychopathology—can contribute to disintegration of the group.

a) The theorist who integrates diversified approaches but neglects personality factors; disintegration of group occurs because personality factors are not attended to

b) The screwball innovator who perceives something new but pushes it too fast, does not inform the group of his thoughts, and soon is without a following

c) The conservative obstructionist whose function seems to be to keep the group in its status quo resting on past achievements

d) The red-tape specialist who issues innumerable memos; disintegration of the group occurs because of emphasis upon detail

e) The opportunistic dictator who does not shun any method to get ahead and then discards whatever and whoever does not suit his purpose

f) The devoted slave who belittles his own role but magnifies the organization in whose service he stands

C-15.3. *The choice of persons addressed in group situations.* The larger the number of people in a group the less there is an opportunity to talk or to reply to all the participants. Selectivity, therefore, has to occur, and individuals tend to show consistent choices as to whom they address in a group gathering.

a) Addresses group as a whole

b) Addresses all people in turn

c) Addresses subfactions of the group

d) Addresses or maneuvers to be addressed by the titular officer of the group

e) Addresses or maneuvers to be addressed by the de facto leader of the group

f) Addresses or maneuvers to be addressed by the person who has the most or least information on a subject

g) Addresses or maneuvers to be addressed by the person with the highest or lowest status

h) Addresses or maneuvers to be addressed by the most active or the most passive person

i) Addresses or maneuvers to be addressed by the spokesman for the majority or the opposition

CC-15.3. *Disturbances.* People afflicted with psychopathology do not possess the flexibility and the freedom necessary for the management of a given situation. In addressing a group or members of a group, they will turn to those persons they feel most at ease with and not to the persons who matter at the moment.

a) In addressing a group, does not respond to questions of individuals but reacts to his own notion of the group as a whole

b) In addressing a group, cannot talk to all at once but must address all people or subgroups in turn

c) In addressing a group talks to one subfaction only, in neglect of other members

d) In addressing a group, always turns to or manages to be noticed by its titular officers and disregards the rest of the organization

e) In addressing a group, regularly turns to or manages to be noticed by the de facto heads and decision-makers in disregard of the titular heads and other members

f) In addressing a group, regularly turns to or manages to be noticed by the cream or the scum of the group, therefore pitching his talk away above or below the level of understanding of the majority

g) In addressing a group, regularly selects or manages to be noticed by persons who are implemental in change of status

h) In addressing a group, regularly selects or manages to be subservient to the most active or most passive persons, neglecting other members

i) In addressing a group, regularly turns to or manages to be noticed by the majority or the minority leader, disregarding his own supporters

j) Addresses or maneuvers to be addressed by the persons who are off key: sexy, drunk, or peeved

j) In addressing a group, regularly turns to or manages to be noticed by misfits and tends to be concerned with them in disregard of the other members

C-15.4. *Switch from passive to active participation.* In group situations, a special technique is required to get the floor or to be noticed.

a) Interrupts others in the middle of sentences or activities

b) Introjects at crucial moments when speaker catches breath or pauses briefly, or comments during recess

c) Waits until others have finished their sentence or action and then begins to speak or act

d) Does not participate actively but comments nonverbally or whispers to others, sufficiently to be noticed but without altering the manifest course of events

e) Does not participate actively but watches or listens only

CC-15.4. *Disturbances.* When people want to assert themselves, inability to obtain the floor, disdain for others, self-concern, and fear are responsible for a variety of disturbances.

a) Disrupts formal talk or ceremony; has to be restrained by force

b) Introjects at intermission, accosts people out in the hall, but cannot comment openly in groups when the subject comes up

c) Waits too long to speak, gets up at the last minute, primarily because he has no technique to obtain the floor

d) Makes noises, grimaces, or becomes otherwise distracting without contributing anything

e) Does not participate at all; is withdrawn

C-15.5. *The mode of speaking in group situations.* The ways of addressing other members of the group or the group as a whole may vary.

a) Makes a few brief, to-the-point remarks

b) Makes brief but irrelevant remarks

c) Makes same remarks over and over while speaking, and repeats them in later discussions

d) Makes long speeches, rambles on, and wanders off the subject matter

e) When called upon to speak, declines

CC-15.5. *Disturbances.* Disturbances in the communicative behavior of the speaker occur when he acts contrary to general expectations, when he says too much or too little, or when his expressions are unintelligible.

a) Makes brief, too-pointed remarks; violates good taste or talks about the unmentionable

b) Makes brief, confused, and unintelligible remarks

c) Makes redundant observations; remarks always on the obvious, often as if it were new

d) Makes long, vague speeches which nobody is able to follow; substitutes quantity for quality

e) When expected to say something, fumbles, stutters, hesitates, and finally sits down without having said anything

C-16. *Responses to quantitative variations in intensity in group situations.* There are people who seek intense experiences, be they in church, on the sports field, in politics, or at war. There are others who can function better in groups when their experiences remain relatively low in intensity.

a) Stimulates or seeks intense experiences:
—Uses material symbols to heighten dramatic effect
—Appeals to people's emotions
—Participates in emotionally loaded gatherings

b) Avoids or prevents intense experiences:
—Strips situation of material symbols
—Appeals to reason
—Participates in gatherings of low emotional pitch

c) Utilizes intense experiences to stimulate group to perform to the limit:
—Seeks groups with high morale
—The coach who utilizes threat of defeat to get the best out of the team

d) Utilizes experience of low stimulus value to reduce group to inactivity:
—Seeks group with low morale
—Brings up boring suggestions in order to have decision postponed

CC-16. *Disturbances.* Too-high or too-low intensity can exert a disintegrating influence upon groups and their members. Communication then ceases to function and groups may dissolve. In contrast to fluctuations in intensity in intentional or political maneuvering, disturbances of intensity due to psychopathology are not volitional in nature.

a) Incites intense experience:
—Extreme destructiveness
—The juvenile delinquent
—The incitor to riot

b) Stifles intense experience:
—Expresses extreme boredom
—Uses abstract discourse without proper reference to real events

c) Uses intense experience to get more out of the group than it can give:
—Troops driven into defeat because of previous exhaustion

d) Dilutes experience to demoralize group:
—The leader who induces everybody to quit because of his own inactivity
—The fearful, ineffectual teacher

C-17. *Position of self in relation to others.* Almost all people express preferences for certain physical arrangements which in part are dependent upon the functions and roles they assume in groups. Some wish to be seen; others try to be inconspicuous. Some desire to be near a certain person; others want to be far away. In placing themselves in certain spots and in timing their arrival and departure, people use a particular kind of environmental manipulation which is designed to control their human relations.

a) Timing and location for establishing or avoiding contacts:
—Location near entrances and exits where a maximum of people walk by
—Location behind a column, so as to be seen by few
—Arrival at the peak of traffic at a party

b) Timing and location for survey, spectatorship, and exhibition:
—Scanning social situations from a distance
—Waiting for people to pass by
—Location chosen to show self in all splendor

c) Timing and location for purpose of control or its avoidance:
—Sitting at the official table or near the executive in order to display importance and power
—Appearance at critical, decision-making moments

CC-17. *Disturbances.* People frequently utilize groups for enacting some of their pathology. This has been particularly true of dictators, kings, and religious leaders who were in a position to live out their pathology by influencing groups. Without the innocent bystander, who gets drawn into such a scheme and becomes an unwitting participant, such action often would be impossible.

a) Timing and location for seeking contact or withdrawal:
—Inability to be alone—the anxious person
—Inability to tolerate the presence of others—certain kinds of schizophrenic patients
—Fear of crowds

b) Timing and location for exhibition and spectatorship contrary to custom:
—The voyeur who watches sexual activities
—The arsonist who gazes at the fire; historically, the Roman emperor Nero who allegedly burned Rome
—The exhibitionist who exposes his genitals

c) Timing and location for power struggle or resignation:
—The argumentative intruder
—The paranoid person
—The passive-submissive person, resigned character who never struggles for power and avoids arousing attention
—Historically, such dictators as Hitler and Napoleon

d) Timing and location for establishing competition and opposition:
—Going to the same place as the rival
—Appearing at a strategic moment in order to detract attention from rival

e) Random location and timing:
—Going with the stream, relying upon luck, seeing what is going to happen with no special purpose in mind

d) Timing and location for establishing abnormal competition or opposition:
—The competitive character who competes even though this is against his interests
—Opposing for opposing's sake: obstructing meetings, suing or accusing people and making their lives miserable

e) Timing and location for purpose of avoiding any commitment:
—The drifter
—The hobo

C-18. *Appealing in group situations.* Initiation of communication within a group network has to rely upon some leverage other than personal gratification. In administrative communication, messages are exchanged in pursuit of an official duty within an organization in which the role system may be highly specialized. In positional communication, the roles of the participants are unknown, but stations are assumed to be manned by people. This type of communication is used primarily for exchanges of messages which occur seldom and sporadically, and where role differentiation can hardly be expected. In personal communication, finally, an interpersonal appeal is made in a group situation (191).

a) Prefers administrative communication:

—Relies upon the organization's official communication channel to transmit a message. Leverage obtained through internal control devices of organization: a waiter giving the chef an order for a customer

b) Prefers positional communication:

—Relies upon impersonal, station-to-station calls to transmit messages. Leverage obtained through appeal to a presumedly responsive person: to the officer in charge; to the oldest member of the group; to the first to arrive

CC-18. *Disturbances.* Application of any of the three forms of communication to situations where it does not apply, inability to use such a form of communication, or consistent adherence to it can lead to disturbances of communication.

a) Applies administrative communication in situations where no prearranged group organization exists; exclusively utilizes administrative communication; or does not know how to function in an administrative setup:

—Person who attempts to organize unrelated people into a team

—People who cannot function in an organization

b) Applies positional communication to situations where people have well-defined roles or are even known by name; or is incapable of using positional communication or uses it exclusively:

—A patient who addresses a letter "to the doctor in charge" after he has been in an institution for six months and knows everybody by name

—Patient who is incapable of accepting substitute nurse when regular nurse is off duty

c) Prefers personal communication:
—Relies upon person-to-person calls to transmit messages. Addresses people by name and tailors messages to fit the individual addressee. Leverage obtained through interpersonal gratification

c) Applies personal communication to situations where personal matters should be ignored; or does not know how to be personal or is so most of the time:
—Patient who expects special rules from doctor because they "get along so well"
—Patient who pretends not to recognize doctor on the street

C-19. *Ways of responding when addressed.* If in a group situation the individual is given the floor, asked a question, or spoken to, he has various ways of responding.

CC-19. *Disturbances.* Disturbances of communication arise when a participant disregards the existence of the group and its goals. He may express this attitude by treating the group situation as a two-person situation, by not responding, or by monopolizing the discussion. Group functioning and goal orientation require a frustration tolerance which many people afflicted with psychopathology do not possess.

When called upon or addressed in public:
a) Says what is on his mind to the best of his ability

When called upon or addressed in public:
a) Blushes, fumbles, stutters; cannot find his words and leaves the audience embarrassed and disappointed

b) Says what the one who asked him wants to hear or particularly does not want to hear

b) Reduces the group situation to a dialogue between the one who asks the questions and himself

c) Says what the leader wants to hear or particularly does not want to hear

c) Takes the opportunity to turn the issue into an accusation or seduction of the leader

d) Says what is popular and the crowd wants to hear, or what is unpopular and the crowd does not want to hear

d) Takes the opportunity to make a propaganda or political speech

e) Tries to please all

e) Responds in an avoidant manner; evades the issue and refuses to commit himself

C-19.1. *Ways of responding when action is called for.* Children learn group functioning first in terms of action and only later in terms of discussions and conferences. In adult life, group functioning usually consists of a combination of action and verbal behavior. In the course of events an individual may be asked to act on behalf of the group, and he may discharge this obligation in a variety of ways.

a) Carries out action as suggested:
—The cooperative, reliable person

b) Carries out action in a way which may differ from the suggested one:
—The research worker

c) Carries out action in a careless and negligent manner:
—The lazy and uninterested person

d) Acknowledges need but does not carry out action:
—The person who wants to postpone action without arousing antagonism

e) Carries out action in a way which goes beyond what is expected:
—The hero who is dedicated to the group

f) Carries out another action altogether but achieves the same goal:
—The resourceful person

CC-19.1. *Disturbances.* When called upon to act, people can respond in several different ways, provided their action implements the goal of the group. If their action does not support the task at hand, group functioning becomes disorganized and breakdown of communication occurs.

a) Does not carry out action as suggested:
—The catatonic person

b) Substitutes for the suggested action another action that does not fit:
—Schizophrenic girl when told to dress up for a social occasion puts on a bathing suit

c) Is incapable of carrying out action:
—The mentally deficient person

d) Mistakes words for action; promises to carry out action, talks about it, but does nothing:
—The playboy who promises to go to work

e) Is perfectionistic and spends too much time and effort on insignificant details:
—The compulsive person

f) Carries out another action altogether and does not achieve the stated goal:
—Some psychopaths
—The autistic person

C-20. *Learning and cooperation in the group.* The intricacies of group participation are learned over a period of many years, in which dominance and submission, individualism and group consideration, opposition and cooperation are mastered.

a) Plays or works side by side with others:
—The nursery school child
—The unskilled worker

b) Interacts and cooperates with others for short periods of time:
—The first-grader
—The semiskilled worker

c) Assumes specialized roles and participates in teamwork:
—The sixth-grader
—The skilled worker in an occupational team

d) Assumes leadership position and responsibility for group:
—The senior in high school and college
—The officer
—The foreman
—The labor leader

CC-20. *Disturbances.* The severity of the patient's mental disturbance is frequently reflected in his ability to participate in groups; the more severe the disease the less the patient is able to participate. Thus, one finds a sliding scale ranging from patients with catatonic schizophrenia and brain disease with no group participation to patients with personality disorders whose difficulties are revealed in inability to assume certain specialized functions.

a) Incapable of group participation other than working side-by-side:
—Psychotic patients in occupational therapy

b) Incapable of group participation for longer than a few minutes:
—The schizophrenic patient who on rare occasions helps in cleaning up

c) Incapable of assuming specialized roles and participating in a team:
—The compulsive patient whose perfectionism interferes with the timing of the team

d) Incapable of assuming leadership and responsibility for group:
—The psychoneurotic patient whose self-centeredness prevents him from assuming responsibility for the group

C-20.1. *Criteria of effective communication in group situations.* The larger a group the slower the feedback and the greater the necessity to prepare messages in terms of language, content, audience, and timing. Any one of the following aspects may be emphasized more than another.

a) Appropriacy:
—Uses language tailored to the situation: optimal length of message, relevant details, and appropriate vocabulary

b) Simplicity:
—Uses clear language, cites examples, avoids verbiage

c) Consistency:
—Uses language to match action; enforcement and exceptions are unambiguously stated

d) Timing:
—Transmits messages at the right moment and informs others when information has become obsolete

e) Distribution:
—Sees to it that messages reach the desired audience

f) Delivery:
—Formulation and articulation of statement in terms of speaking, writing, or signaling is appropriate

CC-20.1. *Disturbances.* Ineffectiveness of communication is more apparent in groups than in two-person situations because the audience as a whole cannot very well steer the communicator and help him along. Enlightening feedback is dependent upon individuals who speak from the audience; but when this happens, speakers affected by psychopathology usually feel more rattled than helped.

a) Uses language incompatible with the situation:
—Makes long-winded explanations where brevity is required
—Omits mentioning strategic details
—Uses vocabulary that is either too general or too technical

b) Uses vague, obscure, or complicated language:
—Uses officialese, federalese, or gobbledygook
—Oversimplifies or talks in outline form

c) Uses language inconsistently:
—Sentences contradict each other
—Exceptions are not noted
—Statements that purport to report facts are not distinctly separated from those that denote opinions or commands

d) Timing of messages is inappropriate:
—Says things too early or too late
—Does not amend or retract messages or does not prepare people for what is to come

e) Distribution of messages and choice of audience is inappropriate:
—Does not reach the "right" people
—Talks over the head of the audience

f) Delivery is inappropriate:
—Talks too loudly, too softly, too long, or too briefly
—Mumbles, or writes illegibly

C-21. *Management of conflicts in group situations.* Some people develop consistent ways in which to manage conflicts with other participants or with the group as a whole. These vary with their needs for security, their desire for leadership, and their exhibitionistic tendencies.

a) Conforms to or opposes the majority opinion and sentiment

b) Conforms to or opposes the minority opinion and sentiment

c) Has noncommittal, stand-by-and-wait attitude toward majority and minority opinion and sentiment

d) Voices solitary individual opinion without seeking majority or minority support

CC-21. *Disturbances.* A well-functioning individual must be able to identify with or oppose majority or minority groups. Inability to identify or oppose, wholly or in part, signals serious disturbances which are likely to interfere with group communication.

a) Inability to identify with majority:
—The delinquent
—Marginal people who have lived all their lives among minorities

b) Inability to identify with minority:
—Snobs and other prejudiced people

c) Nonidentified individuals:
—Displaced children and adults
—Some schizophrenic children

d) Solipsistic, narcissistic individuals:
—Autistic artists
—The hermit

C-22. *Adaptation and control in group situations.* Adaptation in group situations usually means the sharing of control with others. Thus, all members exact some measure of control if they are active participants. Leverage over others can be obtained by denying the satisfaction of some individual needs or by relying upon interpersonal appeal. In addition, there exists a method of exacting leverage which is characteristic of group situations and which operates through manipulation of the need for group membership.

a) Obtains leverage through exclusion or self-exclusion:
—As a prominent member, threatens to resign
—Forces a compromised member to resign

b) Obtains leverage through inclusion:
—Promises other person to make him a member
—Consistently appears in public with a certain member of opposite sex, thus shaping public opinion and forcing engagement

c) Obtains leverage through demotion or self-demotion:
—Reduces other person in rank
—Resigns as officer of an association

d) Obtains leverage through promotion:
—Elevates youthful rebel to the leader of subfaction of the group
—Runs for office

e) Obtains leverage through nonparticipation and passive resistance:
—Gandhi's technique

f) Obtains leverage through oppositional stand:
—By opposing, he becomes somebody that the majority has to cope with

g) Obtains leverage through holding pivotal position:
—In an evenly split group, he throws his weight one way or the other

CC-22. *Disturbances.* Disturbances in the exertion of leverage in group situations may occur when the individual uses himself as a foreign body in the group structure, banking on the fact that others will do everything in their power to restore homogeneity in the group. However, the disturbed person usually overestimates the patience of the other members.

a) Obtains leverage through withdrawal:
—The catatonic schizophrenic

b) Obtains leverage by intrusion:
—The manic and the aggressive person

c) Obtains leverage by sacrifice:
—The social masochist
—The death-defying hero

d) Obtains leverage by crowning himself:
—"His Majesty" in an insane asylum

e) Obtains leverage by holding out and withholding:
—The debt that is never paid
—Hunger strike

f) Obtains leverage through rebellion:
—The aggressive child

g) Obtains leverage by playing both sides:
—The informer

References

1. ABRAHAM, K.: Notes on the psychoanalytical investigation and treatment of manic-depressive insanity and allied conditions. In *Selected Papers*. London: Institute of Psychoanalysis, and Hogarth Press, 1927.

2. ADLER, A.: *Study of Organ Inferiority and its Psychical Compensation.* New York: Nervous and Mental Disease Publishing Co., 1917.

3. ADORNO, T. W., FRENKEL-BRUNSWIK, E., LEVINSON, D. J., and SANFORD, R. N.: *The Authoritarian Personality.* New York: Harper, 1950.

4. AICHHORN, A.: *Wayward Youth.* New York: Viking, 1935.

5. ALEXANDER, F.: *Psychosomatic Medicine—Its Principles and Application.* New York: Norton, 1950.

6. ALEXANDER, F., and FRENCH, T. M.: *Psychoanalytic Therapy.* New York: Ronald Press, 1946.

7. ALLPORT, F. H.: *Theories of Perception and the Concept of Structure.* New York: Wiley, 1955.

8. ALLPORT, G., and VERNON, P.: *Studies in Expressive Movement.* New York: Macmillan, 1933.

9. ARIETI, S.: *Interpretation of Schizophrenia.* New York: Brunner, 1955.

10. Army Medical Service Graduate School: *Symposium on Stress (16–18 March, 1953).* Washington: AMSGS, 1953.

11. ARNHEIM, R.: *Art and Visual Perception—A Psychology of the Creative Eye.* Berkeley and Los Angeles: University of California Press, 1954.

12. ASHBY, W. R.: *Design for a Brain.* New York: Wiley, 1952.

13. Association for Research in Nervous and Mental Disease: *Genetics and the Inheritance of Integrated Neurological and Psychiatric Patterns.* Proceedings of the Association, Vol. 33. Baltimore: Williams & Wilkins, 1954.

14. AULD, F., and MURRAY, E. J.: Content analysis studies of psychotherapy. Psychol. Bull., 52: 377–395 (1955).

15. AYER, A. J., and Others: *Studies in Communication.* London: Martin Secker & Warburg, 1955.

16. BARBARA, D. A.: *Stuttering.* New York: Julian Press, 1954.

17. BARKER, R. G., WRIGHT, B. A., MEYERSON, L., and GONICK, M. R.: *Adjustment to Physical Handicap and Illness: A Survey of the Social Psychology of Physique and Disability.* New York: Social. Sci. Res. Counc. Bull. #55 (Revised), 1953.

18. BAUER, J.: *Constitution and Disease*. New York: Grune & Stratton, 1945.

19. BAVELAS, A.: Morale and training of leaders. Pp. 143–165 in *Civilian Morale* (G. Watson, Editor). Boston: Houghton Mifflin, 1942.

20. BENDER, L.: *Psychopathology of Children with Organic Brain Disorders*. Springfield, Ill.: Thomas, 1956.

21. BERG, C.: The psychology of punishment. Brit. J. Med. Psych., 20: 295–313 (1945).

22. BERG, J. H. VAN DEN: *The Phenomenological Approach to Psychiatry*. Springfield, Ill.: Thomas, 1955.

23. BERGLER, E.: Logorrhea. Psychiat. Quart., 18: 26–42 (1944).

24. BERGLER, E.: Psychopathology of impostors. J. crim. Psychopathol., 5, 695–714, 1944.

25. BERGLER, E.: *The Battle of the Conscience*. Washington: Washington Institute of Medicine, 1948.

26. BERRES, F.: Remedial reading program. University [of California] Bull., 4: 138 (1956).

27. BETTELHEIM, B.: *Love is Not Enough*. Glencoe, Ill.: The Free Press, 1950.

28. BETTELHEIM, B., and SYLVESTER, E.: Physical symptoms in emotionally disturbed children. Pp. 353–368 in *The Psychoanalytic Study of the Child*. Vol. 3/4. New York: International Universities Press, 1949.

29. BEXTON, W. H., HERON, W., and SCOTT, T. H.: Effects of decreased variation in the sensory environment. Canad. J. Psychol., 8: 70–76 (1954).

30. BINSWANGER, L.: *Grundformen und Erkenntnis Menschlichen Daseins*. Zurich: Niehaus, 1942.

31. BINSWANGER, L.: La "Daseinsanalyse" en psychiatrie. Encephale, 40: 108–113, 1951.

32. BIRDWHISTELL, R. L.: *Introduction to Kinesics*. Louisville: University of Louisville, Department of Psychology and Social Anthropology, Research Manual, 1952.

33. BLAU, A.: *The Master Hand*. New York: Amer. Orthopsychiat. Assoc. Res. Monogr., No. 5, 1946.

34. BLEULER, E.: *Dementia Praecox or the Group of Schizophrenias* (1911). (Tr. by J. Zinkin.) New York: International Universities Press, 1950.

35. BLEULER, E.: *Textbook of Psychiatry*. New York: Macmillan, 1924.

36. BLEULER, M.: Research and changes in concepts in the study of schizophrenia, 1941–1950. Bull. Isaac Ray Med. Lib., 3: 1–132 (1955).

37. BODER, D. P.: *I Did Not Interview the Dead*. Urbana: University of Illinois Press, 1949.

38. BOSS, M.: *Sinn und Gehalt der sexuellen Perversionen*. Bern: Verlag Hans Huber, 1947.

39. BOWLBY, J.: *Maternal Care and Mental Health*. Geneva: World Health Organization, 1951.

40. BRENMAN, M., and GILL, M. M.: *Hypnotherapy—A Survey of the Literature*. New York: International Universities Press, 1947.

41. BREUER, J., and FREUD, S.: *Studies in Hysteria*. (Tr. by A. A. Brill.) New York: Nervous and Mental Disease Publ. Co., 1936.

42. BROWN, F. J., and ROUCEK, J. S.: *One America*. New York: Prentice-Hall, 1945.

43. BROWN, G. S., and CAMPBELL, D. P.: Control systems. Scientific American, 187: 56–64 (1952).

44. BÜHLER, C.: *The First Year of Life*. New York: John Day, 1930.

45. BÜHLER, K.: *Sprachtheorie*. Jena: Fischer, 1934.

46. BURGESS, E. W.: The family in a changing society. Amer. J. Sociol., 53: 417–422 (1948).

47. CABOT, P. S. DEQ.: *Juvenile Delinquency, A Critical Annotated Bibliography*. New York: Wilson, 1946.

48. CAMERON, D. E.: *Remembering*. New York: Nervous and Mental Disease Monogr., No. 72, 1947.

49. CAMERON, N., and MAGARET, A.: *Behavior Pathology*. Boston: Houghton Mifflin, 1951.

50. CANNON, W. B.: *Bodily Changes in Pain, Hunger, Fear, and Rage*. New York: Appleton, 1929.

51. CARTWRIGHT, D., and ZANDER, A. (Editors): *Group Dynamics*. Evanston, Ill.: Row, Peterson & Co., 1953.

52. CASSIRER, E.: *The Philosophy of Symbolic Forms: I. Language*. New Haven: Yale University Press, 1953.

53. CAUDILL, W.: Applied anthropology in medicine. Pp. 771–806 in *Anthropology Today* (A. L. Kroeber, Editor). Chicago: University of Chicago Press, 1952.

54. CHANG TUNG-SUN: A Chinese philosopher's theory of knowledge. ETC., 9: 203–226 (1952).

55. CHERRY, E. C.: The communication of information. Amer. Scientist, 40: 640–664 (1952).

56. CLARK, R. E.: Psychoses, income, and occupational prestige. Amer. J. Sociol., 54: 433–440 (1949).

57. COBB, S.: *Borderlands of Psychiatry*. Cambridge: Harvard University Press, 1943.

58. COBB, S.: *Emotions and Clinical Medicine*. New York: Norton, 1950.

59. COLBY, K. M.: Human symbiosis. Psychiatry, 12: 135–139 (1949).

60. Conference on Cybernetics: *Circular Causal and Feedback Mechanisms in Biological and Social Systems*. Transactions of the 6th, 7th, 8th, 9th, and 10th Conferences. New York: Josiah Macy, Jr., Foundation, 1950–1955.

61. Conference on Group Processes: *Group Processes*. Transactions of the First Conference. New York: Josiah Macy, Jr., Foundation, 1955.

62. Conference on a Unified Theory of Human Behavior: *Toward a Unified Theory of Human Behavior.* Transactions of the first four meetings. (R. R. Grinker, Editor.) New York: Basic Books, 1956.

63. CRITCHLEY, M.: *The Language of Gesture.* London: Arnold, 1939.

64. CUTSFORTH, T. D.: *The Blind in School and Society, A Psychological Study.* New York and London: Appleton, 1933.

65. DARWIN, C.: *The Expression of the Emotions in Man and Animals* (1872). New York: Philosophical Library, 1955.

66. DEUTSCH, K. W.: Communication theory and social science. Amer. J. Orthopsychiat., 22: 469–483 (1952).

67. DEUTSCH, K. W.: *Nationalism and Social Communication.* New York and Cambridge: Wiley and Technology Press of M.I.T., 1953.

68. DILTHEY, W.: Ideen über eine beschreibende und zergliedernde Psychologie. In Vol. V, *Collected Works.* Leipzig: Teubner, 1924.

69. DOLLARD, J., DOOB, L. W., MILLER, N. E., MOWRER, O. H., and SEARS, R. R.: *Frustration and Aggression.* New Haven: Yale University Press, 1939.

70. DOLLARD, J., and MILLER, N. E.: *Personality and Psychotherapy.* New York: McGraw-Hill, 1950.

71. DUNHAM, H. W.: Social psychiatry. Amer. Sociol. Rev., 13: 183–197 (1948).

72. EHRENWALD, J.: *Telepathy and Medical Psychology.* New York: Norton, 1948.

73. EMPSON, W.: *Seven Types of Ambiguity* (2d ed.). New York: New Directions, 1947.

74. ERIKSON, E. H.: *Childhood and Society.* New York: Norton, 1950.

75. FARIS, R. E. L.: Cultural isolation and the schizophrenic personality. Amer. J. Sociol., 39: 155–169 (1934).

76. FARIS, R. E. L.: Ecological factors in human behavior. Pp. 736–757 in *Personality and the Behavior Disorders* (J. McV. Hunt, Editor). New York: Ronald Press, 1944.

77. FARIS, R. E. L., and DUNHAM, H. W.: *Mental Disorders in Urban Areas.* Chicago: University of Chicago Press, 1939.

78. FEDERN, P.: *Ego Psychology and the Psychoses.* New York: Basic Books, 1952.

79. FENICHEL, O.: *The Psychoanalytic Theory of Neurosis.* New York: Norton, 1945.

80. FOSTER, L. E., LINDEMANN, E., and FAIRBANKS, R. J.: Grief, Pastoral Psychol., 1: 28–30 (1950).

81. FREUD, A.: *The Ego and the Mechanisms of Defense.* London: Hogarth Press, 1942.

82. FREUD, A., and BURLINGHAM, D.: *War and Children.* New York: Medical War Books, 1943.

83. FREUD, A., and BURLINGHAM, D.: *Infants without Families*. New York: International Universities Press, 1944.

84. FREUD, S.: Obsessions and phobias: their psychical mechanisms and their aetiology. In *Collected Papers*, Vol. I. London: Institute of Psychoanalysis and Hogarth Press, 1924.

85. FREUD, S.: The predisposition to obsessional neurosis. In *Collected Papers*, Vol. II. London: Institute of Psychoanalysis and Hogarth Press, 1924.

86. FREUD, S.: Analysis of a phobia in a five-year-old boy. In *Collected Papers*, Vol. III. London: Institute of Psychoanalysis and Hogarth Press, 1924.

87. FREUD, S.: Notes upon a case of obsessional neurosis. In *Collected Papers*, Vol. III. London: Institute of Psychoanalysis and Hogarth Press, 1924.

88. FREUD, S.: Mourning and melancholia. In *Collected Papers*, Vol. IV. London: Institute of Psychoanalysis and Hogarth Press, 1924.

89. FREUD, S.: *The Ego and the Id*. London: Hogarth Press, 1927.

90. FREUD, S.: *Three Contributions to the Theory of Sex*. (4th ed.), New York: Nervous and Mental Disease Publishing Co., 1930.

91. FREUD, S.: *New Introductory Lectures on Psychoanalysis*. (Tr. by W. J. H. Sprott.) New York: Norton, 1933.

92. FREUD, S.: *The Problem of Anxiety*. New York: Norton, 1936.

93. FREUD, S.: *A General Introduction to Psychoanalysis*. (Tr. of rev. ed. by J. Riviere.) Garden City: Garden City Publishing Co., 1943.

94. FREUD, S.: *An Outline of Psychoanalysis*. New York: Norton, 1949.

95. FRISCH, K. VON: Bees. Ithaca: Cornell University Press, 1950.

96. FROMM, E.: *The Sane Society*. New York: Rinehart, 1955.

97. FROMM-REICHMANN, F.: *Principles of Intensive Psychotherapy*. Chicago: University of Chicago Press, 1950.

98. FROMM-REICHMANN, F., and Others: *An Intensive Study of Twelve Cases of Manic-Depressive Psychosis*. Washington: Washington School of Psychiatry, 1953.

99. GELLHORN, E.: *Physiological Foundations of Neurology and Psychiatry*. Minneapolis: University of Minnesota Press, 1953.

100. GESELL, A. L., and Others: *The First Five Years of Life* (8th ed.). New York: Harper, 1940.

101. GESELL, A. L., and ILG, F. L.: *The Child from Five to Ten*. New York: Harper, 1946.

102. GLAUBER, I. P.: Speech characteristics of psychoneurotic patients. J. Speech Disorders, 9: 18–30 (1944).

103. GOLDSTEIN, K.: *Language and Language Disturbances*. New York: Grune & Stratton, 1948.

104. HART, B.: *Psychopathology: Its Development and Its Place in Medicine*. Cambridge: Cambridge University Press, 1929.

105. HARTLEY, E. L., and HARTLEY, R. E.: *Fundamentals of Social Psychology*. New York: Knopf, 1952.

106. HARTMANN, H., and KRIS, E.: The genetic approach in psychoanalysis. Pp. 1–22 in *Yearbook of Psychoanalysis*. Vol. 2. New York: International Universities Press, 1946.

107. HAYAKAWA, S. I.: *Language in Thought and Action* (1941) (2d enl. rev. ed.). New York: Harcourt, Brace, 1949.

108. HEAD, H.: *Aphasia and Kindred Disorders of Speech*. 2 vols. New York: Macmillan, 1926.

109. HEBB, D. O.: *The Organization of Behavior*. New York: Wiley, 1949.

110. HEIDEGGER, M.: *Existence and Being*. Chicago: Regnery, 1949.

111. HERZ, E., and PUTNAM, T. J.: *Motor Disorders in Nervous Diseases*. New York: King's Crown Press, 1946.

112. HOCH, P. H., and ZUBIN, J. (Editors): *Anxiety*. New York: Grune & Stratton, 1950.

113. HOCH, P. H., and ZUBIN, J. (Editors): *Psychopathology of Childhood*. New York: Grune & Stratton, 1955.

114. HOCH, P. H., and ZUBIN, J. (Editors): *Psychopathology of Communication*. New York: Grune & Stratton. (In press.)

115. HOGBEN, L.: *From Cave Painting to Comic Strip*. 288 pp. New York: Chanticleer Press, 1949.

116. HOLLINGSHEAD, A. B., and REDLICH, F. C.: Social mobility and mental illness. Amer. J. Psychiat., 112: 179–185 (1955).

117. HOMANS, G. C.: *The Human Group*. New York: Harcourt, Brace, 1950.

118. HORNEY, K.: *Our Inner Conflicts*. New York: Norton, 1945.

119. HUNTINGTON, E.: *Mainsprings of Civilization*. New York: Wiley, 1945.

120. ICHHEISER, G.: *Misunderstandings in Human Relations; A Study in False Social Perception*. 70 pp. (Amer. J. Sociol. Monogr.) Chicago: University of Chicago Press, 1949.

121. INGHAM, S. D.: Orientation. Bull. Los Angeles Neur. Soc., 5: 95–106 (1940).

122. International Congress for Psychotherapy: *Report, Zurich, 1954*. Basel: S. Karger, 1955.

123. ISAACS, S.: *Social Development in Young Children*. London: George Routledge & Sons, 1945.

124. JANET, P.: *Psychological Healing*. 2 vols. New York: Macmillan, 1925.

125. JANIS, I. L., and FESHBACK, S.: Effects of fear-arousing communications. J. Abnorm. Soc. Psychol., 48: 78–92 (1953).

126. JASPERS, K.: *Allgemeine Psychopathologie*. Berlin: Springer, 1946.

127. JESPERSEN, O.: *The Philosophy of Grammar*. London: Allen & Unwin, 1951.

128. JOHNSON, W.: *People in Quandaries*. New York: Harper, 1946.

129. JONES, M.: *The Therapeutic Community*. New York: Basic Books, 1953.

130. JUNG, C. G.: *Psychological Types, or the Psychology of Individuation*. 628 pp. New York: Harcourt, Brace, 1923.

131. KAHN, E.: *Psychopathic Personalities*. (Tr. by H. F. Dunbar.) New Haven: Yale University Press, 1931.

132. KANNER, L.: Judging emotions from facial expressions. Psychol. Monogr., No. 3, 41: 1–33, 1939.

133. KANNER, L.: *Child Psychiatry* (2d ed.). Springfield, Ill.: Thomas, 1948.

134. KORZYBSKI, A.: *Science and Sanity* (1933) (3rd ed.). Lakeville, Conn.: Int. non-Aristotelian Lib. Publ. Co., 1948.

135. KRAEPELIN, E.: *Clinical Psychiatry*. (Adapted by A. R. Defendorf.) New York: Macmillan, 1904.

136. KRETSCHMER, E.: *Physique and Character*. (Tr. from the 2d rev. and enl. ed. by W. J. H. Sprott.) New York: Harcourt, Brace, 1925.

137. KRETSCHMER, E.: *Hysteria*. (Tr. by O. R. Boltz.) New York: Nervous and Mental Disease Publishing Co., 1926.

138. KRETSCHMER, E.: *A Textbook of Medical Psychology*. London: Oxford University Press, 1934.

139. KRONFELD, A.: *Perspectiven der Seelenheilkunde*. Leipzig: Thieme, 1930.

140. KUBIE, L. S.: The distortion of the symbolic process in neurosis and psychosis. J. Amer. Psychoanal. Assoc., 1: 59–86 (1953).

141. KUGELMASS, I. N.: *The Management of Mental Deficiency in Children*. New York: Grune & Stratton, 1954.

142. LANGER, S. K.: *Feeling and Form*. New York: Scribner, 1953.

143. LAZARSFELD, P. F., and ROSENBERG, M. (Editors): *The Language of Social Research*. Glencoe: Free Press, 1955.

144. LEE, I. J.: *Language Habits in Human Affairs*. New York: Harper, 1941.

145. Lee, I. J.: *The Language of Wisdom and Folly*. New York: Harper, 1949.

146. LEE, I. J.: *Customs and Crises in Communication*. New York: Harper, 1954.

147. LEIGHTON, A. H.: Psychiatric disorder and social environment. Psychiatry, 18: 367–383 (1956).

148. LEVY, D. M.: *Studies in Sibling Rivalry*. Amer. Orthopsychiat. Assoc. Res. Monogr., No. 2, 1937.

149. LEVY, D. M.: *Maternal Overprotection*. New York: Columbia University Press, 1943.

150. LICKLIDER, J. C. R.: The manner in which and extent to which speech can be distorted and remain intelligible. Pp. 58–122 in *Cybernetics* (H. Von Foerster, Editor). New York: Josiah Macy, Jr., Foundation, 1951.

151. LORENZ, M.: Expressive behavior and language patterns. Psychiatry, 18: 353–366 (1956).

152. McCULLOCH, W. S.: Why the mind is in the head. Pp. 42–57 in *Cerebral Mechanisms in Behavior* (L. A. Jeffress, Editor). New York: Wiley, 1951.

153. McCULLOCH, W. S., and PITTS, W.: The statistical organization of nervous activity. J. Amer. Statist. Assoc., 4: 91–99 (1948).

154. MACHIAVELLI, N.: *The Prince* and *The Discourses*. New York: Modern Library, 1940.

155. MALAMUD, W.: *Outlines of General Psychopathology*. New York: Norton, 1935.

156. MALZBERG, B.: Age and sex in relation to mental disease. Ment. Hyg., 39: 196–224 (1955).

157. MARX, M. H.: *Psychological Theory*. New York: Macmillan, 1951.

158. MASSERMAN, J.: *The Practice of Dynamic Psychiatry*. Philadelphia: Saunders, 1955.

159. MAYO, E.: *The Human Problems of an Industrial Civilization* (1933) (2d ed.) Boston: Div. of Research, Graduate School of Business Administration, Harvard University, 1946.

160. MEAD, G. H.: *Mind, Self, and Society*. Chicago: University of Chicago Press, 1934.

161. MEERLOO, J. A. M.: Problems of displaced people. Pp. 113–136 in *Aftermath of Peace*. New York: International Universities Press, 1946.

162. MEERLOO, J. A. M.: *Conversation and Communication*. New York: International Universities Press, 1952.

163. MENNINGER, K.: *Man Against Himself*. New York: Harcourt, Brace, 1938.

164. MEYER, A.: *The Collected Papers of Adolf Meyer: II. Psychiatry*. Baltimore: Johns Hopkins Press, 1951.

165. MILLER, G. A.: *Language and Communication*. New York: McGraw-Hill, 1951.

166. MORRIS, C. W.: *Varieties of Human Value*. Chicago: University of Chicago Press, 1956.

167. MORRIS, C. W.: *Signs, Language, and Behavior*. New York: Prentice-Hall, 1946.

168. MOSES, P. J.: *The Voice of Neurosis*. New York: Grune & Stratton, 1954.

169. MOWRER, O. H.: *Learning Theory and Personality Dynamics*. New York: Ronald Press, 1950.

170. MULLAHY, P., and Others: *A Study of Interpersonal Relations*. New York: Hermitage Press, 1949.

171. MURPHY, G.: *Historical Introduction to Modern Psychology*. New York: Harcourt, Brace, 1949.

172. MYKLEBUST, H. R.: *Auditory Disorders in Children*. New York: Grune & Stratton, 1954.

173. National Safety Council: *Accident Facts*. Chicago: National Safety Council, Inc., 1955.

174. NEWCOMB, T. M., and HARTLEY, E. L., and Others: *Readings in Social Psychology*. New York: Holt, 1947.

175. NICOLE, J. E.: *Psychopathology—A Survey of Modern Approaches* (4th ed.). Baltimore: Williams & Wilkins, 1947.

176. NIELSEN, J. M.: *Agnosia, Apraxia, Aphasia* (2d ed.). New York: Hoeber, 1946.

177. OSGOOD, C. E., and SEBEOK, T. A. (Editors): *Psycholinguistics: A Survey of Theory and Research Problems.* 203 pp. Int. J. Amer. Linguist., Memoir 10 (Indiana University Publications in Anthropology and Linguistics), 1954.

178. PARSONS, T., and BALES, R.: *The Family; Socialization and Interaction Process.* 422 pp. Glencoe, Ill.: The Free Press, 1955.

179. PETERSON, W. F., and MILLIKEN, M. E.: *The Patient and the Weather: III. Nervous and Mental Diseases.* Ann Arbor: Edwards Brothers, 1934.

180. PIAGET, J.: *Judgment and Reasoning in the Child.* New York: Harcourt, Brace, 1928.

181. PIAGET, J.: *The Language and Thought of the Child* (2d ed.). London: Kegan Paul, Trench, Trubner, 1932.

182. PIAGET, J.: *Play, Dreams, and Imitation in Childhood.* New York: Norton, 1952.

183. PIAGET, J.: *The Child's Conception of Number.* London: Routledge & Paul, 1952.

184. PINEL, P.: *A Treatise on Insanity.* (Tr. by D. D. Davis.) Sheffield, 1806.

185. PODOLSKY, E. (Editor): *Management of Addictions.* New York: Philosophical Library, 1955.

186. PRIBRAM, K.: *Conflicting Patterns of Thought.* Washington: Public Affairs Press, 1949.

187. QUERIDO, A.: Experiment in mental health. World Mental Health, 6: 203–216 (1954).

188. RAPAPORT, D.: *Emotions and Memory.* Baltimore: Williams & Wilkins, 1942.

189. RAPAPORT, D.: *Organization and Pathology of Thought: Selected Sources.* New York: Columbia University Press, 1951.

190. RAPOPORT, A., WEAVER, W., GERARD, R. W., SAMSON, E. W., and KIRK, J. R.: Information theory. ETC., 10: 241–320 (1953).

191. REDFIELD, C. E.: *Communication in Management.* Chicago: University of Chicago Press, 1953.

192. REDL, F., and WINEMAN, D.: *Children Who Hate.* Glencoe, Ill.: The Free Press, 1951.

193. REDL, F., and WINEMAN, D.: *Controls From Within.* 332 pp. Glencoe, Ill.: The Free Press, 1952.

194. REYNIERS, J. A. (Editor): Germ-free life studies. Lobund Reports, No. 1, 1946; No. 2, 1949. Notre Dame, Ind.: University of Notre Dame Press.

195. RIBBLE, M. A.: *The Rights of Infants.* New York: Columbia University Press, 1943.

196. RIDENOUR, L. N.: The role of the computer. Scientific American, 187: 116–130 (1952).

197. RIESEN, A. H.: The development of visual perception in man and chimpanzee. Science, 106: 107–108 (1949).

198. RIOCH, D. McK.: Psychiatry as a biological science. Psychiatry, 18: 313–321 (1955).

199. RUESCH, J.: The diagnostic value of disturbances of consciousness. Dis. nerv. Syst., 5: 2–16 (1944).

200. RUESCH, J.; Social technique, social status, and social change in illness (1948). Pp. 123–136 in *Personality in Nature, Society, and Culture* (2d ed.). (C. Kluckhohn, H. A. Murray, and D. M. Schneider, Editors). New York: Knopf, 1953.

201. RUESCH, J.: The infantile personality: the core problem of psychosomatic medicine. Psychosom. Med., 10: 134–144 (1948).

202. RUESCH, J.: Social factors in therapy. Pp. 59–93 in *Psychiatric Treatment* (ARNMD 31). Baltimore: Williams & Wilkins, 1953.

203. RUESCH, J.: Synopsis of the theory of human communication. Psychiatry, 16: 215–243 (1953).

204. RUESCH, J.: The interpersonal communication of anxiety. Pp. 154–164 in *Symposium on Stress (16–18 March, 1953)*. Washington: Army Medical Service Graduate School, Walter Reed Army Medical Center, 1953.

205. RUESCH, J.: Psychiatry and the challenge of communication. Psychiatry, 17: 1–18 (1954).

206. RUESCH, J.: Transference reformulated. Acta Psychotherapeutica, Psychosomatica, et Orthopaedagogica, Suppl. Vol. 3, 596–605 (1955).

207. RUESCH, J.: Nonverbal language and therapy. Psychiatry, 18: 323–330 (1955).

208. RUESCH, J.: The tangential response. In *Psychopathology of Communication.* (P. H. Hoch and J. Zubin, Editors.) New York: Grune and Stratton. (In press.)

209. RUESCH, J., and BATESON, G.: Structure and process in social relations. Psychiatry, 12: 105–124 (1949).

210. RUESCH, J., and BATESON, G.: *Communication—The Social Matrix of Psychiatry.* New York: Norton, 1951.

211. RUESCH, J., CHRISTIANSEN, C., PATTERSON, L. C., DEWEES, S., and JACOBSON, A.: Psychological invalidism in thyroidectomized patients. Psychosom. Med., 9: 77–91 (1947).

212. RUESCH, J., HARRIS, R. E., LOEB, M. B., CHRISTIANSEN, C., DEWEES, S., HELLER, S. H., and JACOBSON, A.: *Chronic Disease and Psychological Invalidism,* Berkeley and Los Angeles: University of California Press, 1951.

213. RUESCH, J., HARRIS, R. E., CHRISTIANSEN, C., LOEB, M. B., DEWEES, S., and JACOBSON, A.: *Duodenal Ulcer.* Berkeley and Los Angeles: University of California Press, 1948.

214. RUESCH, J., JACOBSON, A., and LOEB, M. B.: Acculturation and illness. 40 pp. Psycho. Mon. Gen. Appl., No. 5, Vol. 62 (1948).

215. RUESCH, J., and KEES, W.: *Nonverbal Communication.* Berkeley and Los Angeles: University of California Press, 1956.

216. RUESCH, J., and PRESTWOOD, A. R.: Anxiety, its initiation, communication, and interpersonal management. Arch. Neurol. Psychiat., 62: 527–550 (1949).

217. RUESCH, J., and PRESTWOOD, A. R.: Interaction processes and personal codification. J. Personality, 18: 391–430 (1950).

218. RUESCH, J., and PRESTWOOD, A. R.: Communication and bodily disease. Pp. 211–230 in *Life Stress and Bodily Disease* (ARNMD 29). Baltimore: Williams & Wilkins, 1950.

219. RUESCH, J., BATESON, G., and KEES, W.: A Problem Child Before and After Therapy. 16mm film. Running time, about 25 minutes. The Langley Porter Clinic, San Francisco, 1955.

220. RUESCH, J., BATESON, G., and KEES, W.: The Child Who Does Not Speak. 16mm film. Running time, about 30 minutes. The Langley Porter Clinic, San Francisco, 1955.

221. RUESCH, J., and KEES, W.: Children in Groups. 16mm film. Running time, about 25 minutes. The Langley Porter Clinic, San Francisco, 1954.

222. RUSSELL, B.: *The Analysis of Mind.* London: Allen and Unwin, 1921.

223. SAINSBURY, P.: Gestural movement during psychiatric interview. Psychosom. Med., 17: 458–469 (1955).

224. SAUL, L. J.: *Emotional Maturity.* Philadelphia: Lippincott, 1947.

225. SCHACHTEL, E. G.: On memory and childhood amnesia. Pp. 3–49 in *A Study of Interpersonal Relations.* New York: Hermitage Press, 1949.

226. SCHILDER, P.: *Medical Psychology* (1924). (Tr. and ed. by D. Rapaport.) New York: International Universities Press, 1953.

227. SCHILDER, P.: *Brain and Personality.* New York: Nervous and Mental Disease Publishing Co., 1931.

228. SENDEN, M. VON: *Raum- und Gestaltauffassung bei operierten Blindgeborenen vor und nach der Operation.* Leipzig: Barth, 1932.

229. SHANNON, C. A., and WEAVER, W.: *The Mathematical Theory of Communication.* Urbana: University of Illinois Press, 1949.

230. SHERIF, M., and CANTRIL, H.: *The Psychology of Ego-Involvement.* New York: Wiley, 1947.

231. SIMEY, T. S.: Mental health and the problem of transplanted persons. Bull. World Fed. Ment. Health, 1: 12–16 (1949).

232. SIMMONS, L. W., and WOLFF, H. G.: *Social Science in Medicine.* New York: Russell Sage Foundation, 1954.

233. SMITH, B. L., LASSWELL, H. D., and CASEY, R. D.: *Propaganda, Communication, and Public Opinion.* Princeton: Princeton University Press, 1946.

234. SNYDER, R. C., BRUCK, H. W., and SAPIN, B.: *Decision-making as an Approach to the Study of International Politics.* Foreign Policy Analysis Project, Series No. 3. Princeton: Organizational Behavior Section, Princeton University, 1954.

235. SONNEMAN, U.: *Existence and Therapy.* New York: Grune & Stratton, 1954.

236. SPITZ, R. A.: Anaclitic depression: an inquiry into the genesis of psychotic conditions in early childhood. Pp. 313–342 in *The Psychoanalytic Study of the Child.* Vol. 2. New York: International Universities Press, 1946.

237. Spitz, R. A.: Psychoanalytische Begriffsbildung und physiologisches Denkmodell. Schweiz. Z. Psychol., 12: 24–39 (1953).

238. Stanton, A. H., and Schwartz, M. S.: *The Mental Hospital.* New York: Basic Books, 1954.

239. Stevens, S. S. (Editor): *Handbook of Experimental Psychology.* New York: Wiley, 1951.

240. Storch, A.: *The Primitive Archaic Forms of Inner Experience and Thought in Schizophrenia.* New York: Nervous and Mental Disease Monogr., No. 36, 1924.

241. Sullivan, H. S.: Conceptions of Modern Psychiatry. Psychiatry, 3:1–117 (1940).

242. Sullivan, H. S.: *The Interpersonal Theory of Psychiatry.* New York: Norton, 1953.

243. Szurek, S. A.: An attitude towards (child) psychiatry. Quart. J. Child Behavior, 1: 22–54, 178–213, 375–399, 401–423 (1949).

244. Szurek, S. A.: Comments on the psychopathology of children with somatic illness. Amer. J. Psychiat., 107: 844–849 (1951).

245. Szurek, S. A.: Childhood schizophrenia; psychotic episodes and psychotic maldevelopment. Amer. J. Orthopsychiat., 26: 519–543 (1956).

246. Tinbergen, N.: *Social Behavior in Animals.* London: Methuen, 1953.

247. Tomkins, S. S. (Editor): *Contemporary Psychopathology.* Cambridge: Harvard University Press, 1946.

248. Travis, L. E.: *Speech Pathology.* New York: Appleton, 1931.

249. Tyhurst, L.: Displacement and migration. Amer. J. Psychiat., 107: 561–568 (1951).

250. Van Riper, C.: *Speech Correction: Principles and Methods* (2d ed.). New York: Prentice-Hall, 1947.

251. Walter, W. G.: *The Living Brain.* New York: Norton, 1953.

252. Warner, W. L., Meeker, M., and Eells, K.: *Social Class in America.* Chicago: Science Res. Assoc., 1949.

253. Werner, H. (Editor): *On Expressive Language.* Worcester, Mass.: Clark University Press, 1955.

254. White, W. A.: *Medical Psychology.* New York: Nervous and Mental Disease Publishing Co., 1931.

255. Whorf, B. L.: *Collected Papers on Metalinguistics.* Washington: Foreign Service Institute, Department of State, 1952.

256. Whyte, L. L.: *The Next Development in Man.* New York: Holt, 1948.

257. Wiener, N.: *Cybernetics, or Control and Communication in the Animal and the Machine.* New York: Wiley, 1948.

258. Wiener, N.: *The Human Use of Human Beings—Cybernetics and Society.* Boston: Houghton Mifflin, 1950.

259. Wiener, N.: Sensory prosthesises. Pp. 203–207 in *Cybernetics* (H. Von Foerster, Editor). New York: Josiah Macy, Jr., Foundation, 1950.

260. WILSON, S. A. K.: *Neurology* (2d ed., ed. by A. N. Bruce). 3 vols. Baltimore: Williams & Wilkins, 1955.

261. WOLFF, H. G.: Life stress and bodily disease—A formulation. Pp. 1059–1094 in *Life Stress and Bodily Disease* (ARNMD 29). Baltimore: Williams & Wilkins, 1950.

262. WOLFF, H. G.: *Stress and Disease.* Springfield, Ill.: Thomas, 1953.

263. WOOD, M.: *Paths of Loneliness.* New York: Columbia University Press, 1953.

264. ZILBOORG, G.: *A History of Medical Psychology.* New York: Norton, 1941.

265. ZIPF, G. K.: *Human Behavior and the Principle of Least Effort.* Cambridge: Addison Wesley Press, 1949.

266. ZISKIND, E.: *Psychophysiologic Medicine.* Philadelphia: Lea & Febiger, 1954.

Index

Where authors are cited on a text page, even though not mentioned by name, they are indexed to that page number.